Way

Stations

to

Heaven

50 Major Visionary Shrines in the United States

Sandra Gurvis

Macmillan • USA

Macmillan General Reference
A Simon & Schuster Macmillan Company
1633 Broadway
New York, NY 10019

An Arco Book

MACMILLAN is a registered trademark of Macmillan, Inc.
ARCO is a registered trademark of Prentice-Hall, Inc.

Library of Congress Catalog Card Number: 96-085541
ISBN 0-02-860576-4

Manufactured in the United States of America

10 9 8 7 6 5 4 3 2 1

Design by Margaret D. DuBois

To the memory of those sacrificed to the folly of religious and racial purity. May there always be freedom of worship.

Acknowledgments —

A book is a collaborative effort, and *Way Stations to Heaven* is no exception. I'd like to thank the following for providing vital information and suggesting various shrines: Holly Bardoe, Mike Harden, John Hein, Rob Lively, Mary Jo Kalchthaler, Sherry Paprocki, Sondra Wegner, and my "tennis pal" who wishes to remain anonymous. If I left anybody out, I apologize in advance.

Pastors, nuns, visionaries, and shrine and church personnel also gave generously of their time and input. Without them, *Way Stations* would not have been possible. Although they're too numerous to mention here, their efforts are deeply appreciated.

Books that provided general information and background about the shrines and sightings were also helpful. These included *Looking for a Miracle* by Joe Nickell (Buffalo, NY: Prometheus, 1993); *Miracles, A Parascientific Inquiry into Wondrous Phenomena* by D. Scott Rogo (New York: Dial, 1982); and *The Supernatural, the Occult, and the Bible* by Gerald A. Larue (Buffalo, NY: Prometheus, 1990).

Lynn Grisard Fulman, Judy Florman, and the lively ladies at the Mary Anderson Center for the Arts in Mt. St. Francis, Indiana put me up and put up with me during various stages of writing. And without the invaluable research efforts of Linda Deitch, I'd still be wandering around various archives.

My family—husband Ron and children Amy and Alex—also provided invaluable support. Although they sometimes slow things down, they're always there when I need them.

My editor Barbara Gilson and agent Bert Holtje gave me the rare and wonderful opportunity to write this book. Not only did it provide me with a "Catholic" education, it greatly expanded my liturgical horizons. And one last thank you—to the higher power who helps us all.

Other Books by Sandra Gurvis

Swords into Ploughshares (Anthology)

America's Strangest Museums (Formerly *The Cockroach Hall of Fame and 101 Other Off-the-Wall Museums*)

The Off-the-Beaten Path Job Book

The following excerpts and/or stanzas have been reproduced with the authors' permission:

"The Anniversary of Man's End" by Allen Demetrius (unpublished poem)

"If It Didn't Happen To Me" by Mary Jo Kalchthaler (unpublished manuscript)

"Jesus Tree" by Ealois Mullins (privately published poem)

Contents

Foreword   ix

Introduction: Happening or Hoax?   xi

Alabama   1
Jasper: Double Exposure at Walker Baptist Medical Center
Sterrett: Medjugorje Pipeline

Arizona   11
Phoenix: Mary Branches Out
Scottsdale: Yuppie Visions at St. Maria Goretti
Sedona: New Age Vortex or Vacuum?

California   23
Chula Vista: A Strange Twist on the Road of Tragedy
Colfax: Mary Visits the Foothills
Los Angeles: Faith Shines Through
Santa Ana: A Mosaic Mystery
Santa Maria: Mary Goes "Krogering" in Earthquake Country
Thornton: Our Lady of Fatima Takes a Hike

Colorado   44
Golden: Double Vision at the Mother Cabrini Shrine
Silverton: Small Town Miracles

Connecticut   52
New Haven: Jesus vs. the Devil in Wooster Square Park

Florida   55
Hollywood: Making Room for Mary

Georgia   60
Columbus: Jesus Christ, Crimestopper
Conyers: Visions by Nancy Fowler
Stone Mountain: Pasta Jesus, Please

Illinois   72
Chicago: The Sorrows of Rosa Mystica
Chicago/Cicero: Weeping Icons Frequent Orthodox Churches
Hillside: Mary Visits a Cemetery

Kentucky   86
Cold Spring/Falmouth: A Woodstock for Catholics

Louisiana   91
Tickfaw: Visions amid the Vegetables

Contents ➤ ➤ ➤

Maine   **95**
    Fairfield: Another Knothole for Jesus

Maryland   **100**
    Emmitsburg: "Vision Night" at St. Joseph's Catholic Church

Massachusetts   **105**
    Medway: Rock of Jesus
    Ware: Mary Cries at Christmas

New Jersey   **113**
    Marlboro: Rough Riding on the Marian Trail
    Paterson: A Chameleon of a Statue
    West Paterson: God Finds a Loophole

New Mexico   **123**
    Chimayo: A "Pit" Stop on the High Road to Taos
    Holman: Jesus Up against the Wall
    Lake Arthur: Heaven on a Burnt Tortilla
    Santa Fe: This Old Madonna

New York   **136**
    Bayside (Queens): Call 1-800-882-MARY
    Hempstead: A Divine Wedding Gift
    Williamsbridge (Bronx): A Jewel in the Bronx

Ohio   **148**
    Barberton: From Magic City to Miracleville
    Carey: Conspicuous Communion
    Fostoria: Rust Stains on Tank or Sacred Image?
    Lorain: A "Contagious" Icon

Pennsylvania   **163**
    Ambridge: Did He Blink?
    Philadelphia: Parochial Vision during the Eisenhower Years
    Pittsburgh: Seeping Beauty

Texas   **173**
    Bellaire: Stampede at the Ayob Home
    Blanco: Tears in a Trailer
    Lubbock: Lone Star Lourdes
    Progreso/Elsa: Mary Appears in an Automotive Context

Virginia   **187**
    Lake Ridge: Stigmata and the Roller Coaster King

West Virginia   **191**
    Holden: Jesus Treed

Bibliography   **195**

When I was first approached about writing *Way Stations to Heaven,* my first reaction was: but I'm Jewish! What could I possibly know about or contribute to a book on mostly Christian shrines and visionaries? But I was told, both by my editor and my agent, that an objective viewpoint was needed. As an uninvolved party, I could bring a sensibility to the project that, say, a lapsed Catholic might not.

So I tentatively contacted a few places. Much to my surprise, I found myself fascinated with the topic, an interest that carried me through the complexity of producing a manuscript of this scope. I learned that the book is not so much about shrines or churches but about people's faith. And I began to understand that although some might find religion to be the opiate of the masses, belief in a higher power, be it Jesus, Mary, Moses, or Buddha, helps take away much of the sting of life.

Obtaining the information was the real challenge. Had it not been for computerized newspaper and magazine archives, I would have been in deep trouble. I used various resources, including Lexis/Nexis, CompuServe, and the Columbus Metropolitan Library networks. Less newfangled local and diocese libraries and Chambers of Commerce also yielded fruitful leads. City halls were helpful, particularly in small towns. More than one mayor and civic official went out of his or her way to provide a needed name, number, or insight.

But that was only the beginning. Not only was I faced with finding the visionaries and/or their spokespeople, but I had to overcome a great deal of initial distrust. Many had been skewered by the media and rightfully so, in a few cases. But it was not my job to crucify or praise, but rather to portray the shrine or organization in an unbiased light. The information had to be accurate and fair, so whenever possible, I let those involved tell their stories through their own words or newspaper/magazine quotes.

This book also presented a test of personal faith. Some sources were downright rude, refused to return phone calls, or made prying inquiries about my religious beliefs. I wasn't questioning *theirs,* but trying to get information. And others attempted to convert me, unsuccessfully I might add.

But just when I would get fed up, I would encounter a Mary Jo Kalchthaler, Mike Slate, or John Hein, visionaries and/or recipients of miracles who were open-minded, kind, and willing to share their experiences. Most priests were equally generous with their time. And shrine personnel, especially those in the gift shops, were especially helpful.

I visited lots of remarkable places along the way. Not only did the folks at Chapel of the Faith Baptist Church in South Central Los Angeles welcome me with open arms and provide terrific information and interviews, but they asked me to give a speech before the entire congregation! And on the other coast, the staff at St. Lucy's Catholic Church couldn't do enough for me, once I overcame their initial hesitancy. Because they refused interviews, I slipped incognito into Nancy Fowler's complex in Conyers, Georgia and into Caritas of Alabama. But people there were gracious and cooperative as well. Sincerity, it seems, goes a long way in the faith business.

Discussions of Jesus on a Pizza Hut billboard and a tortilla invariably draw chuckles and the twirling finger motion around the ear. But I found those who discovered and/or were closely associated with these images to be clear-minded and cogent. They are respectable, upstanding citizens who don't seem much different from most neighbors or co-workers.

I came away with even stronger beliefs. These people are not spewing nonsense, as skeptics or those unfamiliar with different religions sometimes surmise. Rather, they are trying to make sense of their world. And some of the things I heard and saw even I cannot rationalize.

For instance, while down in Georgia, my friend Darlene Patrick Hart and I stopped to see Father Raymond Jasinski, keeper of the weeping Rosa Mystica statue. He invited us downstairs to inspect the statue and while I was taking pictures of it and checking its eyes for tiny holes, Jasinski chatted up Darlene. After we left, she admitted to being spooked by a whole weekend of visiting churches, shrines, and pastors. To me, it was all in a day's work.

But when I got my film back, it looked like that darned statue was *crying*. And its facial expressions appeared to be different, despite many photos being taken from the same angle. So without saying a word, I showed them to my husband Ron, who is also Jewish.

"What do you think?" I asked him as he sorted through the pile.

He tried to disguise his amazement, then quickly handed it back to me. "It's pretty weird, I'll give you that." Still, it's not enough to make me change my religion. So perhaps this was a match made in heaven after all.

Sandra Gurvis
Columbus, Ohio
September 15, 1995

A last thought: In order to obtain the broadest and most varied coverage, the term "visionary shrine" is used for everything from places with healing water, but no actual sightings, to Jesus trees that no longer exist. If I offend any purists, I apologize in advance.

As the millennium approaches, more and more religious sightings and visionary-type occurrences seem to be taking place. A goodly portion center around the Virgin Mary and many visionaries are women, although there are notable exceptions.

The majority of the phenomena listed in *Way Stations to Heaven: 50 Major Visionary Shrines in the United States* took place after 1985. Only one house of worship, the Chapel of the Faith Baptist Church in Los Angeles, was not Roman or Orthodox Catholic. Their window cross, discovered in 1971, can still be seen today.

Much of the recent fervor can be traced to Medjugorje, in the former Yugoslavia. In 1981, six children in the village reported seeing daily apparitions of the Virgin Mary. Despite the dangers of travelling in that war-torn country, millions of tourists heeded their call, experiencing their own revelations, healings, and conversions. Another influence was the Second Vatican Council (Vatican II, 1962–65), which not only downplayed Mary's role in the Church, but removed some of the traditional aspects of worship, such as Latin in services and kneeling before the Eucharist. Many of the faithful, especially older individuals, call for a return to the previous ways.

But *Way Stations to Heaven* is not about theology or religious debate. Rather, it is a guidebook to various sights, shrines, and visionaries in the United States. And although assorted magazines, Mary "hotlines," and academics have made a study of these phenomena, there seems to be no central information base, especially in this country. This book hopes to fill the gap.

Although we know the approximate number of Protestants (80 million) and Catholics (57 million) in the U.S., no statistics seem to be available on how many actually visit these shrines. The very nature of such tourism is ephemeral; people seem to float in and out, sharing stories and experiences. Other individuals roam from place to place, while still others attend a particular site or service frequently. And when an image first appears, thousands or even ten times that can show up. Depending upon what happens to the image, their numbers may gradually or rapidly dwindle.

How to Use This Book

Way Stations to Heaven: 50 Major Visionary Shrines in the United States is meant for everyone, from believers to skeptics and the gradations in between. Each chapter delves into a discussion of the place and how events transpired, providing background details, history of the vision/image, and interviews with the major players (Mary and Jesus were unavailable for comment, however, except sometimes allegedly through the visionaries). Even those who don't plan an actual visit can obtain a great deal of information here.

The "What to Expect" section offers a description of the shrine and, when possible, a gauge of the attitude of the people there. This can be quite useful. For instance, if you're planning to stop by the Christ of the Hills Monastery in Blanco, Texas, you might want to know about their dress code. Other places, such as St. John of God Church in Chicago, may not be practical to visit at all. Not only is the weeping statue gone (an address for more information is provided), but the church is closed altogether. And some places, such as the St. Maria Goretti Church in Scottsdale, discourage visits by nonbelievers.

"What They Say" consists of direct quotes from attendees, doubters, and other participants. Here, people express their thoughts, feelings, and emotions about the shrine or event. Whenever possible, the full spectrum of viewpoints is portrayed.

"How to Get There" is self-explanatory. Along with directions, this section lists mailing addresses, phone numbers, and hours of operation, if available.

Each chapter in *Way Stations to Heaven* is a self-contained unit. A bibliography/source list at the end of the book provides further information.

Common Threads and Differences

Most of us, it seems, want the same thing: a happy family life, good health, peace of mind, work we enjoy. And, along with obedience to various religious tenets and directives, prayers and supplications mostly revolved around these topics. Manifestations such as spinning suns, rosaries changing from silver to gold, fragrance of roses, and inexplicable healings and other changes seemed almost symptomatic of many of these places—a sort of Virgin sighting syndrome or VSS, if you will.

Although they sometimes overlap, the sites themselves seemed to fall into various categories, including the following:

Established churches and shrines. Churches such as St. Lucy's in the Bronx and Our Lady of Consolation in Carey, Ohio offer physical and spiritual healing. St. Lucy's holy water and the Our Lady of Consolation statue have aided countless visitors for decades. Although not officially acknowledged, they are highly regarded and accepted within the mainstream of Catholicism. No miracles of the sun and moon and "doors to heaven" are found here, at least not according to their caretakers.

Other places, like the Mother Cabrini Shrine in Denver and St. Francis Cathedral in Santa Fe, have been faced with visionaries and VSS. Theresa Lopez was the instigator at Mother Cabrini, as was Vangie Peterson at St. Francis, to a much lesser extent. Such situations can be problematic for church officials, who must not only deal with greatly differing viewpoints but also with inquiries from the public and media.

God's little acres. Here, visionaries strike out on their own, acquiring land, buildings, and/or an entourage. Strong personalities such as Nancy Fowler (Conyers, Georgia), Veronica Leuken (Bayside, New York), Alfredo Raimondo (Tickfaw, Louisiana), and others garnered enough support to develop an organized network around their messages and beliefs.

An exception is Terry Colafrancesco. Founder of Caritas of Birmingham, he claims not to be a visionary. But he has constructed quite a tabernacle at Caritas and credits a Medjugorje visionary for some of the happenings on the land.

Appearances on ordinary objects. These invariably attract the most attention and skepticism. The shape of Our Lady of Guadalupe on the floor of an auto parts store (Progreso, Texas); a "Pasta Jesus" on a Pizza Hut billboard (Atlanta); and an image on a soybean oil tank (Fostoria, Ohio) are several examples. The Blessed Mother and her Son also seem to have a fondness for trees (New Haven, Connecticut; Fairfield, Maine; Holden, West Virginia; and others), tortillas (Lake Arthur, New Mexico), and rocks (Medway, Massachusetts).

Weeping statues/icons. Although the Roman Catholics claim some weeping statues (St. John of God, Chicago; St. Elizabeth Ann Seton Church, Lake Ridge, Virginia), the Orthodox Catholics by far have the majority of crying icons, at least in the United States. The fathers at St. Nicholas Albanian Orthodox Church in Chicago; St. George Antiochian Orthodox Church in Cicero, Illinois; St. Paul's Greek Orthodox Church in Hempstead, New York; and others seem to welcome such events. The official Roman Catholic stance appears to be on the same level as that of women priests—nice try, but forget about it.

Statues also blink (Holy Trinity Church, Ambridge, Pennsylvania), change colors (Our Lady of Pompeii, Paterson, New Jersey), and move around (Mater Ecclesiae Mission Church, Thornton, California). In 1979, a wallet-sized portrait of Jesus allegedly bled in Roswell, New Mexico, but the owner died and her surviving relatives refuse to discuss the matter.

Group visions. Every so often a group of faithful will start having visions in, er, *en masse*. Events at the St. Maria Goretti Church in Scottsdale and at St. John Neumann Church in Lubbock, Texas resulted in major outbreaks of VSS, the effects of which are still felt by the churches and the faithful.

At a Greek Orthodox camp in Mercer, Pennsylvania, a bunch of *icons* (nineteen to be exact) started crying in 1988. Only one remains today, and is periodically on display at St. Nicholas Greek Orthodox Church.

Non-shrines. Although neither the Laura Arroyo billboard in Chula Vista, California or the Chapel of the Holy Cross in Sedona, Arizona are visionary shrines per se, enough activity surrounded them to warrant inclusion in this book. The faithful who saw Laura's image on the billboard prayed for the identification of her killer. And the Sedona vortexes stir up lots of spiritual feeling, although some is not exactly Church-approved. The point was to depict as broad a cross-section as possible within the Christian faith.

Real vs. "Fake"?

A main concern seems to be: How can you tell whether a shrine is genuine or not, whether the people are sincere or charlatans trying to brainwash their followers and steal your hard-earned cash? Certain "experts" have made an art of debunking such happenings. Some, such as Shawn Carlson and Joe Nickell, are cited throughout the text and in the foreword and bibliography. James Randi, also known as the Amazing Randi, also has two books, *The Faith Healers* (New York: Prometheus, 1989) and the newer *Encyclopedia of Claims, Frauds, and Hoaxes of the Occult and Supernatural* (New York: St. Martin's, 1995).

Other behaviors may also provide a clue. For instance, those unwilling to share information may have something to hide. Some visionaries also exhibit a high level of paranoia and surround themselves with possessive and rather strange individuals. And listen to what the visionary says: if she praises her relationship to God and her own goodness rather than focusing on spirituality, a certain egotism may be at work.

But, as with most things, the final evaluation must come from within. And since no one has actually seen God (or at least can prove it), we'll just have to content ourselves with our own instincts.

✝ Double Exposure at Walker Baptist Medical Center

Walker Baptist Medical Center
Jasper, Alabama

How It Happened

Like a twice-baked potato, the Walker Baptist Medical Center (formerly the Walker Regional Medical Center) has been through the heat two times. But workers at this large community hospital located in the middle of the Bible Belt seem to take national attention to Jesus-related sightings in stride.

The first incident began with a near-tragedy. On April 9, 1983, 16-year-old Ray Naramore was brought to Walker following a motorcycle accident. The boy was fighting for his life; he'd had a violent reaction to anesthesia. Medics struggled to bring down his 107-degree temperature and stabilize his vital signs.

As his father Joel stood in the hallway praying, he noticed a "glossy and bright figure with a penetrating look" on the door leading to the operating room. "I was leaning against the wall in an almost daze," the elder Naramore told the Jasper *Daily Mountain Eagle*. ". . .The first thing I noticed were the eyes and then I could see the other features. . . . I thought to myself then that somebody was looking over us." Shortly afterwards, the doctors came out and told him Ray had stabilized. The boy eventually recovered.

Although Joel Naramore intended to share the miracle only with friends and family, he did point out the image to one nurse. That's all it took: Soon thousands flocked from far and wide. The local and national press and the then-popular TV show "That's Incredible!" showed up at the door. Suddenly the whole world seemed interested in Jasper, Alabama.

Hospital personnel swear the door changed color and appearance from when it was originally finished and hung. "It is not a hoax," administrator James Armour insisted in *The Star*. "I know

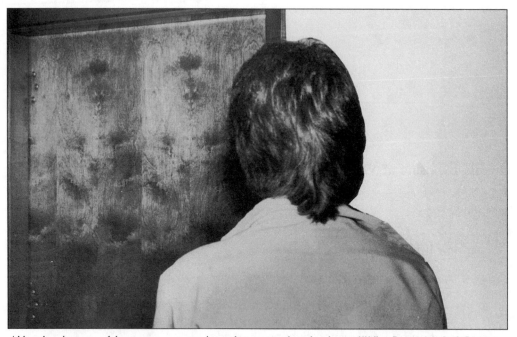

Although a depiction of Jesus was prominent when it first appeared on this door at Walker Baptist Medical Center in Jasper, Alabama, it has faded somewhat over the years. PHOTO COURTESY OF WALKER BAPTIST MEDICAL CENTER.

something happened to the door. We did not do anything to it. There is a phenomenon there that is different."

However, Armour resisted moving the door to the lobby where it could be more easily accessed by the public, expressing the philosophy that if God had intended it to be someplace else, He would have put it there. So every night between 7 and 10 pm, small groups of visitors trooped down the hallway to the operating room for brief viewings. Some kneeled and crossed themselves; others came with the hopes of being healed or helping loved ones do the same.

People claimed to discern eyes, pupils, eyebrows, a nose, and a mouth. Some compared the likeness to the controversial Shroud of Turin, the supposed burial cloth of Jesus Christ that has his image imprinted on it.

Still, there were disbelievers: According to an account in *The Atlanta Journal,* a heavy woman in a wheelchair "scandalized the entire crowd by loudly stating that all it looked like to her was a damn old door." Others, while thinking it resembled *something,* weren't totally convinced it was Jesus.

A second image, said by one employee to also favor actor Chuck Norris, was discovered on an X ray in March 1994. A few months before, a victim of a car crash had been taken to Walker for X rays before being rushed to a Birmingham hospital. The 39-year-old coal miner insisted on anonymity, although his brother and sister-in-law, Dwight and Donna Hicks, spoke extensively to the media. "He had a broken neck," observes Donna. "The doctors said if his neck had been moved half a centimeter one way, he would have been paralyzed and if it had gone the other way, he would have died." In spite of the seriousness of the wreck, the man walked away seemingly intact.

Several weeks later, the man's doctor called him into the office. He showed the man and his family the X ray taken of his upper spine through his mouth. Inside the jaws and superimposed over the bones was an image of a long-haired, bearded man with flowing robes and hands clasped in prayer. Jesus, it seemed, had reared his head again.

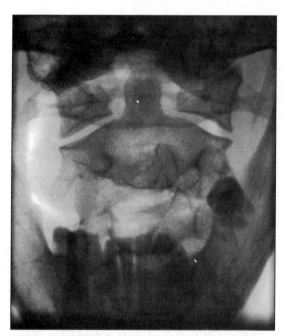

This "Jesus X ray" (or likeness of Chuck Norris, depending upon one's interpretation) at the Walker Baptist Medical Center in Jasper, Alabama, was of the neck and vertebrae of an anonymous coal miner. PHOTO COURTESY OF WALKER BAPTIST MEDICAL CENTER.

"The doctor said the Good Lord had held my brother's neck up for him," Donna Hicks told the *Daily Mountain Eagle*. Although her brother-in-law appeared unmoved by a religious revelation, both Hickses were deeply affected.

"There ain't nobody who can explain why it's there," added Dwight. "I see the image as good as anyone. I don't know how it's affected me, but I wonder about my brother and hope he'll get to church regularly."

"To me, I'd take it as a warning," continued Donna in the interview. "If it were my X ray, I'd be down on my knees 24 hours a day."

According to the hospital, the image was caused by neither malfunctioning equipment nor outdated film. "This film was properly exposed at the proper settings and there's nothing on it that makes me think it might have been tampered with,"

Rita Edwards, director of radiology at Walker, remarked to the *Mountain Eagle*. "I've never seen anything like it."

But compared to the "Jesus door," the X ray was a mere drop in the publicity bucket. It was displayed in the lobby for a few months, then quietly put away. "Mostly people from around Birmingham came to see it," explains Susan Darby, community relations director for the hospital. "It was written up in local papers and the *National Enquirer,* and that was about it." Still, "people did claim to have been touched by the hand of God and one lady fainted when she saw the X ray."

Yet the daily beat of hospital life goes on. "Someone asked me if I thought [the occurrences were] a miracle," Patrick Willingham, CEO of the hospital, said in *The Birmingham News.* "I told them that we have miracles every day here . . . due to the work of our doctors, our nurses, and our staff. But sometimes we have unexplained miracles, where head trauma victims and gunshot victims survive despite all medical evidence to the contrary."

What to Expect

The Jesus door is immediately recognizable by its plexiglas cover. Consisting of mismatched wood grain, it seems to be divided into two halves, with "normal" lumber on the bottom and the image on top. The eyes are the most immediately discernible (at one time, they were said to glow in the dark) but you may have to stare at it for a while to make out the rest of the face. "The image has faded somewhat over the years," observes Susan Darby. Although still in its original location, the door now leads to a chapel for meditation, instead of an operating room.

The X-ray image will jump right out at most viewers. Although radiologists point out that similar shapes have appeared in X rays taken from the same angle, none are quite as distinct. You can see hair, a beard, and a face. Whether it's Chuck or Jesus is anybody's guess.

What They Say

Joel Naramore, Jasper, Alabama: Naramore, who worked as a switchhouse operator in a power plant, seemed to handle the attention with equilibrium. "After all this, I'm not just going to start toting a Bible everywhere and become fanatical about the situation," he stated in an interview in *Powergrams,* his company newsletter. "I'm going to be rational about it and reassess my life.

"People will have to reach their own conclusions about what the door means to them. There will be a lot of critics, but I wanted to tell . . . this story, and let [people] make up their own minds about it. I'm not going to hold back. . . . I am just going to tell it like it happened and hope it becomes an inspiration for them. My experience . . . has a purpose."

Donna Hicks, Nauvoo, Alabama: Hicks was also present the night the Jesus door vision appeared to Naramore. There was no question in her mind that it was real: "I was visiting my mother who had cancer. It affected a lot of people and made their beliefs stronger."

Yet the X ray hit much closer to home. "Nothing like this ever happened to our family, so the image really changed our lives. It showed us that God is with us and made it plain that He was there the night of my brother-in-law's accident. I had faith before; now I have even more."

Lester Puckett, Walker County: "People shout when they see [the door]," Puckett, a guard at the hospital, told *The Star.* "They weep and kneel and pray before [it] and want to reach out and touch it."

The uproar hadn't made his job any easier, such as when three men "ran up from the hospital holding up their arms and shouting, 'Praise the Lord.'"

How to Get There

About 45 minutes from Birmingham, Jasper can be reached via 78W. Walker Baptist Medical Center is located on the outskirts of town, at the second traffic light on the left-hand side.

To get to the Jesus door, take the elevator from the main lobby, get off at the second floor, exit right, and go through the surgery area waiting room entryway. The door is the first on the right and is covered with plexiglas.

Those who wish to view the X ray can inquire at the lobby desk. Visitors are preferred during business or hospital visiting hours. Walker Baptist Medical Center, P.O. Box 3547, Jasper, AL 35502, 205/387-4169.

✝ Medjugorje Pipeline

Caritas of Birmingham
Sterrett, Alabama

How It Happened

Did you know that:

- George Washington had visions of the Virgin Mary and predicted the Revolutionary War, the Civil War, and a third "great peril" due at the end of this century?

- In 1963, Satan supposedly entered the courts and ended school prayer? That since then, unwed birth rates have gone up 218%, student sexually transmitted diseases have risen 300%, SAT scores have taken a nosedive and violent crime has increased sevenfold?

Caritas of Birmingham hopes to "enlighten" visitors and students to these and other points, as well as hark back to a time when a man was sentenced to three months in jail and fined $500 for wanting to take Christianity out of the schools (*People vs. Ruggles,* 1811). They also organize excursions to Medjugorje via BVM (Blessed Virgin Mary) pilgrimages and sell related books, audiocassettes, and videotapes. And their own properties have become a destination point for visionaries, prayer groups, and some priests. Some of their monies allegedly go for aid to war-torn Bosnia-Herzegovina.

"The Catholic textbooks have become too liberal in their interpretation of issues such as sexuality and abortion," observes a volunteer who asked to remain anonymous. One of about 30 residents who lives on the grounds, he gives tours to visitors and pitches in wherever needed. According to him, parochial books "describe things like contraception in great detail, then waffle on the issues of right and wrong."

To combat this, the organization is gearing up to form its own publishing company. Caritas already prints and distributes a newsletter with a circulation of over 220,000. Although it is free, subscribers are encouraged to become "Field Angels" and mail in donations. And for $50, you can purchase a piece of their 35,000-square-foot Tabernacle (offer expires December 8, 2003, when all names will be sealed in a cornerstone).

A few years ago, the $1.3 million Tabernacle, apparition site, travel agency/information center, and attendant buildings were but a cow pasture. Then in 1986 Birmingham businessman and frequent Medjugorje flier Terry Colafrancesco founded Caritas (Latin for "love of all people") with the intent of promoting pilgrimages to then-Yugoslavia. According to *The Birmingham News,* Colafrancesco was building up a brisk enterprise.

One of the Medjugorje schoolchildren who since 1981 had been receiving messages from Mary, Marija Pavlovic made the acquaintance of Colafrancesco during his visits there. In 1988, when he learned she was to donate a kidney to her brother, he suggested the procedure be done at Birmingham's University Hospital, and opened his home to both Pavlovics.

In seeming anticipation of Marija's arrival, Colafrancesco purchased a 90-acre field next to his property. According to *The Birmingham News,* he mowed around an evergreen tree where she was later to have a vision. He placed a crucifix and Madonna statue on the site and installed a public address system.

Marija Palovic allegedly had a vision at this tree at Caritas of Birmingham. The field was conveniently prepared for her arrival. PHOTO BY SANDRA GURVIS.

Described by the Rev. Joseph A. Pelletier as "the most serene and deeply spiritual of the seers" and by *The Atlanta Journal and Constitution* as a Kristy McNichol look-alike, Marija, who was then in her early twenties, proceeded with business as usual. She had visions at Colafrancesco's home, in his field on Thanksgiving Day, and even at the hospital during surgery. They related to the themes of great commitment, faith, prayer, and fasting as well as threats of catastrophe caused by neglecting God. And although she stayed less than two months, pilgrims came by the thousands.

It wasn't even a matter of actually seeing the visionary: The field was now considered holy by osmosis. Pilgrims accepted communion and priests heard confessions. Masses were held. "God doesn't take his blessings back," Reverend Larry Kubera told *The Birmingham News.* "The blessing is not because of any individual." Caritas, it seems, had become a sort of Medjugorje spinoff.

But Colafrancesco had detractors. Neighbor Bob Lucky, disturbed by the public address system, took direct action. "It got where I couldn't watch television in my house during the summer, so I invented an air horn for 'em," he told *The Birmingham News*.

Another neighbor, Jim Tanner, became suspicious when Colafrancesco began to groom the field months before Marija's arrival. He told the *News* he overheard Colafrancesco ask Marija if she was going to have a vision by the tree the next day. But he also expressed belief in the Pavlovics' sincerity: "I don't think it's right for [Colafrancesco] to manipulate her and her brother like that."

The Diocese of Birmingham prohibited construction of a church and the holding of Mass on Caritas grounds. Although Bishop David E. Foley issued a statement recognizing Colafrancesco's "deep devotion to Medjugorje," he added that Colafrancesco and those at Caritas are "a group of pious people who have set this business up."

But Caritas has taken root, reaching out to a greater and greater sphere of believers. The organizers keep in touch with Pavlovic, who is now married. "Marija visited us a few months ago, but she was pregnant so we kept things private," explained the tour guide. Private retreats as well as visiting icons, such as one from France that presumably exuded oils and fragrance, keep things humming.

They also accept Visa and MasterCard.

What to Expect

The organization tries to keep a low profile, particularly in the media. But visitors will find an incredibly tranquil atmosphere amid abundant greenery that may cause reflection in even the most truncated souls. And the volunteers are friendly.

The Tabernacle alone is worth the trip. Made of red mountain stone and lacy-looking glass and fronted by a winding staircase, it rises amidst gently curving hills. The inside and outside are replete with statuary from aging churches; encased in the foundations are old rosaries, medals, and scapulars donated by the faithful. "The construction workers, many of whom were non-Catholic, found a great sense of peace here and performed their jobs admirably," observes the volunteer. The apparition site across the street is eerily placid and on sunlit days, almost blindingly lush.

Despite the external serenity, the inside is a hive of activity. Acronyms abound: along with BVM Pilgrimages, there's OLPG (Our Lady's Prayer Groups), OIM (Operation Introducing Medjugorje), ATIS (Automated Telephone Information Systems), and others.

Computers, a printing facility, and an up-to-date travel agency round out operations.

Those who wish to extend their stay can participate in five-day retreats. The schedule includes prayers, services, and treks around the grounds. A base price covers meals in addition to hotel reservations and transfers. "Many of our visitors go on to Medjugorje," adds the volunteer.

What They Say

Kelli Hewett, Birmingham, Alabama: A reporter for *The Birmingham News* during Pavlovic's 1988 visit, Hewett recalls Colafrancesco as being very evasive with the media. "There was no getting past him," she recalls. During one of Pavlovic's visions, "He had us wait outside his house in the rain and freezing cold. You could sort of see something was happening but couldn't tell exactly what."

She found the onrush of pilgrims to Sterrett disconcerting, "almost like a mania. Suddenly we were inundated with busloads of visitors and inquiries from travel agencies. And these were supposedly educated, upper-middle-class people. Yet nothing was substantiated."

Mike O'Neal, Birmingham, Alabama: According to *The Atlanta Journal and Constitution,* O'Neal was a pilot and former FBI agent who, with his family, planned to move from Chicago to Birmingham to be part of the Caritas community. "I read a book about Medjugorje and I knew it was true," he said. "I told my wife, 'I have a feeling this is bigger than we can imagine.'"

He planned to "live the messages" of Our Lady which came courtesy of the Medjugorje visionaries. Part of his inspiration, he said, was that some of the silver links in his rosary had turned golden. The changing represents "a door. You can stand there and look at the door, or you can walk through it."

His new calling took him around the country to spread the Caritas message. "I was an FBI agent for 20 years. I worked kidnappings, bank robberies, and extortions. Nobody ever told me then that I was an answer to a prayer."

Frans Labranche, Abita Springs, Louisiana: "There is an aura of peace present," Labranche told the *Birmingham Post-Herald.* A deacon, he helped hand out the Eucharist (consecrated bread) to the faithful during gatherings. "The people are not pushing or shoving." Pavlovic's appearance "is a special way to pay reverence to the Blessed Mother. We're not expecting a miracle . . . most of the people are here to be together, to pray, and to ask the Virgin Mary to intercede with her Son."

How to Get There

Caritas is located about 20 miles south of Birmingham. Take I-280E to County Highway 43 and turn left. Go about six miles and look for a "100 Our Lady Queen of Peace Dr." sign on the left-hand side. Open seven days a week. 100 Our Lady Queen of Peace Dr., Sterrett, AL 35147, 205/672-2000.

✝ Mary Branches Out

Immaculate Heart of Mary Church
Phoenix, Arizona

How It Happened

On December 12, 1989, an unidentified man spotted a strange-looking yucca branch outside a bar at the corner of Van Buren and 11th Streets. What made this particular limb special was that it appeared to be shaped just like popular depictions of Our Lady of Guadalupe and the date just happened to coincide with the feast day of this patron saint of Mexico. Never mind that the poor little stalk was shot at, made fun of, and eventually ripped from the mother tree in the poverty-stricken, primarily Hispanic neighborhood. This only reinforced the faith of thousands of believers who came to bask in the presence of Our Lady, and ensured it a place of honor at the Immaculate Heart of Mary Church in Phoenix.

Our Lady of Guadalupe has special meaning to Hispanic peoples and their forbears. In 1521, when the Spaniards conquered Mexico City, the Aztecs were enslaved. "They felt as if they had nothing to live for," historian Leonard Anguiano of the Mexican-American Cultural Center in San Antonio explained in the *Phoenix Gazette.* A few years later, Our Lady of Guadalupe appeared before a visionary, telling him to build a temple on the spot where she stood, and the Indians were "filled with hope again."

The church remains today, where it continues to draw great numbers of pilgrims. "It is an especially inspiring sight to the poor and oppressed," Anguiano continued. The Blessed Mother is "always a ray of hope when things seem the worst."

So it seemed to follow with the yucca branch. Within hours of its discovery, the base of the plant was transformed into a makeshift shrine, surrounded by votive candles, hand-hewn crosses, flowers, and baskets of donations. Hundreds of people mobbed the site, causing traffic congestion and general mayhem. The scene was also hazardous to the plant's health as "people were plucking away the blossoms, leaves, and bark," recalls Father Tony Sotelo of Immaculate Heart. The final insult occurred when two self-described "guerrilla artists" severed the bough, much to the distress of the crowd.

Although the pranksters were arrested and the branch recovered, Sotelo wanted to turn over a new leaf. "When the police returned the branch to me, we decided to move it to Immaculate Heart," he remarks. "We already had a shrine, so this just added to it." On January 22, he led a procession that crowded into the small chapel, placing the twisted bough at the foot of a life-sized statue of Our Lady of Guadalupe which sits atop a pile of rocks. People came from as far away as Colorado and Mexico to pay their respects.

Even some in the Diocese of Phoenix expressed their support. According to Primo Romero, director of the Spanish-speaking office there, the outline of the Virgin Mary in a dried stalk can be a symbol to believers that "she hasn't abandoned them," he commented in the *Gazette*. In the neighborhood where the limb was found, "it's easy to feel forgotten. So here comes this sign that helps [people] believe God remembers His promise that the poor shall gain heaven. It gives them a sense of peace. . . ."

The scoffers, including the two "artists," may be barking up the wrong tree. "One thing that upgrades a saint is persecution," Tod Swanson, assistant professor of Christian studies at Arizona State University, told the *Gazette*. "The detractors play a large role in upgrading a holy object's status and turning it into a shrine."

An offshoot of the branch is a revitalized enthusiasm for the Church. "When you're battling the problems of drugs, domestic violence, and dropouts, how can you fault something that brings joy and renewed faith?" adds Sotelo. "It's not my place to say whether it's a miracle, but it's brought people closer to God and that's good enough for me."

What to Expect

Because the faithful were a bit too enthusiastic, taking delicate sprouts as part of their devotions, the branch now stands out of reach to the right of Our Lady's head. It really does appear to mirror the statue's exact dimensions. A large photograph of the original yucca tree and a plaque commemorating Our Lady of "the Corner" complete the tableau.

Father Sotelo welcomes all comers to his small (about 500 people) but homey house of worship, with its simple wooden pews and twin white stucco towers. "Initially we had a big rush, but the novelty has worn off," he observes. Still, people continue to stop by and attendance has increased along with Sunday Masses, which are up to seven from four in 1989. "The truly spiritual things aren't spectacular but take place in a quiet way."

What They Say

Amanda Pulido, Phoenix, Arizona: Although Pulido had her doubts about finding Our Lady in a yucca branch, the experience moved her to tears. ". . . When I got there and saw all these people . . . who would never be near a church in the middle of the week . . . I had a really good feeling," she confided to the *Phoenix Gazette.*

Of the detractors, she observed, "If we want to pray aloud to a yucca plant, we shouldn't have to make any excuses. I would no sooner kick a Muslim kneeling towards Mecca or stomp on the sacred burial ground of the Indians. . . . We live in a country [with] freedom of religion. And my ways, no matter how crazy they may seem to you, must be respected."

Dick Croell and Carol Dohm, Denver, Colorado: "We are very devoted to the Blessed Mother and would not be surprised by anything she would do to get her message across," Croell said in the *Gazette.* He and his fiancee Dohm had just returned from Medjugorje. "Nothing happens by accident. Things always happen for a reason. Maybe this branch grew in this particular shape to bring attention to the Church and to Mary. Whatever it is, it is a good force."

Father Thomas O'Brien, Phoenix, Arizona: As head of the Diocese of Phoenix, O'Brien was less enthusiastic. "Unfortunately, we have a society that does not respect God or the values being taught in our religious institutions," he told *The Arizona Republic.* "There is a hunger . . . for an experience of God's presence. . . . People are looking for signs that God is here. When society begins to be oppressive in terms of religious experiences, people will find ways to overcome that oppression. Their hunger must be fulfilled."

How to Get There

The Immaculate Heart of Mary Church is just off I-10 in Phoenix. From the east, take the Jefferson/Washington exit and go west on Washington, where it's at the corner of 9th and Washington. From the west, take the 7th St. exit, cross Jefferson, and go east on Washington. The easiest access is through the west door of the church. Hours are 6 a.m.–6 p.m., except for Sunday when it's open until after the 7:15 p.m. Mass. 909 E. Washington Ave., Phoenix, AZ 85034-1093, 602/253-6129.

✟ Yuppie Visions at St. Maria Goretti

St. Maria Goretti Church
Scottsdale, Arizona

How It Happened

Every Thursday night, a group of twenty- and thirty-somethings meet at the St. Maria Goretti Catholic Church. They supposedly welcome all to their prayer circle, but "if [people] come to be spectators and see all the visionaries and talk to me, they're barking up the wrong tree," the group leader, Rev. Jack Spaulding, warned in the Associated Press. "This hasn't turned into a three-ring circus."

Well OK, but why Scottsdale—one of the most affluent communities in the country—and why a bunch of self-proclaimed yuppies? The core group of nine visionaries and Spaulding, who also claims to have conversations with Jesus and Mary, got together in the late '80s. Spaulding, whose symbol is "truth" (more on that later), started receiving messages while in Medjugorje and began to be approached by young people who informed him that they, too, were hearing Big Voices from Upstairs.

Many had degrees, high-powered jobs, and marriages. Yet they gave up the trappings of supposed success to help the Virgin Mary "meet the Devil on his own ground," Spaulding said in *Our Lady Comes to Scottsdale,* a book on the St. Maria Goretti happenings authored by Father Robert Faricy and Sister Lucy Rooney, themselves experts on Medjugorje and claimed apparitions. The visionaries' goal: to turn the hearts of the youth of America towards Jesus and Mary.

Through himself and the visionaries, some of whom had accompanied Spaulding to Medjugorje, "If we . . . with God's help [can] convert . . . anybody can," Spaulding said. "The kids kid around— that they have committed every sin in the book. So anybody who comes can't say, 'Oh, you were always so holy.' No they weren't."

Mary supposedly manifests herself from a statue in the church to four of the women. First she glows, assumes a human form, then steps out of the statue as a dark-haired, blue-eyed white female between the ages of 18 and 25 with great skin. The visionaries describe her as Our Lady of Joy. A picture published by the church resembles a sort of celestial Julia Roberts bearing an armful of white roses.

Like Father Spaulding, each visionary is said to represent a virtue of Jesus's heart. As individuals, the nine are responsible for these symbols:

Divine love and mercy. That would be Gianna Talone-Sullivan, who holds a doctoral degree in pharmacology and at the time was divorced. Along with daily conversations with and visits from Jesus and Mary, the former whom she described as "incredibly handsome," Gianna also endures nightly assaults from the Devil. "She can wake up with bruises on her body," says the book. "Jesus has told her this is for purposes of redemption, to help others to be saved, and for Gianna's own greater strength."

She has the distinction of being the first whom Jesus and Mary visited in Scottsdale and appears to have the greatest number of visions. She also claimed to have a dream in which she "saw" the other women and men who were to become visionaries. Gianna gave up her day job in management for a pharmaceutical company to work in a Catholic hospital in Phoenix, and recently reappeared as a visionary in Emmitsburg, Maryland (see page 100).

Humility is Annie Ross's sign. An escapee from a marriage to a Turkish Moslem, she began hearing voices and having visions in 1989. Mary "asked" her to write various messages, an experience Annie describes with a "Wow!"

Since she "learned from Our Lady that to be humble is to serve the Father unconditionally," she has since given up her beloved flower-arranging business, a request supposedly made by the Lord. Apparently no such restrictions have been made on her upcoming nuptials to a longtime family friend.

Strength and faith. Siblings Wendy and Steve Nelson were raised in South Dakota and Nebraska, moving near the Goretti church several years ago. A former sorority girl at Arizona State University, Wendy (strength) left all that jazz to dedicate herself to prayer groups and Mass.

She had also lived and worked with the Missionaries of Charity in Phoenix, an organization sponsored by Mother Teresa that deals with underprivileged children. After hearing voices, she too turned over her life to Jesus. As for milestones like marrying or joining a religious order, "I leave it to divine inspiration. . . . They [Jesus and Mary] decide."

Although Steve (faith) dreamed of becoming a rodeo star, Jesus and Mary put that scheme on hold. "At first, he said to himself . . . they could not possibly ask him to give up his calf wrestling and roping," comments the book. He attended medical technology courses at a community college with possible plans to train as a fireman. Or he might become a priest. As for his self-described "direct plug-in to God," he intends on using his "sinfulness" to help people. "If they took me as more than what I am, what good would I be for them?"

Suffering. Susan Evans has seen plenty of that. According to the book, she developed lupus and scleroderma (skin disorders), fibromyalgia (chronic muscle and joint pain), and hearing loss in addition to emotional and spiritual distress. Physicians may not always be sympathetic to her ailments, so the Lord is her doctor. "If you dwell on your suffering, which is easy to do, you are going to hurt more," she remarked in the book. "But to pray and be filled with His peace, His love, His joy, then your suffering is easier."

Hope is the byword for former sales representative Mary Cook. "When I was 25, I had the big sports car, was making money, trying to impress with clothes," she confided to the Associated Press. Then "I decided it wasn't worth it—the drinking, the traveling, wheeling and dealing." So Mary became a waitress, then worked with the teen program with the Goretti parish, finally landing a job with the preschool there. Like Gianna, she receives messages which Father Spaulding sometimes reads to the prayer group.

Courage. The youngest, James Pauley, still lived at home when he joined the group. He was included because Gianna had seen him in her fateful dream and, according to the book, Spaulding told him he was "one of Mary's children," although James didn't "know exactly what that means." So he dutifully went to Mexico to work among the poor and became involved in the parish's teen program. He had yet to experience visions or interior locutions.

Compassion. Like James, Jimmy Kupanoff hadn't seen the Blessed Virgin in the "flesh" although she has "spoken to him a few times, in clear words, in his heart." A major in communications, he was one of the first in the group to make the 1987 pilgrimage to Medjugorje.

Joy. Last but certainly not least is Stefanie Staab, a graduate of Arizona State University who works as an accountant. Having grown up among several divorces and remarriages, Stefanie credits Mary with putting her (Stefanie) on the road to piety. Yet although she claims to speak with Mary regularly, she still skis, does target shooting, listens to jazz (Christian, of course), and jogs. "I feel like a lady-in-waiting sometimes, kind of waiting for [Jesus] to tell me what to do."

Although the archdiocese hasn't exactly tried to stamp it out, they stated that the happenings "are explainable within the range of ordinary human experience." However, they commended the visionaries' devotion to the Church as well as Spaulding's efforts, allowing the prayer groups because they encouraged faith.

Attendance at the St. Maria Goretti groups continues to spiral into the thousands. And even though no one there is talking, it's a good bet the "Scottsdale Yuppies" will continue to draw in the faithful.

What to Expect

Located in the chic and sunny suburb of Scottsdale, the exterior of the St. Maria Goretti Church looks more like a landing dock for a spaceship than a traditional Catholic shrine. With over 2,500 families, it boasts two priests as well as assorted assistants, secretaries, receptionists, and a music director. Along with the several prayer groups, active programs include marital, bereavement, and teen counseling and several schools. Many of the services and programs take place in the large tabernacle.

However, strangers—particularly those who aren't total believers—are looked upon rather suspiciously. So if you want to ingratiate yourself with Spaulding and the visionaries, act as if you've been there before. The church is open most hours to those who want to wander in and look around, and prayer groups are held in the taber-nacle on Thursdays at 7:00 p.m.

What They Say

Father Jack Spaulding, Scottsdale, Arizona: "From the beginning, I knew this was bigger than I could control or handle," Spaulding said in the book. "My spiritual director . . . says, 'Who are we to say that God can or can't act?' We have to allow things to unfold in their timing. But I had been praying, 'Lord, help me to understand,' by which I meant 'Lord, help me to control.' All of us see that what is asked of us is the 'yes' of obedience—the kind of obedience our Lord has, blind, just saying 'yes'."

Father Ernest Larkin, Phoenix, Arizona: As head of the Dio-cese commission investigating the visionaries, Father Larkin voiced this in *The Catholic Sun:* "We don't think that these are hoaxes or that there is any attempt to deceive anybody. We simply maintain that there is not enough evidence to say that these are miracles. We're not saying that it's impossible that these are miracles, we're just saying that it's impossible to conclude that these are miracles."

Sister Mary Therese Sedlock, Phoenix, Arizona: Also part of the commission, Sister Mary Therese expressed her beliefs more succinctly in the book. She felt parishioners might be placing too much emphasis on the visions and messages instead of "just living a life of faith and the spirit of Jesus." Of Father Spaulding and the visionaries she observed, "I felt they lacked a certain openness."

How to Get There

From downtown Phoenix, take I-10E to Rural Rd. and turn left; it will become Scottsdale. From Scottsdale, turn right to McDonald and take a left at Granite Reef. The church is on the second block. St. Maria Goretti Church, 6261 N. Granite Reef, Scottsdale, AZ 85250, 602/948-8380.

✟ New Age Vortex or Vacuum?

Chapel of the Holy Cross
Sedona, Arizona

How It Happened

Although it's not a visionary shrine per se, Sedona *is* a mecca for mystical revelations. "This is the only city in the U.S. that has 80 channels but no TV station," local author Jim Bishop quipped in the *Los Angeles Times*. Along with half-a-dozen or so power spots or "vortexes," there is the Chapel of the Holy Cross, a futuristic Catholic shrine conceived in 1932 and finished almost twenty-five years later.

According to author Richard Dannelley, author of several books about the area, all religions come from the same source, anyway. "The great cathedrals in Europe are on points containing the primary energy pattern of the universe," he explains. "Jesuit priests used dowsing rods to discern the layout of the church."

The Native Americans discovered the towering red rocks and mesas first, claiming them as sacred, "the place where the Great Spirit Mother birthed the human race," states the *L.A. Times*. Then the movie people came, filming Zane Grey's "Call of the Canyon" in 1920 and countless films, TV shows, and commercials since.

In 1980, the vortexes were brought to public attention by dueling authors Page Bryant and Richard Sutphen, who wrote books and conducted tours in the Sedona area. Each claimed to have "discovered" the mystical power of the red rocks themselves. And in August 1987, the town became a magnet for 10,000 New Agers, who, after checking their Mayan calendars, came to celebrate the birth of an era of "harmonic convergence."

The population has more than doubled from 5,000 in 1980 to over 14,000, with the influx being mostly New Agers, artists, and retirees. Property values have gone into outer space as well. Claims of healings, visions, clairvoyance, telepathy, and contact with spirits and extraterrestrials have made the buttes the butt of many jokes. Dannelley half-jests that he leaves extra copies of his material in a vehicle outside his house, "just in case I'm abducted by aliens." And the *Times* article observes that the "woo-woo foo-foos" and "moon puppies" declare the imminence of various spaceship sightings, such as the one in which Ashtar, Prince of the Universe, is supposed to land at Bell Rock Vortex looking for virgins.

Yet despite the divergence of various beliefs, "there is a lot of Christian activity," observes Bob Anderson, deacon at the Chapel of the Holy Cross. "And although a small group of people worship the vortexes, the majority follow traditional faiths. Even though some Catholic New Agers make the religion dovetail with whatever is happening at the vortexes, the Church doesn't see it that way.

"Most of us find New Agers to be wonderful people and very friendly," he continues. "So much of the antagonism is overblown and inevitably draws publicity. Sedona is a melting pot from all over the country."

Yet the Chapel of the Holy Cross has an eclectic history itself. Artist Marguerite Brunswig Staude first came up with the idea in the '30s while visiting the newly completed Empire State Building. "When viewed from a certain angle, a cross seemed to impose itself though the very core from the structure," she wrote in the Chapel's descriptive pamphlet. She showed her design to architect Lloyd Wright, a relative and associate of Frank Lloyd Wright. A model was made "to be built in Budapest on one of the hills overlooking the Danube. [World War II] soon put a stop to this dream."

After the war, however, Staude discovered an ideal location in Sedona, on a 250-foot crimson sandstone spur with twin pinnacles jutting from a 1,000-foot wall. "This was to be the pedestal wherein to plant our cross." The chapel was completed in 1956, and was to be "a national shrine where God can be worshipped as a contemporary. . . . [to] bring Him closer to each and every one of us. . . ."

The Chapel has about 150,000 visitors a year. "It is a very special, spiritual place in a beautiful setting," adds Anderson. But only in Sedona would a man ride all the way from Nova Scotia on his bicycle seeking God and find exactly what he was looking for.

What to Expect

With its towering buttes, Indian ruins and crafts, parks, and bustling arts community, Sedona is a fascinating place. Dozens of treks to the spectacular formations by bus, jeep, llama, van, or hot-air balloon are available.

New Age dabblers and devotees can choose from metaphysical bookstores, crystal shops, holistic healers, Tarot card readers, meditation booths, contacts for trance channelers, UFO groups, and other interests within the outer limits of the human experience. Although the mystical atmosphere may be subject to constant fluctuation, the physical climate is temperate all year round.

A serpentine concrete ramp leads to the Chapel of the Holy Cross. The outside is a spectacular combination of the best of nature and modern architecture. The interior is a basic Catholic church with wooden pews, a marble altar, and metal statuary, some of which is Staude's sculpture. Although some Masses have been held there in the past, the chapel is not a parish but is affiliated with the Diocese of Phoenix.

What They Say

Richard Dannelley, Sedona, Arizona: A lifelong resident of Sedona, Dannelley has made a study of origins and effects of vortexes and medicine wheels. Stone altars consisting of circles and spokes at the designated vortex point, medicine wheels supposedly help channel energy and can be used for various ceremonies. "All of this is related," he asserts. "Human DNA is in the shape of a vortex. The Native Americans used medicine wheels, putting rocks in the form of a circle and a cross, which indicates Christ-consciousness."

Traditionalists often look at so-called rock worshipers with suspicion, he continues. "But Christ was born in a cave and the center of Judeo-Christianity is a rock in Jerusalem." And if that's not enough proof, try taking a picture of a vortex with a camera. "Color print film picks up vibrations not visible to the normal human eye. Pictures show balls or fields of energy coming from the rocks."

Joe Berna and Robert Kirkpatrick, Sedona, Arizona: Both Christian preachers, Berna and Kirkpatrick take a firm stand. "New Age Mecca?" Berna, a Southern Baptist, fumed in the *L.A. Times.* "It's a spiritual battleground!" He cautioned against confusing psychic visions, crystals, and belief in goddesses with the New Testament. New Agers "are looking in the wrong place and finding the wrong God."

"We're not battling with people, but with a demonic phenomenon," added Kirkpatrick, who formerly ministered to Sedona's Wayside Chapel. "New Agers are POWs in Satan's camp."

Bob Gillies, Cocomo National Forest, Arizona: Gillies and his fellow rangers expend much effort disassembling medicine wheels that obstruct the park's scenic views. One 200-foot circle on Schnebly

Hill Road consists of lava chunks and seems to reappear overnight, thanks to the mystics. "We've really got better things to do," he told the *Times.*

He is also concerned about the effects of candle smudges on pre-historic symbols and paintings in various caves. "I'm not here to debate [the mystics'] beliefs," he observed. "No one is denying them the right to meditate. But a medicine wheel is just as unacceptable as if someone were to erect a Star of David or a cross or spray-paint 'Jesus Saves'. . . . This is everybody's land—not just yours or mine."

How to Get There

From Flagstaff, take Alt. 89A south to Arizona 179 (about 25 miles) and you'll be in the whirlpool traffic of Sedona. To get to the vor-texes, mesas, and buttes, just follow the vibes or the tour guides.

The Chapel of the Holy Cross is off 179, about three miles from the intersection of 89A and 179. It sits upon rock and literally crosses Chapel Rd. It is open seven days a week, 9 a.m.–5 p.m. closed Christmas, Easter, and Thanksgiving. Chapel of the Holy Cross, P.O. Box 1043, Sedona AZ 86339, 602/282-4069.

✝ A Strange Twist on the Road of Tragedy

Billboard at Intersection of Broadway and Main
Chula Vista, California

How It Happened

The facts are cold and brutal. On the night of June 19, 1991, nine-year-old Laura Arroyo ran to answer a knock on the door of her family's San Ysidro condominium. That was the last time anyone saw her alive—her fully clothed, battered body was discovered shortly after dawn the next morning. After beating and stabbing her repeatedly, her killer or killers dumped her in an industrial area of Chula Vista, five miles away from the seemingly safe row of condominiums.

The death horrified the community. People were afraid to let their children outside, and donated thousands of dollars toward a reward for information about the crime. The police combed the neighborhood repeatedly, interviewing everyone and locating no leads, at least according to newspaper accounts. It seems no one had seen anything unusual at all.

However, a few weeks later, Frank Sanchez, president of Martin Outdoor Advertising, began receiving calls about a religious sighting at a blank billboard at the corner of Broadway and Main in Chula Vista, not far from where Laura was found. "At first, I heard the image was of Virgin Mary," he recalls.

But within a matter of days, the play of illumination and shadow seemed to turn into a likeness of Laura Arroyo, and the uproar began. By the end of the week, people flocked to the billboard, jamming the business district with foot and automobile traffic. Those wanting a closer look paid $3 to park in an empty field nearby.

An estimated 30,000 showed up every evening, according to Chula Vista police. And most were convinced they saw Laura's winsome features in the lights cast on the white billboard at night.

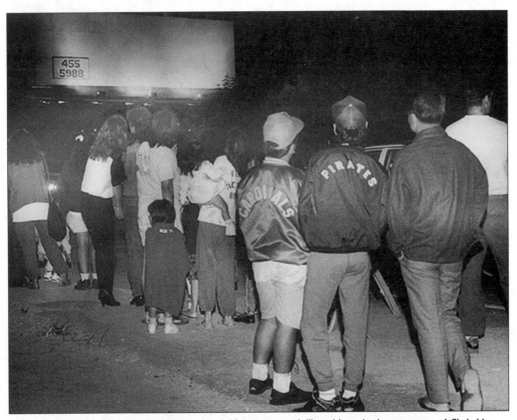

Nine-year-old Laura Arroyo was brutally murdered. Her image on a billboard brought the community of Chula Vista, California, together. PHOTO BY ION MOE OF THE CHULA VISTA STAR NEWS.

Others believed the dead girl was attempting to provide clues to the whereabouts of her murderers; still others claimed to see the killer's countenance on the billboard as well. Although many of the faithful were Latino Catholics from the South Bay, California area, people arrived from as far away as Arizona.

Sanchez was faced with a dilemma. The deluge also attracted food vendors and other curiosity seekers, and "was creating a huge safety hazard," he says. "It began to take on the atmosphere of a party. The reasoning was, 'Why stay at home and watch TV when we can go to the board?'"

Children were dashing between cars, and according to the *Los Angeles Times*, Chula Vista officer Merlin Wilson worried that "it's just a matter of time before we have some kind of an incident out there . . . [like] someone get[ting] run over or something."

So, based on police recommendations, the company temporarily turned off the lights, replacing the bulbs with higher-intensity ones a few days later, in hopes the image would disappear. However, "people still claimed to see Laura, and kept on coming," observes Sanchez. Plus he'd gotten to know the Arroyo family, and they were encouraged by the sighting. "And it gave others hope."

Finally, after meeting with police, and with the approval of the Arroyos, a color picture of Laura and the modest message "In Memoriam—Laura Arroyo" with the number of a special hotline were plastered on the 14-foot-by-38-foot billboard. Although it was only supposed to be up for 60 days, it remained in place for close to a year, costing Martin Outdoor $1,500 to $1,800 a month in revenue. And even though the numbers flocking to Broadway and Main gradually diminished, the billboard served as a makeshift shrine to the memory of Laura, cluttered with religious candles, handwritten notes, and flowers. Laura's father, Luis, tended the area, making sure it was neat and clean.

Still, it "is not a tombstone [or] a memoriam in perpetuity," Sanchez told *The San Diego Union Tribune*. "It's an advertising vehicle. It served a purpose during a very serious situation."

Today it's business as usual at Broadway and Main. The billboard is back in action as a vehicle for commercial enterprise, featuring a consortium of seasons' greetings from local merchandisers and other messages of the moment. And no progress appears to have been made on the Arroyo case; police are still looking into it. But Laura is not forgotten—not by her family nor by her school friends and teachers, who a few months ago paid homage to her during what would have been Laura's sixth-grade graduation.

A local merchant claimed his daughter saw a similar image on the blank billboard before the Arroyo killing. So perhaps the apparition was a work of collective imagination—or a foreshadowing of what was to come. But the reality is that the Laura Arroyo murder remains unsolved. Like the origins of the sighting, no one has a clue.

What to Expect

There's not much to see here, save for strip malls, gas stations, and lots of traffic. But the locals willingly share stories and observations about the Arroyo killing. And just passing by the board gives an eerie feeling, a mixture of sadness and awe. Police and Laura's family still hope someone will come forth with new information.

What They Say

Luis Arroyo, San Ysidro, California: At the time of the sighting, Luis was employed by a tow truck company. "They told me at work and I went over to the billboard right away. Everyone was crying, although some people tried to make money from it."

He visited every night. "I light the candles that people leave there and talk to Laura," he said in the *Times*. "I ask her to help us find the person who hurt her. I know that God will allow her to talk to us, if only once, so we can catch [this] terrible person. She was a little girl. How can somebody do something like this to a child? She wasn't old enough to hurt anybody."

Today the close-knit Arroyo family, who emigrated from Mexico, still lives in the same condominium; Luis now paints cars for a living. "Sometimes you see what you want to see, but the fact that thousands of people saw the same thing made me believe," he observes. "I think Laura was trying to tell us something; her brothers and my wife felt it was really her. The sighting made me feel that people truly cared and would help." Although he is disillusioned with lack of police progress on the case, he still searches for answers: "Someone knows something."

Frank Sanchez, Chula Vista, California: "The way the lights hit the board, you could envision a silhouette; the makings of eyes and hair. It was eerie." Although others speculated that a previous ad might have "bled through" the painted-over billboard, "nothing underneath the image corresponded to the girl's appearance."

Changing the lights only created "a new kind of shadow, an image closer to that of Christ. It was kind of scary. I mean we're talking about what's supposed to be a plain white surface, although we know the mind can play tricks."

Sanchez was relieved when the Arroyo family agreed to put Laura's picture up on the board. "People were praying for a solution and trying to help, but things had gotten out of control."

Michelle Becker, Chula Vista, California: Becker visited the billboard several times and took her husband and two nieces. "I see the little girl in the middle and a woman on the right side, . . ." she told the *Times*. She pointed out Laura's dark hair.

"I know they changed the lights today, but I still see it, so I don't think it is the lights. In my heart I really do hope it is the little girl and she is trying to say something to us. I think it is a great strength to her family."

How to Get There

A suburb of San Diego, Chula Vista can be accessed from both Interstates 5 and 805. Take Main St. exit from either; go east from I-5, west from 805. The site is about 3½ miles from 805.

✝ Mary Visits the Foothills

St. Dominic's Catholic Church
Colfax, California

How It Happened

On Thanksgiving Day, 1990, to accommodate the holiday routine, Mass started at 9:00, an hour later than the usual 8:00 a.m. "Normally, our regular attendance is about 20," recounts Ed Molloy, coordinator for St. Dominic's, a small community church located in the Sierra foothills. "But some [congregants] were inspired by a recent trip to Medjugorje, so we had nearly 50." Built in the early '50s, the diminutive church has a warm, airy interior and stained-glass windows.

After several decades of the Rosary, the parishioners dispersed, leaving Molloy alone with the pastor in the rear of the church. "We were discussing some maintenance problem or another, when he popped up with 'Do you see what I see?'," continues Molloy. "Sure enough, there on the front wall by the altar was a beautiful silhouette of the Blessed Mother."

Although Molloy and a few others present at the time discounted it as an interesting phenomenon and claimed to forget all about it, a well-known priest happened to be traveling through the parish. Along with the regular attendees, his followers saw the image during Sunday services and "within days we were receiving hundreds of calls," says Molloy. Channel 10 in Sacramento soon stopped by, and in Molloy's words, "a deluge of the faithful and the curious began to pour into Colfax," a tiny burg (pop: 1,000) mostly known for excellent skiing and camping.

Thousands showed up daily to visit a church that could comfortably hold 300, waiting in lines a quarter of a mile long for a glimpse of the multicolored image. Parking spaces across the street escalated to $10 each; the California Highway Patrol and Porta-Potties became presences as well. Madonna Richeson, owner of the pre-image–monikered Madonna's Classic Kitchen, found her business doubling. She placed her hand on the wall on top of the image and professed not to see a shadow: "It was like my hand wasn't there," she told the *Los Angeles Times*.

The uproar continued to escalate. Tie-dyed shirts inscribed "I Saw the Light—St. Dominic's Church" were peddled at $12 each. Although the vendor maintained that $2 went to feed the needy, he didn't go into which "needy" the monies would benefit. Another merchant offered image-themed key rings and bumper stickers while television camera crews and photographers discussed the best angle, lighting, and aperture to capture a vision for the viewers and readers at home.

Things were further complicated by time constraints. At best, the image only lasted an hour a day, appearing above a statue of Christ. Onlookers alternately described it as the Virgin Mary holding the infant Jesus, a figure 8, or a snowman. Depending upon the light, hues would change from pink and orange to white and blue.

Within a few days of the first sighting, various "experts" weighed in with opinions. "It's an obvious and simple physical phenomenon," Al Rhomberg, a self-described Sacramento physicist, told the *Los Angeles Times*. "It's something you'd see with any stained-glass window." He went on to describe the image as sunlight reflecting through the window, bouncing off a recently adjusted light fixture, and striking the wall. Covering or removing the light fixture or blocking the window would surely erase it. "Or quicker still, just tap the fixture with a stick and the image will move."

James Phelps, a Cal State physics professor, also examined the image. "This isn't even a first class illusion," he told the *Times*. "Any real optics person would turn up his nose at this."

The lights *had* been modified, but not in the way naysayers hypothesized. In September, "a plastic diffuser from one of the six hanging light fixtures came crashing down between two of our parishioners," explains Ed Molloy. God must have been watching, because no one was hurt: "Those things are heavy and could have split someone's head in two." Molloy and his crew checked all the lights and found several more out of place, finally securing all the diffusers by wrapping fine wire around the fixtures. "But that was almost three months before the image appeared in the church."

Still, the first cloudy day seemed to prove the cynics right. The vision was a no-show and thousands of pilgrims left disappointed. And although he'd mentioned the possibility of canonical commission, Bishop Francis Quinn of the Sacramento Diocese had to agree with Professor Phelps that the image was merely a refraction of light.

It was a sad day for the faithful. "Their world is impoverished just a bit by the disappearance of the apparition," editorialized John Seelmayer in the Nevada City *Union*. "And in a world where skepticism about religious faith all too often translates into skepticism about the existence of any goodness, the disappearance of the vision may provide more fuel for those who doubt almost everything they see."

Yet Ed Molloy and others at the church remain convinced more than mere physics is at play. Some assert that the added faith derived from Medjugorje may have encouraged the formation of the image.

"There's no problem with the how," says Molloy. "It's the why. Why not when the church was first built? If fixing the light is the cause, then there were at least 11 Sundays when it could have been seen by upwards of 300 people. But it wasn't, probably because it wasn't there. It gives one pause." Another hidden blessing may be that now that the critics and thrill-seekers are gone, the parishioners can enjoy their inspirational light show in comfort and peace.

What to Expect

The image can still be seen during late fall and winter months, sometimes even occurring when it's overcast. Sunny days from around Thanksgiving until mid-February provide an incredible sight: starting about 9:30 a.m., indistinguishable blobs of color on the wall form into an 1½-foot-by-3-foot likeness above and over the shoulder of the statue of Jesus on the right side of the altar. As the sun rises and goes westward, the picture moves eastward but, oddly enough, shifts up instead of down, mirroring the sun rather than doing the opposite, which is the normal law of physics.

Because morning mass is said daily, the church will still likely be open at 9:00. But it's best to call first.

What They Say

Ed Molloy, Colfax, California: Ed Molloy is the man to see regarding any aspect of the occurrence. This World War II veteran and computer buff has dealt with press inquiries; organized crowd control and arranged for services when the pastor was ill during the height of the deluge; and kept things moving along, even when a group of rowdy teenagers vandalized the church for no apparent reason.

Photographs, he feels, don't do the image justice: "They lack the depth that is sensed visually. The [likeness] to me is a sort of holographic silhouette in fluid colors. It shows the outline that we of the faith normally recognize as the Blessed Mother holding her child." He also claims to have experienced a tremendous smell of roses while in the chapel. "It has happened three times, and there were no flowers present. It almost floored me."

Yet Molloy has neither visions nor conversations with Jesus and Mary and acknowledges that the image may just be a natural phenomenon. But he believes it's here for a purpose. "God is the author of the light, and Mary's spirit is doing what she needs to do. People are looking to feed their souls."

Darlene Pagtakhan, Union City and Annette Bolden, Davis, California: Pagtakhan and her husband Chris drove nearly three hours in hopes of getting into the small chapel for daily rosary service. "I think it's real, maybe," she said in *USA Today.* "I think it's her. It's happened before but it's always been someplace far away. This is the first time I've been close enough to come."

"It's very beautiful," added Bolden, who was on her third visit. "Whatever it is, it has brought people together for a good purpose—spirituality. I would say it's a miracle."

Frida Hoffman, Weimar, California: "I have been at this parish for 12 years, and nothing like this has ever happened," observes Frida Hoffman, who is in her 70s. She maintains that the image has much to do with the revitalization of the parish. "Every Friday night, you see families saying the Rosary. There are young people, with lots of children, more than I've encountered in any other church."

You don't have to go to Medjugorje to be spiritually renewed, she theorizes. And perhaps the fair-weatheredness of the image was divinely inspired as well. "If we have too many people, the building will collapse. There's a reason why things happen the way they do."

How to Get There

Take I-5N to 80E and get off at the Colfax exit. Circle around to the right towards town (crossing the freeway). The church is located at the corner of Auburn Ave. and Oak St. Hours vary. St. Dominic's Catholic Church, 58 E. Oak St., Colfax, CA 95713, 916/346-2286.

✝ Faith Shines Through

Chapel of the Faith Baptist Church
Los Angeles, California

How It Happened

Late in August 1971, Mrs. Mable Davis and her young daughter, Pat, arrived at the Chapel of the Faith Baptist Church for afternoon children's choir practice. No one else showed up, not even the pianist. Discouraged, Mrs. Davis went to make a few phone calls to try to drum up participants. "She was about ready to give up on the whole thing," recalls Pat, now in her 30s. "The church was under-going a lot of turmoil," facing a declining membership. The pastor, Rev. Roy Williams, was away at a Baptist convention, so things were even quieter than usual.

Suddenly Mable Davis heard a great cry from Pat in the choir rehearsal room at the back of the church: "Look, Mommy, there's a cross in the window!" Mable immediately recognized what was later described as a "great gleaming glowing cross" and changed her tune, as did the entire congregation: Soon thousands of people showed up at the Chapel of the Faith every day around 4 p.m. when the cross was in its blazing glory. Church attendance swelled from 60 or 70 to about 200. And Mable Davis not only had her pianist but a volunteer organist as well.

Naturally, the scene had detractors. Some pointed out that if the cross was truly a miracle, it would always be seen rather than only being visible during a certain time. Others claimed it was the result of a prismatic effect in which the image bounced off the glass when a spot source of light was pointed towards it. Still others remarked it looked more like a German cross than a representation of Jesus.

Yet people wondered why that particular church—a small con-gregation in a poverty-stricken area—had been chosen, rather than a larger, more prosperous house of worship. No other in the church-intensive area had been so blessed. "We checked," says Alelia Williams, the Reverend's widow. And the window itself was nothing special—purchased from the Jones Lumber Company in Watts, it hadn't even been customized for a church. Materials came from a variety of distributors, while the glass itself was translucent rather than clear, allowing for the penetration of shadows of objects.

Gang members troll outside the Chapel of the Faith Baptist Church in South Central Los Angeles, but within lies a bounty of faith and a window cross. PHOTO BY SANDRA GURVIS.

Broken a few years later, it was replaced with the same type of glass. The cross still remained visible.

Church members took care not to exploit the phenomenon. Although Mrs. Davis and other congregants organized walk-through tours, Reverend Williams forbade selling pictures or other depictions of the cross on church property, insisting that crowds remain orderly and deferential. "My husband had a conservative attitude," recalls his widow. "He respected [the image] but felt interpretation should be put on the Bible rather than the cross itself." When present, the Reverend gave a sermonette to visitors. "He wanted to bring people to Jesus, and always said, 'That window is not going to save anybody; they must turn to Christ for themselves.'"

Still, a few of the faithful got carried away. One discarded her crutches, while another threw away his eyeglasses, and still another passed out. An individual clad in white robes declared herself anointed by God and proceeded to try to do the same, with oil, to others in line. And naturally, the media came to call: newspapers, television, *The National Enquirer.*

As associate minister Floyd W. Stanford told the latter: "For . . . years we prayed for a larger congregation. Suddenly the shining cross has brought us the answer to our prayers." And although the church never actively solicited funds or advertised, for the first time, they no longer had to struggle for nickel and dime donations.

Although the cross is mostly remembered by the older congregants, today the Chapel of the Faith Baptist Church has an active, marvelous-sounding choir; an enthusiastic minister (the Rev. Louis C. Hall); and devoted congregants. On any given Sunday, the parking lot is filled with newer-model cars, and most of the well-dressed attendees reside outside of South Central. By simply being accepted, the cross seems to have worked its own magic.

What to Expect

If you know where to look, you can usually see the cross, especially on sunny days. (A cross also allegedly appeared in a similarly textured bathroom window, but little was made of it). It can jump out at the viewer during late afternoons, but if it's not immediately obvious, go over by the window and look for a "pillow"—a rectangular shape with concave sides and pointed corners. The cross is just to the left of it. Someone's usually willing to show you where to stand.

Folks at this church are warm and welcoming, but it's often closed during the week. So call before coming out, and if it's a Sunday, expect to work a visit around church school and worship. You might find the services more inspiring than the cross itself.

What They Say

Patricia "Pat" Davis Ray, Lancaster, California: "When I first saw that cross as a kid, it was blazing away, like it was the end of the world," recalls Pat Ray of that fateful first encounter. "Even though I've moved away and had my share of problems, I still find myself coming back to this church. Now we're getting into generations of families and I see kids in diapers growing up. I prayed for things to change here, and finally they did.

"Today's world is a lot more complicated than in the '70s. Life is harder and people are more frightened." Now in her mid-70s, Pat's mother Mable is ill "but still trusts in the Lord."

George Seals, Los Angeles, California: A deacon at the church, George Seals was initially skeptical and somewhat taken aback by what has been called the "cross flap." "It came up so suddenly, I just went along with it. Nobody had ever noticed it before, and I wondered why."

Now, twenty-five or so years later, he remains adamantly neutral. "I don't knock it or praise it, but I do see it as a sign."

Oreatha Greer, Los Angeles, California: In contrast, Oreatha Greer believed wholly and helped usher in the thousands who visited Chapel of the Faith. "It was definitely a blessing, I felt like [our church] had been chosen, and this was all we had strived for.

"Some had a bad attitude, but a few of those changed when they saw the cross. If didn't come from God, where did it come from?"

How to Get There

Chapel of the Faith is located at the corner of 80th and S. San Pedro Sts. in South Central Los Angeles. Take the 110 freeway to the Manchester exit (from the south) or the Florence exit (from the north). Both streets run into S. San Pedro; if coming from the south, turn left, from the north, turn right. 7931 S. San Pedro St., Los Angeles, CA 90003, 213/751-2123.

✝ A Mosaic Mystery

Our Lady of the Pillar Roman Catholic Church
Santa Ana, California

How It Happened

Every morning around 7 a.m., Irma Villegas goes to Mass. Through rain, shine, and the fog that can shroud the beautiful mountain-surrounded town of Santa Ana, she and several of the faithful—most of whom only speak Spanish or variations thereof—say the rosary amidst the eerie hush of Our Lady of the Pillar. With an interior devoted to representations of the Holy Mother—stained-glass windows, statuary, paintings, mosaics—this church seems like a logical place for the Virgin Mary to put in an appearance.

And she did, according to Irma Villegas and others. One November morning in 1991, Villegas was praying as usual, and "saw this light at the altar. I kept on seeing it, and it took my eyes over there." She points to the left portion of a huge, 30-foot mosaic of Mary which dominates the wall behind the altar. "There were the faces of Jesus and Mary, Jesus and Mary, back and forth."

Eventually, only the image of Mary remained: "At first I didn't say anything. I was so moved, I was crying with happiness." Having gone to Mass every day since age 7, she has derived great satisfaction from religion. "My family believed me. They know this is what I do."

But the vision persisted and a few weeks later, word got out. "Other people noticed it too, and started coming to church," continues Villegas. "You could see more of Mary, her body, her hands, her long-sleeved dress." The clergy were last to know: Father James D. McGuire, assistant pastor at that time, found out about the image via the local paper.

He has never spoken to Irma or the others about this matter, the first reported sighting of the Blessed Virgin in Orange County, an area which boasts some 750,000 Roman Catholics. "I didn't want to interfere," he explains. "The Bishop has waited, because you want to give this thing time, a chance to prove itself. It's normal procedure in the Catholic Church." If an image is genuine, "it will endure."

But news and camera crews and pilgrims weren't about to sit around for the requisite hundred or so years. And the hubbub upset church routine. "A lot of commotion like this is not conducive to a spirit of prayer and reflection," Father McGuire told the *Los*

Visitors looking hard enough might glimpse the faces of Jesus and Mary in the mosaic at Our Lady of the Pillar in Santa Ana, California. PHOTO BY SANDRA GURVIS.

Angeles Times in 1991. The church, located in a primarily Roman Catholic, Mexican neighborhood, boasts a weekend attendance of 9,000 to 10,000 and hardly needed any more traffic.

Still, *something* seems to be in that mosaic, because on a sunny day when the light shines through the stained-glass window and casts a warm glow, a faint outline can be discerned. Villegas has claimed, at various times, to have seen permutations of Jesus, his family, and of course Mary. Villegas says it's like "the negatives of a photograph" and where she kneels—two or three pews down on the right, facing the altar—offers the best seat in this house of God.

Villegas postulates that the purpose of the image is to encourage humanity to pray the rosary more and, through Mary, to try to help save the world. She also points out that multiple appearances by the Blessed Mother—especially so close to the millennium—might signify that The End is near. "A lot of people have seen her," she insists. "If you open up your heart and want to believe, you will." But for the church fathers it was—and is—business as usual.

What to Expect

This is one big church. You'll need to get close to the front of the cavernous interior (especially to the right of the altar) even to get an idea of what Villegas is talking about. The left half of the mosaic, which depicts Mary as shown in a vision to St. James in 42 A.D., is where the image has been sighted. Look below the word "Gratia," near the head of a gold-flecked angel.

Unless you're fluent in Spanish or Irma Villegas happens to be around, don't expect much help from the congregants or the ladies whose only purpose seems to be tending the dozens of flowers surrounding the various statues. And if it's foggy or overcast, you may see nothing at all.

What They Say

Father James D. McGuire, O.A.R., Lamont, California: Now stationed at another parish, Father McGuire is not as skeptical about the idea of an appearance by Mary as he initially seems. His former post "would be appropriate, as Our Lady of the Pillar is the patroness of Latin American countries and the congregation is largely Hispanic. The church bespeaks Mary."

On the other hand, "I got the impression many people didn't perceive [the image] although a few in Irma's particular spot claimed they saw something." Yet "religious groups keep coming to view the mosaic and give their devotions to the Blessed Mother."

Msgr. Lawrence J. Baird, Orange County Diocese, California: As spokesman for the diocese, Msgr. Baird takes a harder line. "If such an alleged vision is taking place, that would have to be what we commonly call a miracle, and miracles do happen," he said in the *Los Angeles Times.*

"But in something like this—and there have been many, many such cases reported—we try to explain things first through natural causes. And in this case, there doesn't seem to be any reason to suggest it is more than that." He expressed concern that such sightings "trivialize" Catholics' basic belief in Mary as the Mother of God.

Mila Grant, Santa Ana, California: Grant, an office manager, also went to view the image at Colfax (see page 27). "I was able to see [Mary] six times in three days when she was appearing there," Grant told the *Times.* "I haven't seen her today [at Our Lady of the Pillar], but I believe she is here. . . . And I hope to be fortunate enough to see her again. If I do, it would be icing on the cake."

How to Get There

From Los Angeles, take I-5 South to 17th St. in Santa Ana and turn right. Go to Bristol and turn left, then go right on 6th. You can't miss Our Lady of the Pillar Church on the left-hand side. Open seven days a week. 1622 W. 6th, Santa Ana, CA 92703, 714/543-1700.

✝ Mary Goes "Krogering" in Earthquake Country

Cross of Peace Project
Santa Maria, California

How It Happened

OK, so people found it difficult to take Carol Nole seriously when she started spreading the word in 1988. The Virgin Mary allegedly told her to construct a cross "on the north side of town, on the hill directly in line with the back of Scolari's market." Along with being 75-feet high, the cross "will have one-foot holes inset with stained glass, golden in color, where the nails were."

"You've got to wonder why the Virgin Mary's dealing in such trivia," Gerald Larue, professor emeritus at USC, observed in the *Los Angeles Times*. "If she's finally going to speak to someone, why doesn't she say anything more profound. . . ."

Naysayers who thought that Nole's six-month stretch of visions would go the way of Reaganomics were in for a shock. Today the Cross of Peace, Inc. not only has permission from the Catholic Church to conduct an annual Mass, which according to Nole's spokesman-husband Charlie pulls in an estimated 6,000, but "we have about 8–10,000 people a year who visit us and attend our prayer meetings. And at least 25 families have moved out here to be nearer to the cross." A church review conducted several years ago neither denied or confirmed the claims.

And the numbers are growing. For along with healings, miracles of the sun, and rosaries turning to gold, this group is convinced they've found a safe haven in Santa Maria from the Big One: an earthquake that will spread from Oregon to California to Mexico. "A few hours before it happens, there will be a huge crucifix in the sky," predicts Charlie, who previously sold real estate before going into the religion business full-time. "The cross will stay for 101 days." As a result of the quake, "millions of lives will be lost, and there will be riots and disorder."

According to Charlie, "Santa Maria was originally a river bottom. When an earthquake shakes, the 20 feet of sand that is underneath will absorb the damage and save the buildings."

Not surprisingly, Father Gregory Coiro of the Archdiocese of Los Angeles responded with "a healthy dose of skepticism," according to the *Santa Barbara News-Press*. Not only are forecasts of doom increasing as the millennium approaches, but "it's not hard to predict [that] an earthquake is coming to California in the future . . . people begin to attach greater importance to [prophecies] than the occasion might warrant. People who get worked up about such private revelations foretelling destruction are somewhat foolhardy."

But they *are* persistent. In 1988, when Carol received her 29 messages, the faithful began praying on the 1,500-foot-long hill, which according to Charlie "is a perfectly shaped image of Our Lady of Fatima when seen from an aerial view." The owners of the land, who use it for cattle-grazing and weren't interested in selling, posted "No Trespassing" signs.

"They have turned down several offers . . . made . . . much in excess of its value," Charlie said in the *Santa Maria Times*. So the intrepid group gathered across the street, praying at the foot of the hill along a public highway. "We had up to 1,500 people there each weekend. The state became concerned that there might be an accident so in September of 1990, we moved to St. Joseph's Church in Nipomo."

All went well until the next summer, when an article in the *Los Angeles Times* described the scene as having a "festival air . . . with its snack bar, gift shop, and the faithful scurrying about, sharing stories about divine inspiration." Along with a video describing the messages and project, visitors drove by the hill and attended Mass at the church. Concerned that the meetings implied Church endorsement, the pastor asked the Cross of Peace to leave. The group moved to its current location, an office on Preisker Lane.

Despite the many obstacles, the Noles remain convinced that the cross will happen and when it does, it will be a refuge in the coming chastisement. "Carol and I have given our lives to this project, and we'll keep it going as long as the Lord and Mary let us."

What to Expect

The group meets for prayer at the Preisker Lane location every Tuesday night from 7 to 9 p.m. On Saturdays and Sundays, larger gatherings are held at nearby Preisker Park. "They come by the busloads, so people need to make arrangements in advance," adds

Charlie. The annual Mass is usually held around March 24–25 to commemorate the anniversary of Carol's messages, and features well-known speakers, such as Joanne Petronella, dean of the International Institute of Ministry in Anaheim, California. The Preisker Lane information center has a large gift shop selling books, rosaries, plaques, and other religious items.

Located about 2.8 miles east of Highway 101 on Highway 166, the hill isn't much to see—yet. "But the fact that it's a perfectly shaped icon shows us we've got the right place," observes Charlie.

What They Say

Msgr. John Rohde, Santa Maria, California: "I feel very strong about [the messages]," Rohde, who previously served as the Noles' spiritual adviser, told the *National Catholic Register.* "A lot of powerful things have happened to people who have come up there. I feel something is going on and I have no reason to suspect they're not authentic."

Father Gregory Coiro, Los Angeles, California: Coiro believes today's society is more open-minded about otherworldly visitations. "In the past, if you told people you heard a message from the Virgin Mary, many would consider you insane," he said in the *Times.* "But . . . with the New Age movement and the fascination with the supernatural, there's more of an acceptance of this kind of thing."

Sharon Wittson, Orange County, California: A nurse, Wittson claims to have heard messages from Jesus that a major temblor—8.4 on the Richter scale to be exact—is on the way. Still, "heaven has not told me the date," she said in the *Santa Barbara News-Press.* Also involved with the Cross of Peace project, she claims that she was directed to Santa Maria to stockpile food and supplies there. To doubters such as Father Coiro, she responded, "Everyone has a right to their opinion and God has given everyone free will."

How to Get There

Santa Maria is about a one-hour drive from Santa Barbara. Take 101N and get off at Broadway. The first street is Preisker Lane; it's in the Gateway Business Park. The Cross of Peace, Inc. is open from 9 a.m. to 5 p.m., Wednesday through Sunday. 2015-H Preisker Ln., Santa Maria, CA 93454, 805/349-7003.

✝ Our Lady of Fatima Takes a Hike

Mater Ecclesiae Mission Church
Thornton, California

How It Happened

The Mater Ecclesiae Mission Church is one of two satellite churches under the jurisdiction of St. Anne's Church in Lodi. With no regular clerical staff, God's little outpost in Thornton, California hardly seemed the place for a raging religious altercation. But bitter accusations have flown between priests and parishioners, with suspicions continuing today. All because a statue allegedly moved and cried.

Produced at a factory in Lisbon, Portugal and brought to the Bay Area in 1968, the icon in question was a 4-foot, 60-pound Our Lady of Fatima. Purchased by a Portuguese grain farmer in memory of his son-in-law who was killed in a tractor accident, the statue was donated to the mission church. In 1981, thirteen years after this Madonna's arrival in Thornton, miracles began to be reported.

Our Lady, it seemed, couldn't stay put. Starting in March of that year, she began to "move" from the left side of the church to the altar. "One day, June 13, I was in the church by myself. She was in her place," Manuel Pitta, a longtime Thornton resident and volunteer who cleans the church, told *The Sacramento Bee*. He left the church for a short while but "when I got back, she was by the altar and the rosary was still moving back and forth."

Most of these activities took place on the 13th of the month, coinciding with the anniversary of the original Our Lady of Fatima, who first materialized in Fatima, Portugal on May 13, 1917, before three children. The legend is that the apparition of the Virgin Mary reappeared for six months in a row on the 13th, requesting prayers for the conversion of Russia and predicting a world war.

According to several accounts, a small group of church regulars sealed the statue in flowers; she relocated without disturbing a single stem. They bolted her down; she managed to arrive at her destination with the fasteners intact. Whenever she was put back, she shed tears.

She also tilted her head and changed the position of her hands at various points in time. "Miraculous photos" came to light, including one with what appears to be a picture of Jesus resting on her shoulder. Although she "wept" at a wedding in front of 350 people, no one actually ever saw her move. And in September 1981, a

The Catholic Church thought this photo taken of the weeping statue at the Mater Ecclesiae Mission Church in Thornton, California, was a fake, but some of the faithful disagreed. PHOTO USED WITH PERMISSION.

permanent, fenced-in home near the altar put an end to her commute.

By now, however, people were travelling to see her. They came by the thousands, from all over the U.S. and Canada. Kept open seven days a week, the church was mobbed, especially on the 13th of every month and Sundays. Bus loads lit candles and prayed; miraculous "recoveries" were reported but not substantiated. And at $2 a candle, donations paid for a new roof and air conditioning for the church and the wrought-iron fence around Our Lady.

But by 1983, after a year-long investigation, Bishop Roger M. Mahoney, then head of the 150,000-member Diocese of Stockton, declared the entire phenomenon a hoax. "The alleged extraordinary events . . . do not meet the criteria for an authenticated appearance of the Virgin Mary," he stated at a press conference. Our Lady's movements "could occur by somebody picking up the statue"; the tears "could be explained by condensation or by someone applying fluid. . . ." An unnamed witness who touched the liquid on the statue's face seemed to back up the latter. It was oily and sticky, "certainly not the texture or consistency of human tears."

But perhaps most damning was the Church's reaction to the pictures. Investigators sent the Jesus/statue photo to a forensic science laboratory in Oakland. A report came back that the bearded male figure next to Our Lady was "images [sic] cut out of commercially available sources," according to the bishop. He called for a return to the church's "normal operation" and discouraged all pilgrims, save for regular worshipers.

Consisting mainly of parishioners and the faithful, the crowd greeted the news with hostility, especially when the bishop and the five priests accompanying him debunked the photographs. "It's not true," an unnamed devotee objected to the McClatchy News Service. "I never lie. A priest from Petaluma comes to take pictures, and Christ is on them." "Not true, not true . . ." another moaned. "They don't have faith."

Although most of the traffic has died down, a few parishioners still hold services and take communion, holding firm to the belief that miracles are occurring. And the occasional priest, mystic, and curiosity-seeker still stops by.

Today, most meetings take place in people's homes, with various "revelations" privately published in religious tracts. These include predictions relating to the Roman Catholic Church and modern-day America as well as a pending Armageddon between now and the year 2000. If time is running out, perhaps that's why Our Lady continues to be restless.

What to Expect

Nowadays, things at the church are rather quiet. Thornton is a tiny, out-of-the-way place; the largest metropolis is Sacramento, a half-hour's drive in decent traffic.

The church itself is an unimposing, one-story building. Inside are plain wooden pews and a simple altar. The exception is the Our Lady statue—normally surrounded by flowers, pictures, and candles, on special days she is adorned with crowns, rosaries, and dressy robes. Her eyes are eerily red-rimmed and she has an incandescence that doesn't seem wholly attributable to porcelain. Still, any spookiness might be credited to the zeal of those around her.

What They Say

Manuel Pitta, Thornton, California: Pitta, who also worked as a custodian in a school and emigrated to the U.S. from Portugal in 1949, tells of being intimidated by priests for his beliefs. During the height of their investigation, "I was called at home on Friday at 1:00 a.m. and was told to go to the diocese office in Stockton on Monday," he recalls. "Naturally, it made me nervous."

When he arrived, he was taken into a room with a big conference table. "The priests locked the door and informed me that the face of Jesus had been cut out and superimposed on the photo [of Our Lady]."

Pitta swears he didn't even notice the double image until someone pointed it out after he'd taken the picture of the statue. "[The priests] called it the work of the devil and said that if I didn't agree, they could put me in jail." Shortly after that, Pitta had his first "encounter" with Mary.

Although he felt railroaded by the clergy, Pitta shows little resentment. "They haven't bothered me since then and the saints visit me every Saturday."

Reverend Cornelius de Groot, Lodi, California: "No one has ever seen the statue move," de Groot, the pastor at St. Anne's Church, told *The Sacramento Bee.* "The only factual information was that it was found in different places in the church. . . . Drops of liquid were seen on the face, which I have seen and others have seen. I don't know whether there is a natural explanation for it."

Bishop Donald W. Montrose, Stockton, California: The current head of the diocese has visited the mission church several times. "I spoke to a women's group there and a parishioner who goes to the chapel regularly told me about a photographer who used special lighting to take pictures of the statue," he observes. "[The parishioner] also found glue and other supplies in the restroom."

Also, "it concerned me that people were getting a blessing without the presence of [an ordained] priest. Although they may think they're in the company of a saint or Jesus Christ, they're simulating confession and absolution." As a result, communion, confession, and other holy ceremonies at the mission church are attended by a priest.

The bishop concurs with the findings of the 1983 investigation. "Most people—especially priests—who visit are pretty consistent about disbelieving." Just in case, however, he reads the tracts sent by the Thornton group every month.

How to Get There

From Sacramento, take I-5 south, then exit at Thornton. Turn left, then go a short distance until you get to Sacramento Blvd., which is designated by a small market and the town library. Veer left on Sacramento Blvd.; the Mater Ecclesiae is just on the right.

The mission church may be locked Monday through Thursday; it's more likely to be open on weekends. Still, call before coming out; don't expect Our Lady to let you in. 26553 Sacramento Blvd., Thornton, CA 95686, 209/369-1907.

✝ Double Vision at the Mother Cabrini Shrine

Mother Cabrini Shrine
Golden, Colorado

How It Happened

Until 1991, the Mother Cabrini Shrine was primarily known as a place where America's first citizen saint, St. Francis Xavier Cabrini, lived and initiated her good works of establishing schools, hospitals, orphanages, and child care centers around the world. Housing a convent, a chapel, a grotto, a mountaintop statue and other icons, a camp house/retreat, and a native spring, the Shrine attracted a steady stream of the faithful and others seeking quiet renewal in the foothills above Denver.

Then Theresa Lopez, a local homemaker who at one time allegedly pleaded guilty to a felony charge of check fraud, claimed to have had a conversation with the Virgin Mary at the shrine. Recently returned from Medjugorge, Lopez reported visions there as well, in addition to visions on the surface of a Colorado lake.

According to various news accounts, Lopez offered up a description of Mary as someone wearing a golden gown, surrounded by a pink sparkling glow, with a voice resembling wind chimes. Mary had instructed Lopez to deliver a message of faith, communion, and continued Mass. Meanwhile, Lopez has not only acquired an entourage but a group of bodyguards to protect her from what she claimed were death threats.

On December 8th, 1991, the day of the Feast of Immaculate Conception, an estimated 6,000 people from all over the U.S. converged at Mother Cabrini to share Lopez's vision. They came in chartered jets, vans, and buses, buying commemorative T-shirts at $20 each, partaking of bottled holy water labeled "for spiritual health." They waited outside in the freezing cold to enter the snow-covered grounds of the shrine.

Once there, they gazed at the sun on the mountaintop, hoping to see the Blessed Virgin, or at the least, spinning lights. Some knelt near the shaking, staring Lopez. "On the Richter scale of Virgin sightings, this would be . . . a 4 or 5," Carl Rashke, religious studies professor at the University of Denver, told the Associated Press.

Although some claimed to view Mary, angels, or the gates of heaven, the only thing others received was extensive eye damage. "It's a physical fact that if you look directly into the sun, it can harm and kill cells in the retina," states Dr. Lawrence Winograd, a Denver ophthalmologist. The retina "works on the same basic principle as a magnifying glass—you put it under the light and intense heat will be generated."

His explanation for the eruptions of color is similarly clear-cut: "The cells in the retina are having a last hurrah before they die. And the injury is usually permanent; there is no treatment." Victims may not only have continuous "spots" before their eyes but may experience a loss of sight.

Winograd and other local physicians encouraged both secular and Catholic newspapers to publicize warnings about what direct sunlight can do to the retina. Unfortunately, they were too late: Dozens of people filled optometrists' and ophthalmologists' offices with complaints. One woman, who went up to Mother Cabrini with her two-year-old handicapped son, burned both her retinas, ruining her central line of sight. "I go up there to pray with one disabled member of my family and come home with two," she told *Newsweek*.

The Denver archbishop expressed concern about the gatherings and advised the faithful to stay away. Still, the diocese, which covers over 300,000 Roman Catholics in northern Colorado appointed a committee of clergy and lay people to inquire into Lopez's claims.

At about the same time, Veronica Garcia, another homemaker and friend of Lopez, professed to have had celestial visitations as well. "They were told to keep away from each other because their visions were so different," says a source who knows both women. "Theresa's mostly dealt with [Our Lady of] Fatima, while Veronica's concentrated on divine mercy." Both women's spiritual advisors called for the separation to avoid confusion, contradicting messages, and the appearance of a conspiracy.

"If people [are] following Theresa or me, they are following the wrong thing," Garcia, a Denver secretary, told the *Rocky Mountain News*. "Their faith is supposed to be in Jesus Christ and God."

A subsequent investigation, however, revealed that the Church had no belief, at least in Lopez. "From the information available, there does not appear to be evidence which would indicate a supernatural origin for these alleged events," opined Roman Catholic Archbishop J. Francis Stafford in a prepared statement in May 1993. He warned Catholics against participating in services dedicated to the visions, gatherings that usually took place at Mother Cabrini on the second Sunday of each month.

Still, "No one challenged Veronica, because Theresa was the primary visionary and that's the only one [the church] usually questions," explains the source.

Lopez has moved to Rome to be in seclusion with her son. "Theresa is obedient to the Church and wants to remove herself from the controversy. But she was amazing. . . . One day she came into our office and wrote several messages [from the Virgin Mary] on a piece of paper. They came out fully formed, as if Theresa had instant recall" of her conversations with Mary.

Veronica Garcia has continued with her own writings and devotions, focusing on those who have strayed from the Church but want to come back to God. "She's very low-key," observes the source. "And there's a good possibility the Church will continue to leave her alone," especially since Garcia claimed to have been told by the Blessed Virgin that her visions on Cabrini would end in December 1994. Unlike Lopez, Garcia has published her findings in several volumes and continues to be fairly accessible to the public.

Things seemed to have settled down at the Mother Cabrini shrine, although a dedicated group heads up the hill every second Sunday. Still, it might be advisable to meet God's direct line of vision with a pair of protective lenses.

What to Expect

The shrine is located on 900 acres near Lookout Mountain and attracts tens of thousands of visitors from around the world. The minute you step out of your car, you can begin devotions: close to the parking lot are small, candlelit shrines and a spring of miraculous water discovered by Mother Cabrini herself. According to the Shrine's brochure, she tapped her cane, told the sisters to dig, and water trickled out. "The spring has never stopped running and has never frozen," says the brochure.

Then you can climb the non-Led Zeppelin "stairway to heaven." Nearly 375 steps head towards the pinnacle of the Mount of the Sacred Heart, where a 22-foot statue of Jesus Christ overlooks the skyscrapers of Denver, gleaming whitely against the brilliant Colorado sunshine. "Erected in 1954, it is the result of the nickels, dimes, quarters, and pennies [donated] by the grateful and prayerful friends of Mother Cabrini," the brochure goes on.

Before you begin, however, you can have your picture taken near a large crucifix. A gift from an appreciative family whose son was miraculously cured of polio thanks to "prayerful intercession" (the brochure's words) by Mother Cabrini, it is one of many places to pause and reflect. Others include the mysteries of the rosary and the stations of the cross, which resurrect Jesus's final journey.

On top, visitors can read about the life and times of Mother Cabrini ("a saint who died at the age of 67 years and . . . founded 67 missions") and view the glass-covered "Heart of Stone," preserved in perpetuity thanks to the efforts of a Catholic postal workers' union. Cabrini herself arranged this heart-shaped outline of large white stones surrounded by a smaller stone cross and crown of thorns.

But perhaps most compelling (or at least recently so) is a small circle of rocks that marks the spot where Lopez and Garcia had their visions. Groups of pilgrims still flock there and although you won't likely see Lopez, you might encounter Garcia, who occasionally visits, or perhaps have an experience of your own. After that, it's all downhill.

What They Say

Michelle Lobato, Colorado Springs, Colorado: The following are excerpts from a letter written by Michelle Lobato to a local bishop describing her 4-year-old son's behavior at the shrine: "Without questions, Jimmy walked down the hill, passed the bush and put his hands on the chain link fence below. He stood there looking into the sky for about 30 seconds or so, then he . . . said, 'Do you see her?'

"I then asked, 'Can we see who? Who do you see?'

"Pointing to the sky, he said, ". . . It's the Blessed Mother. She's there . . . She's wearing pink. She has a rosary in her hands. . . . She has a towel-thing on her head. . . . There are stars under her feet. I see colors. . . .'

"Jimmy wasn't at all afraid," the letter continued. As his mother and several others approached the boy, he assured them that Mary would guide them to righteousness. "I turned to look at the people behind me and their eyes were full of tears. So were mine. . . . I was numb."

Richard and Betty Kersteins, Lakewood, Colorado: Although Betty was always devout, Dick had been somewhat skeptical until he went to Medjugorge a few years ago. "I then did a complete turnaround," he says.

Both Kersteins were present in 1991 when Theresa Lopez had her first visions at Mother Cabrini. "Someone was carrying a statue of Fatima up the hill and the gown suddenly turned gold," recounts Betty. "Then it seemed that all the other statuary and crosses were turning gold. Everywhere you looked, it was gold."

On another Sunday, Dick and several hundred others glimpsed an image of Mary waving to them. "Although what I saw was faint, others stated they heard her call, 'Come to me,'" says Dick.

Even now, visions come thick and fast for the faithful. "We get lots of Canadians and Native Americans, and they basically report the same types of things," he goes on. "A lot of us believe the renewal of the U.S. Catholic Church will come out of Denver."

Robert H. Feeney, Denver, Colorado: "It's not as if we have a manual, or somebody on staff waiting all his or her life to handle an alleged apparition," Feeney, a spokesman for the Diocese of Denver, told the Associated Press. "Every step of the way, it's brand new."

How to Get There

Located 15 miles west of Denver, the Mother Cabrini shrine can be reached by taking exit 259 from 70W. Go straight and follow the signs to the shrine. Mountain temperatures fluctuate, so wear layers of clothes. Also watch for signs warning about dangerous snakes. Hours vary. Mother Cabrini Shrine, Golden, CO 80401, 303/526-0758.

✝ Small Town Miracles

Christ of the Mines Shrine
Silverton, Colorado

How It Happened

Silverton has devolved from a booming mining camp in the 1870s to a struggling tourist attraction with maybe 450 residents during the winter season. Nestled in the rugged San Juan Mountains, it represents the halfway point between the cosmopolitan lure of Durango and the skiing and hiking meccas of Telluride and Ouray. With quaint storefronts, unpaved streets, and one way in and out (via Route 550), it seems a miracle that this town—which gets 250–300 inches of snow a year—has survived at all.

Some folks give the Christ of the Mines Shrine partial credit for Silverton's continued existence. This 12-foot, 7-ton statue of Jesus Christ with his arms outstretched to a span of nearly 15 feet overlooks the town. And things had been much worse before. "During the 1950s, the mining industry hit rock bottom," recounts longtime resident Gerald Swanson. "There wasn't a working mine anywhere." People were moving out and businesses closing faster than a mountain snowslide.

Swanson and a few other members of a Catholic men's club cooked up the idea of a shrine in 1958. "We wanted to honor the miners and the Sacred Heart of Jesus," he continues. "We also hoped that in some small way it would help."

So with little more than faith and a knowledge of the area, they found a nook on Anvil Mountain that could be readily seen from the highway and was fairly easy to get to, at least after the ice melted. Club members and then-parish priest Father Joseph Halloran went to the local courthouse and discovered the site belonged to the county, which willingly donated the land. It wasn't being used for anything, anyway.

The club organized the funds and human resources to obtain the regionally quarried stones and pay for Carrara marble from Italy, where the statue was sculpted. It was a bargain—the icon itself only cost $5,000—but compensating for shipment from Italy and assembling the various pieces (not to mention getting them up the mountain) proved to be more of a challenge.

Still, everybody chipped in. "We obtained materials for the base and surrounding alcove from an old brewery and Father Halloran recruited the county crew to assemble and put the statue on its pedestal," remarks Swanson. Even non-Catholics donated time and money. "Here, everyone watches out for everyone else."

Shortly after the statue's dedication, the lower reaches of the town's biggest mine, the Sunnyside, opened and proved to be profitable, marking one of Silverton's most prosperous periods. High-grade gold and other minerals were found there.

There were other marvels as well. "We wanted to plant a stand of trees behind the shrine, but were told by the U.S. Forest Service and others that nothing would grow there," says Swanson. But the new parish priest, Father Joseph McGuinness, insisted on purchasing 1,000 spruce and Scotch pine seedlings and trying anyway. After being hand-watered for a month, the little trees took root. "Now we have a mini-forest behind the shrine and it gives it a little class," adds Swanson with a smile.

But perhaps the most stunning happening was on June 4, 1978. A high-altitude lake above the Sunnyside workings broke through the mine. Water rampaged through the underground tunnel and lower portal, demolishing everything in its path, filling the mine with debris and silt, overturning cars, and smashing equipment.

On this particular Sunday evening, however, no one was present, not even the night watchman. "This was a miracle in itself, as someone is usually around, working in the office and doing repairs," explains Swanson. Given the history of mining disasters, the lack of injuries was extraordinary.

Still, even the good vibes generated by Christ's upraised arms couldn't prevent the mine from closing in the early 1990s. Sunnyside was sold to a Canadian company with different interests. The price of equipment and Environmental Protection Agency requirements made costs skyrocket, while the market for gold and other precious metals declined. "Shutdowns are happening everywhere; we weren't the only ones affected," comments Swanson.

Still, Silverton chugs along, bolstered by tourists from the Durango & Silverton Narrow Gauge Railroad, which runs several times a day during the warmer months. An estimated 200,000 visit the town every year, and 225-plus enterprises, many of which are shuttered during the winter, open for business. So although life isn't always easy or prosperous, it does go on. The Christ of the Mines shrine isn't the source of spinning lights or visions, but its effects seem grounded in the day-to-day business of survival in the mountains.

What to Expect

Although there was lots of foot traffic in the '60s, actual pilgrimages seem to have declined, at least from outsiders. Perhaps it's because the shrine is easily seen from the road and also well-lit at night, quite an impressive sight in the dark mountains.

However, the half-mile trek up Anvil Mountain may be worth the effort, if only to get fresh air and view the surrounding masonry and the detail work on the beautiful marble statue. It also provides a chance to commune with nature and may be as physically close to heaven as one can get.

What They Say

Father Joseph McGuinness, Mancos, Colorado: The shrine was already complete when Father McGuinness was assigned to the parish in 1961. "Many attributed the reopening of the mines to the intercession of the Lord," he says.

"For a while, we tried to keep a ledger of all visitors, but interest died down," he admits. "Now, many people don't even know it's there." Still, up until a few years ago, groups of nuns and bishops traveled from nearby towns to make an annual trek to the Christ of the Mines.

There seems to be a reciprocity, however, between the shrine and the people of Silverton. "The locals take care of it, for instance, repairing it when vandals shot off the fingers of the statue." And although he feared the nearby spruce and pines might be liberated for Christmas decorations, not a one has ever been touched.

The portion of Anvil Mountain where the shrine is located used to be a major avalanche and rock slide area. "But there hasn't been a slide since the shrine opened."

Gerald Swanson, Silverton, Colorado: An enthusiastic booster of Silverton, Swanson runs a local gift shop and is restoring a period bed-and-breakfast. "Although we've had a hodgepodge tourist business, the economy has been stable," he says. "I believe that as long as the Christ of the Mines statue stands, we'll be monitored by a Supreme Being. It's comforting to know someone is watching over us."

How to Get There

Those brave enough and/or comfortable with mountain driving can take the San Juan skyway (U.S. 550) to Scenic Drive and go east. The shrine is on the left, about a half-mile up on Shrine Rd., which in some parts is known as West 15th St. Since Silverton is a tiny place, it's nearly impossible to get lost. Visitors from the railroad can ask for the best directions to the shrine. The natives are friendly and might even take you there. Direct all inquiries to the Silverton Chamber of Commerce, P.O. Box 565, Silverton, CO 81433, 303/387-5654.

Connecticut —

✝ Jesus vs. the Devil in Wooster Square Park

Wooster Square Park
New Haven, Connecticut

How It Happened

The guy with the pointy tail seemed to arrive first. For years, Wooster Square Park, which adjoined St. Michael's Catholic Church, had a so-called "Devil Tree." It had a 5-foot-long scar with three prongs that resembled a pitchfork; no one seems to know how the satanic sycamore got that way. And the area had become the site of drug deals, muggings, and other crimes.

Then one summer night in August 1992, a nearly blind young woman was walking through the park with her father. Although the anonymous visionary could only discern light and dark, she stopped suddenly and, according to *Yankee* magazine, cried, "Daddy, am I crazy or am I seeing the Lord?" A short distance from the Devil Tree, a giant crucifix had appeared within the shadows of another old sycamore. With a branch span of nearly 20 feet, the head, legs, arms, and torso of Jesus were visible under a street lamp.

The girl and her father returned with a camcorder and word soon spread. People began dropping by the park at all hours. Thousands of pilgrims left flowers, notes, and religious items at the tree's base, wearing down the grass around it. Some camped out all night at park benches, marveling over the phenomenon. "The street light was not new, the tree certainly had been there a long time," observed *Yankee*. "Why had it taken a blind girl to see this?"

Perhaps equally remarkably, "crime in that area seemed to stop," remarks Rob Lively, an associate professor of religion at the University of Maine. "The streets around the park were safer and people weren't as afraid to go there. The tree helped restore a sense of community."

In fact, self-appointed tree guides willingly delineated Christ's various body parts to the uninitiated or skeptical. Some people claimed to glimpse the Easter Bunny, Virgin Mary, and/or children playing at Jesus's feet while others viewed nothing but clusters of suppurated bark. "Maybe we're not holy enough to see it," one woman told a reporter. "Maybe I'll start going to church more and come back."

As the night deepened, the vision of Christ hanging from the cross became clearer, creating a spooky effect. "This image is not as benevolent as many others," adds Lively. But that didn't discourage the creation of a circus-like atmosphere; blasting car horns, shouting pedestrians, religious arguments among families. Flashlights shone on a knee, a hand, the beard. Still, the crowds were respectful.

Neighbors claimed the image, which consists of clusters of defined grooves and ripples, was created by lightning. And although many were familiar with the Devil Tree, nothing like this had ever happened before. "The tree was struck . . . right where Jesus is now," a man identified as Walt told *The Yale Daily News Magazine*. "That's why we can see him like that. . . . You know where lightning comes from, don't you?"

The priest at St. Michael's refuses to comment. So if good and evil *are* doing battle in Wooster Park, the Jesus Tree is on its own.

What to Expect

Although the crowds have almost stopped in recent months, the area around St. Michael's has become diverse and community-minded. Still, going into the park alone at night when the image is clearest may not be wise. Flashlights and large companions are recommended.

With a circumference of about 10 feet, the Jesus Tree is relatively easy to identify. Located directly across from St. Michael's and under a street light, it may also have offerings at the base. The tree's bottom two branches extend outward, creating the "cross" part of the crucifix. Jesus is rather distinctly defined on the trunk and his head is tilted down with a sad expression.

The glorified rake a few feet away pales in comparison. And who but the boldest would have the chutzpah to visit Lucifer's lair in the dark, anyway?

What They Say

From an account in The Yale Daily News Magazine, *New Haven, Connecticut:* "A group of four young guys stroll up to the tree, laughing. 'I don't see no Jesus,' says one.

'Where is he? Does he talk?' says another.

One of the young guys examines the flowers and the candles flickering at the base of the tree. 'What is this . . . voodoo?'

Eventually they can think of no more jokes and, in a tight group . . . walk away. . . . One [looks] back over his shoulder on his way out. He keeps his eyes fixed on the Jesus Tree for a few seconds as he takes quick steps out of the park."

Rob Lively, Wilton, Maine: At the tree and other sites, "People talk about AIDS, racial strife, abortion, drugs, war. At church they nod off during the sermon. What brings people is a mystery that has been taken away from the modern church." Regardless of whether it's real, "It means something to the people who come. It brings them closer together and adds significance to their lives. That's what matters."

How to Get There

Take I-95 to New Haven, get off at the Long Wharf exit (one way). Take a left on Water, then turn right on Olive and go two blocks. Turn right on Chapel and the park (located at Wooster Place) is the green space on the left. Late April is a particularly nice time to come, as there is a local cherry blossom festival and the trees in the area are in full bloom.

Florida —

✝ Making Room for Mary

Our Loving Mother's Foundation/Home of Rosa Lopez
Hollywood, Florida

How It Happened

Even Rosa Lopez admits she's an unlikely visionary. "Sometimes I think God chose me by mistake," she told the *Chicago Tribune.* "I feel I'm not clean or pure enough. But I know that Mary and Jesus want to see that all are redeemed."

Before she first started seeing the Virgin Mary in Conyers, Georgia in 1992 and later in her bedroom in Hollywood, Florida, the married, middle-aged Cuban woman with two grown children suffered from health problems and was bedridden. Not only did she claim to be healed of maladies ranging from colitis to hepatitis to hernias, but she began taking Polaroids of miraculous visions that supposedly appeared in her home and back yard.

At first, however, she kept the revelations to herself. "Jesus and Mary were preparing her heart and soul for what was to come," explains Susy Ikhwan, who initially volunteered to type up the various messages. "They asked her to keep it a secret, although of course her husband Armando knew what was happening, however difficult it was for him to accept it. He didn't see anything she saw, so he thought she was going crazy." Plus, Rosa began decorating their bedroom in 20th Century Shrine, with rosaries and statues, and claimed Mary sometimes spent the night there. It was enough to strain any marriage.

Within a few months, however, he literally shared her vision. "[Mary] was in the window," he told the *Tribune.* "I passed my hands in front of the vision and I still saw it. I went back to the bed and peeked with one eye. And it was still there."

In early 1994, Mary "gave" Rosa permission to spread the word and soon the afflicted, the infirm, and those seeking spiritual

55

enlightenment began appearing on the family doorstep. "You can't say no; they've come from so far away," Armando continued. "The house isn't mine anymore; it's the Blessed Mother's." Even their children, Cari and Alex, began delivering holy water to the ill. Obtained from a fountain fueled by an ordinary garden hose in the yard, it is supposedly blessed, although its curative powers have yet to be documented.

Amazing things happen at the home of Rosa Lopez in Hollywood, Florida. Note the two "hearts" in the photo.
PHOTO COURTESY OF OUR LOVING MOTHER'S FOUNDATION.

According to Ikhwan, as many as 50 people file through on an average day, although the main event is on the 13th of the month. At that time, Mary allegedly appears in Rosa's former bedroom, in what has come to be known as the apparition room. About 1,500 or so pilgrims converge upon the blue-and-white house in the primarily Protestant, working-class neighborhood.

Messages center around a return to prayer, Mass, and saying the rosary. Rosa told the *Tribune* that she once saw Jesus "holding an eight-month aborted baby in his arms and [he] handed it to his mother. Great painful moments are approaching the world. . . . Only prayer will save you from all that is coming." The revelations are delivered in English and Spanish via loudspeakers.

"At first, we had a lot of trouble with the neighbors and the city," admits Ikhwan. "But now the streets near the house are closed on apparition day and the neighbors don't say much anymore." Police direct traffic and ambulances provide aid to those affected by the intense South Florida heat. The issuance of parking tickets has also helped.

The Church was also quite clear about its stand. In November 1994, Miami archbishop Edward A. McCarthy issued a statement against "promoting or in any way encouraging these so-called private revelations that have not been authenticated by the Holy See."

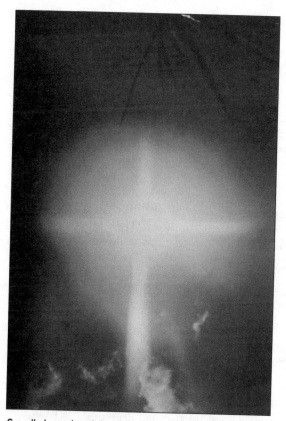

So-called miracles of the sun and moon occur at the home of Rosa Lopez in Hollywood, Florida. PHOTO COURTESY OF OUR LOVING MOTHER'S FOUNDATION.

But Ikhwan believes they might change their minds. "We've contacted the diocese and they say they're investigating, although we haven't heard anything yet."

Lopez's followers aren't waiting for them to get around to it. They've already organized Our Loving Mother's Foundation, with Ikhwan as president. The Foundation disseminates a monthly newsletter with Mary's messages as well as videotapes of the "mystical lights" around the Lopez home.

The volunteer organization uses donations and other funds for the newsletter and free handouts such as rosaries, scapulars, and religious literature. The Foundation also helps with the Lopez mortgage. "Before the apparitions, Rosa and Armando rented out the two other bedrooms," explains Ikhwan. "They were on a fixed income and had to meet the payments." Now Mary has taken up the slack.

City officials expressed concern that, since the Conyers apparitions have become less frequent, tens of thousands of the faithful might migrate to this small tract home in Florida on the 13th of each month. Lopez is worried as well. "All this is too much for such a small heart," she said in the *Tribune*. But Mary has settled in for the duration and allegedly refuses to move the apparition site. Naturally Rosa Lopez has faith in her celestial boarder: "Mary will provide."

What to Expect

The Lopezes get visitors from all over the world but prefer they wait until the 13th. On that day, pilgrims get a tour of the house and apparition room. All but a few gather outside and wait for the 11:45 a.m. service, at which time Rosa receives her message. Only the terminally ill are allowed in the apparition room during the rosary prayers: "Jesus anoints the sick there through Rosa's hands," states Ikhwan.

The message is then read aloud and Rosa circulates among the crowd and may do the laying on of hands if so moved. People have claimed to see what has become standard at such sites: rosaries changing colors, spinning suns and moons, crosses in the sky, profiles of Mary. Some of these are documented in the Foundation's blurry videos, which are accompanied by a soundtrack of wavering religious music. Those wanting the experience of illegal substances without actually ingesting any, getting arrested, or damaging themselves and their unborn children might find it worth the $10 plus $2.50 postage.

The interior of the house is also plastered with Polaroids of sky images of Jesus, Mary, and the gate to heaven. The Foundation hopes to knock out a wall of a bedroom to make space for more pilgrims.

Devotions can be made outside at various statues and the fountain. Still, "Rosa is always there for people," adds Ikhwan.

What They Say

Mary D., Delray, Florida: "My husband was an alcoholic for many years. I petitioned the Blessed Mother at Rosa's house to help [him] stop drinking. He became sick with very high blood pressure and sought help on Dec. 27, 1994, at Fair Oaks Hospital in Delray. His blood pressure returned to normal and he stopped drinking. He has been sober since Dec. 27 and does not even crave a drink. This was truly a miracle."

Bonnie P., Hollywood, Florida: "On March 24, 1995, I came to Rosa Lopez who put Holy Water on my left side which has been paralyzed from a stroke since April 4, 1993. Rosa removed my sock, brace, and shoe and wiped holy water on my leg and foot. She prayed over me. I stayed for about an hour. After I returned home I felt as if I could walk and I did with the aid of God and my cane, no brace and no shoe. I continued to walk around my home."

Dead German Tourists, a Miami rock band, Hollywood, Florida: According to the *Tribune*, the band was ensconced a few blocks away from the Lopez home during a recent apparition day. Along with playing popular songs, they provided a local radio station with updates of the happenings. One of the members, who calls himself Flipper, decided to visit the Lopez home and meet Rosa.

Name changed by request.

Her prayers made him unsteady, he reported. "I felt like I was gonna go down. It was a religious experience. We may come back."

How to Get There

Take I-95 to Hollywood Blvd. Go west on Hollywood to 441 (SR 7). Turn right on 441 to Johnson St. Turn left on Johnson to 66th Ave and turn right on 66th to Arthur St.; the house number is 1301.

The site opens at 8:00 a.m. on the 13th for services, which begin at 11:45 a.m. The newsletter recommends that you bring chairs, umbrel-las, refreshments, and a container for holy water. It also pro-vides detailed directions and tips for avoiding parking tickets. Send a self-addressed stamped envelope to Our Loving Mother's Foundation, P.O. Box 653237, Miami, FL 33265-3237, no phone.

Georgia ⎯

✝ **Jesus Christ, Crimestopper**

Tree of Unknown Genesis, 2731 N. Lumpkin Rd.
Columbus, Georgia

How It Happened

The gnarled, weatherbeaten tree in Margaret Richardson's front
yard may have always been odd-looking. But no one knew exactly
how otherworldly it actually was until Bishop Barbara Shepard of
the Word of Wisdom Christian Center happened by one evening in
April 1994.

"You have to understand, there's a lot of gang warfare in our
area," Shepard explains. "We had a meeting at our church and
decided to pray about it." Someone threw a tissue on the ground
"and we stomped on it, like we were stomping on the devil. I could
see the devil's face on the ground, and I prayed that I wouldn't see
it any more."

Shepard passed by Richardson's house on her way home from
church, as she had many evenings before. But this time something
was different: "As I drove towards the house, I saw an image. It was
Jesus. It was bright, shining, facing the Jehovah's Witness Kingdom
Hall across the street. For a second, it was blinding." It took her a
few passes around the block to figure out that the image had
emanated from Richardson's tree.

Shepard got out of her automobile and rang the doorbell. No one
answered. She lingered a while, hoping someone would show up.
"But I sensed the presence of sickness, and didn't think anyone
would come," she states.

Since it was after midnight, a policeman stopped and asked her
what she was doing on private property. "I showed him the tree. He
said in the 25 years he'd traveled down this road, he'd never seen
anything like it."

Shepard returned the next night when Richardson was home. "I'd been at the hospital with my daughter who had asthma," Richardson recalls. "And there was this lady standing across the street. She came to the door and said, 'Do you know what you've got in that tree in your yard?'"

Richardson went outside and Shepard, who was with her grand-daughter, showed her the image. "I recognized it right away," says Richardson, a regular churchgoer. "It looked like Jesus holding a lamb. It was pretty and had a gray glow you could see for miles."

As any student of human behavior knows, two or more individuals pointing and staring at something are bound to draw attention. Before another Sunday rolled around, Richardson had people trampling through her and others' yards, and TV crews and journalists knocking on her door.

They came from all over; during its peak, the tree attracted up to 2,000 onlookers a night. "Folks weren't mean, but they didn't pay much mind to what they were doing," observes Richardson of her ruined flowers and inconvenienced neighbors. "They just wanted to see the tree."

The faithful brought their own floral offerings, laying them at the base of the tree. There were reports of healings. Richardson herself was visited by a woman who claimed to be cured of paralysis after putting her hand on the tree. Every night at dusk, groups gathered and prayed, often singing and testifying until 4 a.m.

Soon the police were called to direct the crowds and traffic. "It was like mushrooms growing out of the ground," Sergeant W.E. Allmond told *The Atlanta Constitution*. "Bling! They were there." At times officers blocked Richardson's street to through vehicles and onlookers had to view the tree from behind barricades.

Not everyone was thrilled. "It's like a waste of taxpayers' money for the police to babysit a tree," Jerald Bellamy, a member at the Jehovah's Witness Kingdom Hall, grumbled to *The Constitution*.

A few weeks after the image went public, a vandal sprayed black paint on the tree. Although it obscured the face of Jesus somewhat, the faithful still came, until, as mysteriously as it arrived, the likeness went away. "The image only lasted about two months, and hasn't come back since," adds Richardson.

But while the tumult was going on, a more tangible miracle was occurring. According to both Shepard and Richardson, crime dropped dramatically in the area. "It hasn't stopped by any means, but the image seemed to draw people together, both black and white," observes Shepard. "There was a closeness that hadn't been there before."

Adds Richardson, "Some preachers said that God wouldn't come in a tree. But when I saw rough-looking kids outside at 2 a.m. in bandannas talking to each other, I knew differently. More than one told me the image gave them something to believe in, that it changed their lives."

"That night, I didn't want to go to bed with a picture of the devil in my head so I prayed for a sign from Jesus," says Shepard of her discovery. "God works in mysterious ways."

What to Expect

Margaret Richardson handles intermittent inquiries with humor. "If that was Jesus in my yard, he's welcome to come back any time," she remarks of the play of shadow and light that caused such an uproar. "There was some talk about people from the city chopping down the tree, but they'd have to get permission from the owner, since it is a rental property."

If you do stop by her house, however, don't expect to see anything more than an ancient, tangled tree. And it might not be wise to tarry. Richardson probably won't complain but the neighbors, fearing another stampede of the faithful, might call upon a higher authority—the cops—to save their lawns instead of visitors' souls.

What They Say

Barbara Shepard, Columbus, Georgia: Shepard was a pastor for nine years before taking on leadership at the Word of Wisdom Christian Center, a nondenominational organization. During the time of the image, "so much happened spiritually," she asserts. Along with a decrease in gang problems, "many people came back to Jesus, including those with heavy drinking and drug problems.

"Although people have mocked me, the image strengthened my faith, which was strong to begin with. It also revealed who truly believed in him as well as those who supported my ministry."

Margaret Richardson, Columbus, Georgia: Richardson got feedback from all sides about her tree. "People asked me, 'How do you know what Jesus looks like?' I told them, 'Well, the tree resembles pictures from my childhood and the Bible.' Some people thought I was crazy, but I have faith, and that's what I saw."

Richardson's daughter-in-law remained unconvinced. "She was standing there talking about how nothing was there and people were getting mad at her. So she had to leave."

Olitha Jones and onlookers, Columbus, Georgia: Jones told *The Constitution* that she saw three separate images, including a sheep, which others interpreted as the folded arms of Jesus.

"That's a calf," said Henry Mims.

"It's a lamb," Jones replied.

"It's a tree!" said Tony Smith.

How to Get There

About a two-hour ride from Atlanta, Columbus can be reached via I-85S. Then take I-85S to the Victor Dr. exit and turn right. Go down three or four lights to N. Lumpkin Rd. and turn right again. Richardson's tree is in the front of her yard, which is across the street from the Jehovah's Witness Kingdom Hall. Send written inquiries only to Margaret Richardson, 2731 N. Lumpkin, Columbus, GA 31903.

✝ Visions by Nancy Fowler

Our Loving Mother's Children
Conyers, Georgia

How It Happened

Nancy Fowler, a soft-spoken, seemingly retiring, overweight housewife and former nurse, has baffled scientists, faced the skeptics, and wowed believers. By 1987, the married mother of two had glimpsed hell, "a dark, black, fiery hole," she told *The Atlanta Journal and Constitution,* and heaven, an "immense room filled with white-robed, winged angels."

She became conversant in the various forms of spiritual communication: apparitions, seeing beings in a bodily state; imaginative visions, often referred to as "wide-awake dreams" in which the real world has vanished; intellectual visions, direct communications from God that are not viewed at all; and inner locutions, the obtaining of fully realized messages without using any of the five senses. Many of Fowler's messages echo those of Fatima—conversion, prayer, reparation, sacrifices—but are also strongly anti-abortion, the act of which is equated with murder.

She has also had several close encounters of the satanic kind. According to *To Bear Witness That I Am The Living Son of God,* a book written by her followers about her experiences, Lucifer tried to strangle her while she was driving on the highway, disguised himself as Mary and in other forms, and in general made a nuisance of himself during her locutions.

But Fowler continued to "communicate" with Jesus and Mary, the latter of whom even allegedly advised her to go on a diet. Religious statues and pictures replaced a stereo system in her living room, and the triangular shelves in the corner where she had many of her visions were built according to Jesus's specifications (he *had* been a carpenter). The space was renamed the Apparition Room and soon became Vision Central. A singing bird outside the window "signaled" Mary's presence.

A native of Cambridge, Massachusetts, Fowler soon found herself with a spiritual advisor, a scribe who faithfully recorded her locutions (his name also appeared in messages from Jesus), and other supporters. She located a piece of ecclesiastically prime real estate: The Farm, several sparsely treed acres in Conyers, about 20 miles outside of Atlanta. According to *To Bear Witness,* Jesus pointed her towards a small house with a big back yard and a hill, not surprisingly to be called Holy Hill. A nearby well was also declared "holy" although the local health department warned it might be contaminated with coliform bacteria.

Although she didn't actually build it, they came anyway. People from all walks of life gave up the fast-paced, garish secular world for Our Loving Mother's Children, as her group came to be called. And thousands of others visited on the 13th of each month, when Fowler had her visions. They arrived in buses, wheelchairs, and cars, often parking in lots quite distant from the site. This worked minor miracles for the Conyers economy: hotels and restaurants sprang up, seemingly overnight. However, some not-so-grateful locals sported bumper stickers stating, "Eat, Drink, and See Mary."

The faithful bore camcorders, 35mm cameras, and Polaroid One Steps, which are particularly successful in capturing what looks like a doorway superimposed over the sun. Although some might interpret this as the "Golden Door" cited in Revelation 4:1, a group called the Georgia Skeptics produced identical pictures in a number of nonreligious situations, including that of a lone 50-watt halogen spotlight in a dark room. "The Polaroid's iris had the exact same shape (straight vertical sides, curved top and bottom) as the Golden Door," observed Joe Nickell in his book, *Looking for a Miracle.*

After hearing Fowler's message over a public-address system, pilgrims also professed to see the sun dancing and spinning as well as the face of the Virgin Mary in the sky. Occasionally, someone would claim to smell roses. The faithful knelt in front of pictures of Mary, accompanying their devotions with prayer and song. And they vowed that the water in the well had healing properties.

On June 13, 1993, the normally media-shy Fowler agreed to something that would make many visionaries shudder—she submitted to a battery of medical and scientific tests. She "placed no restrictions on the tests that could be performed," stated a Loving Mother pamphlet, "Why Do You Test Me?" A group of scientists, ranging from a professor of neuropsychophysiology (whew!) at the Catholic University of Bolivia to neurologists to a psychiatrist to EEG technicians to a radiation scientist and others, was assembled. Under the unblinking eye of a camera crew, Fowler's EEG was measured during her visions.

According to the pamphlet, the brain activity during this time was that "normally associated with deep sleep or coma." While Fowler was seeing Jesus, the delta measurement was 3, with a recurring pattern of 333. For Mary, it was 4 or 444, and for the Prince of Darkness it was 6, or 666. And if that's not enough, another scientist detected the appearance of ionized radiation while the Virgin Mary was "visiting" Fowler, and very little activity before or after.

The physicist even evaluated a crucifix on the wall of the Apparition Room while Fowler claimed Christ was present. "When he moved the probe to the heart of Christ, the electrical energy began to pulsate, as if the cross was alive," according to the brochure. "When Nancy said that Jesus said to her, 'That is all,' the electrical activity ceased."

On the other hand, when author and vision-buster Joe Nickell placed a stethoscope to the same statue, he heard nothing. He has also pointed out that you can hold your own thumb to an icon and feel a pulse.

Whether or not people choose to believe, Jesus and Mary's messages come through loud and clear to Nancy Fowler: Pick up your rosaries and pray.

What to Expect

The Farm is a simple, bare-bones operation. Spread out over its 30-some acres are the one-story white clapboard house; a barn which serves as a communications center for Our Loving Mother's Children and sells English and Spanish books, videos, and holy cards; the Holy Hill/well; and other unmarked structures. Walkways are partitioned off with chicken wire. Piles of folding chairs rest against the buildings, while signs direct pilgrims to go here and stay away from there.

Even the walkways of The Farm at Conyers are supposed to inspire religious experiences. PHOTO BY SANDRA GURVIS.

Still, volunteers are friendly and eager to welcome newcomers. Inside the barn, videos of Fowler run continuously and pictures of "miracles" (as in, "See Mary over by that tree?") plaster the walls and various scrapbooks. Despite its humble appearance, Our Loving Mother's Network has a sophisticated information dissemination system: you can get their monthly newsletter, the *Journal of Reported Teachings and Messages at Conyers,* via regular mail, fax (404/413-1656), or through most electronic information services and the Internet (e-mail address for the latter: p01475@psilink.com). There is also a telephone network, with a new recorded message on the 14th (404/498-1891, touch-tone; 404/922-8885, rotary).

A combination of a "Brady Bunch"–style den and a chapel, the Apparition Room in the main house still has a stone fireplace and decorated ceiling fans. Statues of Jesus and Mary replace the usual TV and gallery of family portraits. Total silence is a must; people come here for serious prayer and not to sprawl in a Barcalounger. (The pews and metal chairs aren't conducive to relaxation, anyway.)

The well at Holy Hill only allows one gallon of water per visitor, and you're reminded that during the walk back, you'll have enough time to say an entire round of the rosary. Services are held at 3:00 p.m. on Sunday and on the 13th of every month. Although in October 1994, Fowler stated Mary's appearances would be limited to that date once a year (the anniversary of Fowler's first vision), the latest *Journal* reports an ongoing dialogue and messages.

What They Say

Rev. Peter Dora, Atlanta Archdiocese: So far, the Catholic church has yet to make inquiries at Conyers. "We fully acknowledge that

Although the water at The Farm at Conyers, Georgia, allegedly has healing properties, visitors are limited to one gallon each. PHOTO BY SANDRA GURVIS.

people are seeking something they don't seem to be finding else-where," Dora told the Associated Press. "In the same breath, we are concerned about the damage this could do to these believers if it turns out to be false." So the ever-vigilant Loving Mother's Children encour-ages those who have experienced conversions and healing to write to the Archbishop of Atlanta (680 W. Peachtree N.W., Atlanta, GA 30308-1984). And don't forget to send a copy of the letter to Joy at the Conyers address (see below).

Sammy Deaton, Lawrence-ville, Georgia: Deaton lost his wife Mary to a heart attack in 1992. He went to Conyers on the 13th a few months later and "got right in front of the Apparition Room. I looked up at the sun at about 11:45 a.m. I saw all kinds of colors coming from the sun. I put my right hand over my right eye, and an "M" appeared in my eye. . . . I saw a cross flash in the sky." He glimpsed an apparition of Mary during another visit. "She appeared to me in a brown picture frame. Her clothes were shining brown." He interpreted the color as mourning for the loss of his wife: "That was why she appeared in a picture frame to me. [Jesus and Mary] let me know that [my] Mary was with them."

Duquela Dickerson, Tampa, and Karen Horne, Pittsburgh: Both women were present during a recent visitation. "We thought we would just come for the blessing, not necessarily to be healed," Horne, a victim of multiple sclerosis who has been wheelchair-bound for five years, told *Time.*

"The doctors told us three weeks ago that there is nothing they can do," added Dickerson, whose 4-year-old daughter had been diagnosed with inoperable brain cancer. "I just came to pray to the Lady. She's got a son, so she knows the pain of having a child pass away."

How to Get There

From Atlanta, take 20E and get off at Highway 138 (exit 42). Turn left (over the expressway) and go down a few miles to White Road. Turn left again; look for a small sign "The Farm" on the left (street address: 2332 White Rd.). If you plan to go on the 13th, arrive early. Although events usually begin around noon, traffic backs up quickly and parking's at a premium. Our Loving Mother's Children, P.O. Box 309, Conyers, GA 30207, 404/922-0885.

✝ Pasta Jesus, Please

Pizza Hut Billboard
Stone Mountain, Georgia, and about 20 other places around Atlanta

How It Happened

It has been compared to a Muppet, the Cowardly Lion, Leon Russell, Willie Nelson, the creature from the movie "Alien," and Jim Morrison, but it was Jesus to an Atlanta-area woman who prefers to be known only as "Simpson." In May 1991, Simpson claimed to see an image of Jesus "straight from Michelangelo" on a Pizza Hut billboard while she filled up her tank at a Texaco station.

"I was very conflicted about singing in the church choir," recalls the fortysomething fashion designer, vegetarian, and single mother of two grown children. "There was a lot of dissension within the group, and it just didn't seem natural or real." As she pumped gas, she had a private conversation with the Lord: "I was thinking, OK, God, this is it. If you want me to stay and participate, give me a sign.

"Just then a still, small voice inside me—what we Christians call the Holy Spirit—told me to look up. As I was wondering who said that, I saw the pizza billboard, and it took my breath away. I mean, nobody really knows what Christ looks like, but it was definitely the version that everybody recognizes." Held aloft by a fork and nestled among the spaghetti, sauce, and oregano were a crown of thorns, two deep-set eyes, a nose, and a beard. Something very unusual was happening above the words "Spaghetti Junction" and it wasn't just the bargain meal of $1.29 (choice of Personal Pan Pizza, spaghetti, ham and cheese sandwich, or single trip through the salad bar).

Perhaps a Higher Authority was also lending Pizza Hut a hand. Domino's had opened *its* first 50-seat Express! in Atlanta a few weeks before and the reduced prices were Pizza Hut's way of "saving" the lunchtime congregation. Pizza Hut displayed about 70 billboards in the locally-targeted ad campaign; about half were pizza and the remainder, spaghetti.

Still, Simpson waited a few days before notifying the media of her discovery. She took her daughter India and a girlfriend to see it. "It

A Pizza Hut billboard in Stone Mountain, Georgia, was a major topic of conversation when Jesus was spotted in a forkful of pasta. PHOTO COURTESY OF AUSTIN KELLEY ADVERTISING.

took my friend a half an hour to recognize the image. Then suddenly she went from praying quietly to speaking in tongues—something she'd never done before."

Once word got out, it seemed like "almost overnight it went nationwide," recounts Simpson. "People were waiting for me at work, and I got tons of calls and letters." CNN phoned, as did the Arsenio Hall show. Based on the image, Simpson also decided to stay in the choir. "There was some question about my wanting to go for a singing career, but I decided to use my voice for God."

The onslaught of fascinated motorists affected the nearby businesses as well. Prior to the sighting, an ill-placed highway median divider at Coleman Watley's Jiffy-Lube served as a deterrent for those who wanted an oil change. Not so the faithful. They gladly maneuvered around to get a look at the billboard, and while there got their cars serviced, too.

Personnel at the Texaco station where Simpson made her discovery were less pleased. "People couldn't get gas," owner Chris Bradshaw Jr. complained to *The Atlanta Constitution*. "All at once the lot was full . . . and we couldn't do no business." Although the same billboard was at about 20 other locations, the Memorial Drive posting received the most attention and traffic, including busfuls of churchgoers.

Pizza Hut denied any attempt at subliminal suggestion. The photo was strictly a stock shot supplied by the Wichita headquarters to franchisees. "I think anybody who would think we would send a photographer and a food stylist into a room with a plate of steaming spaghetti and . . . fashion [a] face is really stretching it," Roger Rydell, then-director of public affairs, told columnist John Kelso.

Austin Kelley Advertising, who handled the local account, found the brouhaha not only amusing but a blessing. "We got great press at zero cost," observes vice-president Suzanne Harkness. "We couldn't have paid for that kind of exposure. People are still talking about it." If there is a hidden symbol, it's in the words "Spaghetti Junction." "To Atlantans, it means the intersections of 285 and 85. You look down at it from an aerial perspective and it resembles a plate of pasta."

Within weeks, the Memorial Drive sign was replaced by a recruiting slogan for the Marines. The remaining billboards became objects of interest and curiosity until they, too, were torn down as part of a regular rotation. "We kept them up longer than originally planned," adds Harkness.

Although cynics poked fun and swore that all they saw was an incentive to chow down, Simpson remains firm in her beliefs. "It showed me that Christ is real. Here in Stone Mountain, the Ku Klux Klan capital of America, blacks and whites were hugging and praying and forgetting their differences. And it provided me, an average person, with the opportunity to spread the word of God. It just has to be a miracle." Meanwhile, Pizza Hut never did develop that vegetarian dish she'd been hoping for.

What to Expect

Unfortunately, the only record of the billboard can be found in fading newsclips and in the archives of TV stations and Austin Kelley Advertising. And the smaller the picture, the harder it seems to discern the image. But perhaps one day, the spiritual spaghetti may be resurrected and rise again. (Should that happen, look for the furrowed forehead in the middle of the forkful of pasta.)

What They Say

Donna Carmichael, Atlanta, Georgia: "I guess you could make it what you wanted to make it," Carmichael told *The New York Times*. "If you wanted a religious experience, you could probably have one, but you really would have to be in some kind of state of mind to [be driving by] . . . and see that on a billboard."

Danny Harrison, Atlanta, Georgia: "It was very easy for me to see," Harrison said in the *Times* story. "Of course, I believe in miracles anyway, so I didn't find [it] that unusual. The miracle was that people declared it as being the face of Jesus instead of any old face."

Billy Bradshaw, Stone Mountain, Georgia: As a partner in the family-owned Texaco station where Simpson first saw the image, Bradshaw caught flak from all angles. "Even though it brought out a lot of weird people, I'm a Christian so I personally believed in it. But I didn't recognize the face, although a lot of others around me did, including the media and my fellow workers." Some even felt a presence, but all he ever saw was a forkful of spaghetti. "I'd be lying if I said anything else."

How to Get There

From downtown Atlanta, take I-85N to I-285E and get off at the Memorial Dr./Avondale Estate exit. Turn left at the light, and go down about two miles. The billboard is on the corner of Memorial Drive and Village Square St. and currently advertises Krispy Kreme doughnuts. Talk about anti-pasta. . . .

✝ The Sorrows of Rosa Mystica

St. John of God Church
Chicago, Illinois

How It Happened

In 1947, in Sankt Ulrich, Italy, the Virgin Mary allegedly appeared, with three swords, then three roses across her chest, to Pierina Gilli, a local peasant. From there, a bustling industry grew, producing statues that supposedly wept and creating a popular stopoff for religious tours. Replicas of the Rosa Mystica—as the rose-bearing Virgin was called—"sell like hot cakes," the daughter of the gift shop owner informed a *Chicago Tribune* reporter. Gilli, who died in 1991 and whose family greatly prospered from believers' donations, was also "told" by the Blessed Virgin to have coins stamped and statues carved in Mary's honor. Mary, it seems, had joined the age of commerce.

The post World War II-period, however, had been much less fortunate for the St. John of God Church in Chicago. Previously fueled by income from South Side stockyards, this once-flourishing parish of 10,000 had by 1983 dwindled to about 500 elderly souls led by a Father Raymond Jasinski. The largely Polish population had been replaced by Hispanics, who preferred their own churches, and blacks, who (although they sent their children to the convent school) were mostly non-Catholic. As jobs and former residents disappeared and graffiti, gangs, and poverty encroached, the church's debt spiraled. Even the nuns who ran the school became afraid to answer the door.

Enter John Starace, the Rosa Mystica's society's U.S. director. A priest who lived in Brooklyn and who in fact had been thwarted in establishing a Rosa Mystica shrine in upstate New York, Starace was affiliated with a diocese in India but had never ministered to a parish there. Starace claimed to have been in the presence of over 90 weeping statues around the world. And when he met Father Jasinski at a religious retreat in 1983, he likely recognized a hot prospect.

According to Stephen Roszell, a filmmaker who produced the 1992 documentary "Rosa Mystica," Starace "promised the statues would cry, making the church a national shrine and bringing the Poles back to the neighborhood."

Now in the private possession of a priest, the Rosa Mystica statue, formerly of St. John of God Church in Chicago, can still appear almost tearful at times. PHOTO BY SANDRA GURVIS.

And thanks to the generosity of one of the few remaining wealthy parishioners who was also present at the retreat, two statues were purchased, one for St. John's and the other for the man's home. ("In one article in the *Tribune*, [the man's wife] is quoted as having said that, 'My husband is at that point of life where he either gets involved with statues or with younger women and . . . [he] chose statues,'" remarked one of the nuns, Sister Fulgenta Piasecki, in the movie.)

Two weeks after the statues were unpacked, on May 29, 1984, Jasinski and several other witnesses saw the St. John's Rosa Mystica weep. Her tears flowed so copiously that Sister Ambrosette Kopacz,

73

an elderly nun, wanted to wipe them from the 39-inch wooden statue. Church custodian Siggy Urbanski tasted them and declared them salty "like human tears."

"After that, things began to happen so fast, the message spread so fast, that at noontime on the busiest street corner everybody was passing this message of the Virgin crying," Sister Fulgenta told Roszell. "We called nobody."

"They were coming in throngs," added Urbanski. "The whole aisle was filled all the way out to the doors. The heat at the main sacrificial altar was 135 degrees, at least, from all these candles being lit."

Various rationales for the waterworks ranged from warnings about the end of the world to a call for the cessation of gang activity to an admonishment about not enough people saying the rosary. Alleged miracles included the reported levitation of one woman who abandoned herself to religious ecstasy, as well as an assortment of undocumented cures. Even an investigation by the Archdiocese of Chicago skirted around the source of the fount, eventually refusing to rule out natural causes, although it stopped short of identifying the weeping as a miracle. And with the thousands of visitors came donations. It appeared that Starace's predictions had come to fruition.

Then as abruptly as they began, the tears stopped, although people tarried throughout the summer, hoping Rosa Mystica would cry again. In mid-July, a "laughing gunman" entered the church and shot the statue, nicking the robe around the shin area. The perpetrator, a 23-year-old outpatient of the Illinois Mental Health Center, was declared not guilty by reason of insanity. Although about 30 people were present, no one was harmed and damage to the statue was minimal, small marvels in themselves. According to Father Jasinski, the gunman recovered and is now a devout Catholic.

But another form of erosion was taking place, as the *Chicago Tribune* began to delve into Starace's history. "Basically, he was exposed as a hoax," says Roszell. Starace's affiliation with so many weeping statues served as damning evidence, as did his checkered background and refusal to speak with the press. He also disassociated himself from Jasinski and the others at St. John's, much to their embarrassment. "His central role in the weepings was downplayed over time," although by then, the number of visitors to the church dwindled greatly.

Still, in spite of everything, a handful insisted on believing. "The archdiocese wanted the parish to forget about the statue and reach out to the neighborhood," continues Roszell.

"There also were efforts to consolidate St. John with other failing churches, but Father Jasinski chose to focus on Rosa Mystica instead."

Today, St. John of God is closed. On top of everything else, "the interior had various structural problems and repairs would have cost several thousand dollars," states Father Francis Cimarrusti, who served at the parish after Jasinski left. The school is now a shelter and learning center used by various Catholic charities.

The archdiocese is considering dismantling the sanctuary and moving it to Marysville, Kansas, where it will become part of another parish. According to Cimarrusti, sections from the stained glass windows were given to Loyola University for a new building. And, after being moved into a corner by Cimarrusti ("where it was originally intended to go," he says), the statue is now in the possession of Father Jasinski, who has retired to Georgia.

"To my knowledge, neither it nor the other statue ever wept again," comments Roszell. The privately owned statue also cried in 1984, around the same time as the other, but this information was kept quiet until several months after the fact. (Starace was supposedly present during both weepings.) The owner died less than a year later.

Roszell, a non-Catholic, went to St. John's final Mass. "Many prosperous former parishioners came and commented what a pity it was that no one could save the church," he says with a trace of irony. Instead of waiting for a miracle, they might have tried to create their own.

What to Expect

Basically, there's nothing to see except a shell of a building in a high-crime area. Although the former convent school is used sporadically, people there won't be likely to have much information. This shrine might perhaps best be thought of as a testimonial to the old adage, "God helps those who help themselves."

Although the statue's in a shrine in his basement, Father Jasinski, who considers himself its guardian, hopes one day to return it to a place of glory inside a Catholic church. "But certain conditions need to be met. If it's God's will, it will happen." The other statue remains privately owned.

What They Say

Sister Ambrosette Kopacz, Chicago, Illinois: Now retired and ill, Sister Ambrosette was one of the statue's biggest supporters. "Did the statue cry?" she asked rhetorically in Roszell's movie. "Yes, because I wiped the tears of the Blessed Mother. . . . I was asking for more handkerchiefs because the sisters and the people in back of me were calling, 'Touch her, touch her with mine.' . . . And I was so happy about [it] that I said, 'Mary, never leave me. I'm with you.'"

Danny Marcinkowski, Chicago, Illinois: The movie's principal narrator, Marcinkowski spent much of his time at the church, doing odd jobs. "Jesus never went to places . . . of wealth and places of prosperity," he observed. "He always went to . . . peasants and the down-and-outs or even just walking, roaming. . . ."

Of the crowds facing the statue, he remarked, "I seen [sic] these people, they were coming in, dropping to their knees. . . . And we didn't have a rug there. They fell—with their hands together in prayer. They came like . . . a duck landing in water. . . . It was incredible."

Eugene Kennedy, Chicago, Illinois: "Many people sneer at this kind of phenomenon," the former Maryknoll priest, author, and psychologist remarked in the *Tribune.* "But maybe they should look at what they believe in. After all, it's not unusual to see a sophisticated scientist put up a high-rise building without a 13th floor.

"The truth is that we just don't know the nature of the mystery very well. Most people never realize the transcendent moments in their lives and they want a little sign. . . . A weeping statue isn't very much" when people are looking for something to believe in. "The mission of faith is to say . . . that it is an ineffable mystery."

How to Get There

Those wishing for a private viewing of the Rosa Mystica statue can write Father Raymond Jasinski at 3625 Range Way, Loganville, GA 30249.

✛ Weeping Icons Frequent Orthodox Churches

St. Nicholas Albanian Orthodox Church
Chicago, Illinois

St. George Antiochian Orthodox Church
Cicero, Illinois

How It Happened

Using salt crystals, Shawn Carlson, an astrophysicist at the Lawrence Berkeley Laboratory in California, claimed he could make a picture cry. He informed *Newsweek* that he had found "six ways to gimmick a painting" with a method that was "very simple, requiring no detailed knowledge of physics. It could have easily been done hundreds of years ago," even with liquids other than water.

The crowds who witnessed crying icons at two separate Orthodox churches in the Chicago area might not be so easily convinced. Both were depictions of the Virgin Mary; both wept fragrant oils and were detected by the attendant priests; both were interpreted as a commentary on the woeful state of the world and as a call to return to God.

Approximately 250,000 Orthodox Christians live in the Chicago area. The urban bouillabaisse there has over 90 Orthodox parishes. Divided along national lines, including Greeks, Russians, Albanians, Serbians, Ukrainians, and others, each denomination has its own hierarchy and individual organization.

The first icon, at St. Nicholas Albanian Orthodox Church, was discovered on December 6, 1986, on the feast day of the church's patron saint, St. Nicholas, by the Rev. Philip Koufos and several parishioners. The gold and scarlet icon, painted by New York City artist Constantine Youssis in the early '60s, depicts Mary holding the baby Jesus. Fluid "was coming up from between [Mary's] fingers and from her eyes, which were welling up," Koufos told *People* magazine. "I had seen other weeping icons, but never one that large or with so much moisture."

Thousands mobbed the 250-family church to view the canvas-on-wood portrait. St. Nicholas temporarily eliminated its coffee and rolls social hour after Sunday services, although it attempted to honor its party commitments at the adjacent banquet hall. "God didn't tell us, 'Hey, I'm coming, don't rent the hall,'" John Koltse, then president of the board of directors, commented to the *Chicago Tribune.* Conveniently located across the street from a shopping mall, the church accommodated its own Christmastime rush by staying open twelve hours a day.

Still, visitors journeyed from as far away as Sri Lanka and Pakistan, according to a jubilant Koufos, who told the *Tribune,* "Everyone is pitching in. Already she [the icon] is working her wonders." Volunteers stationed themselves at the doors, ushering the long lines which snaked through the banquet hall leading to the sanctuary. Armed security guards were hired and candle orders tripled. Yet "people have been very reverent and very quiet and sober."

Cotton wadding on the floor captured the streaking tears, which Koufos described to *The New York Times* as consisting of "a very thin, oily sweet substance very similar to the chrism we use to baptize children or unction for the sick."

The Greek Orthodox Archdiocese of North and South America, which has jurisdiction over the Chicago church, wasted no time in investigating and acknowledging the event. "Truly it is a miraculous sign that this occurred on the Feast Day of St. Nicholas," Archbishop Iakovos, head of the New York-based diocese, said in a prepared statement. "The weeping icon is a vivid testimony that even in our highly developed age of science, technology, and rampant knowledge there still remains spirituality and devotion."

By February 1987, the church had seen an estimated 300,000 visitors and Father Koufos and his volunteers were worn out. So the hours and days of operation were reduced, with services set at specific times. "We're trying to be compassionate to everyone, including our own parishioners," he told the *Tribune.*

Still, the crowds continued through July, when the icon stopped weeping. Although the painting seeped moisture for a few months in 1988, the tears had basically ceased and haven't been seen since. Yet the church still has outside visitors who come by to pay their respects.

In an almost "Twilight Zone" case of parallel circumstances, a painting at St. George's Antiochian Orthodox Church began to cry on April 22, 1994, during the feast of *its* namesake, St. George. It was the eve of Lazarus Saturday and the beginning of Holy Week. Senior pastor Father Nicholas Dahdal, visiting priest Father Douglas Wyper, and a few parishioners were preparing for services when Wyper noticed a small rivulet of fluid trickling from Mary's eyes.

"THE MIRACULOUS LADY
OF CICERO, ILLINOIS"

This painting at St. George Antiochan Church in Cicero, Illinois, began to weep in April 1994, much to the delight of the congregation and believers. PHOTO COURTESY OF ST. GEORGE'S.

Part of a screened partition, the fourth portrait from the left, the painting depicts a sorrowful Mary holding a rather mature-looking baby Jesus. "Her eyes were red and puffy, like she'd been crying for a while," adds Dahdal. By midnight, four streams were running down Mary's face, and hundreds crowded into the medium-sized church, which boasts a flock of about 1,000 families.

Less than four days later, in the middle of the usual media blitz and crush of the curious/faithful, a major religious leader of the Antiochian church, known as the Right Reverend Bishop Basil, stopped by to affirm or debunk the phenomenon. He inspected the painting front and back, and—just to be on the safe side, because as he told the *Tribune,* "we know from the Scripture that Satan can do miracles"—performed an exorcism. This basically simple affair involved him blessing the icon and pronouncing, "I banish thee Satan, in the name of Jesus Christ." *Then* he declared it a miracle and the image was named "The Miraculous Lady of Cicero, Illinois."

As with St. Nicholas's, Dahdal and his congregation were inundated with visitors and interview requests. "Although it turned our lives upside down, it's also been inspiring," he states. The suburb of Cicero cooperated as well: local police helped direct traffic and a contractor donated labor and materials to make the church wheelchair accessible. The mayor even issued a proclamation honoring the parish.

Both churches claim not to need the coins and cash which are often left on altars and in other conspicuous places. "We do not want money," Father Koufos told the *Tribune.* Built in 1961, "[St. Nicholas] was paid off years ago." St. George does not even pass a collection plate or set out a donation box, although an estimated 5,000 pass through the church a day.

Neither church attempts to impose its beliefs. "Miracles aren't there to convert, just to confirm the faith," observes Dahdal. "We've had clergy from all denominations, and I think every nun in Illinois has visited us." As of this writing, the icon still weeps, and pilgrims flow in as well, seeking the sense of peace and comfort that it seems to convey.

The only fly in the divine ointment may be the refusal of both churches to submit to scientific testing. Koufos, who has a doctorate in archaeology and inspected St. Nicholas's for leaky ceilings and dripping pipes to make sure the icon was legitimate, alleged that analysis of the tears would verge on blasphemy. "It is not a very religious procedure," he told *The New York Times*.

Besides, "even if one determines their exact content, what does it prove?" wonders Dahdal. "How can you tell whether the liquid is made by man or the hand of God?"

What to Expect

Although St. Nicholas is small, it's ornate and elaborately decorated, heavily adorned with pictures of various saints and angels. Part of the iconostasis, a decorative wall, the 5-foot-by-3-foot image is located at the front of the church where the congregation faces east. Tributes of plants, flowers, and candles surrounding the icon double as a barrier, protecting the painting. According to Father Koufos, pilgrimages and healings are still common: people weep, kiss reproductions of the picture, cross themselves, and pray.

The icon at St. George helps separate the altar from the pews. Along with eight other dry-eyed icons, this painting arrived at the church from Greece in 1983. That was also the year St. George was converted from a Dutch Reform to an Antiochian Orthodox church. With roots back to the time of Christ, Antiochian faithful "are primarily descendants of countries of the Middle East, including Jordan, Syria, Lebanon, Egypt, and Palestine," explains Dahdal.

Although not as heavily ornamental as some Orthodox Christian churches, St. George's boasts gold-tipped chandeliers and bronze doors. Cotton swabs are also available to collect moisture from the icon; according to church authorities, people have been healed when anointed from the tears.

What They Say

Frances and Frank Kraus, Chicago, Illinois: In 1987, when the St. Nicholas icon was weeping, the Krauses visited the church to pray for their son, who was hemorrhaging from an unknown illness. Frank Krause was blind and when a priest saw his white cane, he offered him a cotton swab with oil from the icon. But Frank shooed him off. "It's not for me," he cried, according to an account in *People* magazine. "I don't care if I get my sight back. I came for my son who is dying."

The priest gave the Krauses a flower that had been touched by the icon. "I feel better now," Frances said. "I feel calm." She crossed her son with the flower at the hospital and the next day, the bleeding, which had necessitated 60 pints of transfusions, stopped. "I believe this was a miracle," Francis told *People.*

Reverend Constantine Nasr, Oklahoma City, Oklahoma: Although he was skeptical, Father Constantine Nasr of the St. Elijah Antiochian Orthodox Christian Church in Oklahoma City made the pilgrimage to Cicero anyway. "We have doubts because we are human beings," he remarked to the *Saturday Oklahoman & Times.*

"It took me a long time," he said of his first encounter with the St. George icon. "To witness the weeping . . . is something baffling. To explain, it's like your lips have been shut. I sat down. I did the prayer. But being doubtful like Thomas, I just didn't know what to do."

So he lit candles for his congregation and friends, and watched people file past the icon. As he meditated upon life and its trials, "his faith was strengthened," stated the article.

He became a believer. "I did not want to leave. It's like a heavenly place. And like, you forget where you are; you forget your business. You are in a different world—like a supernatural experience."

How to Get There

Saint Nicholas: From downtown Chicago, take the Kennedy expressway going west. Exit at Harlem Ave., turn left and go to Diversey Ave., where you'll make another left. When you reach Narragansett turn right, go one block, and turn left into the church parking lot. (It's across from the Brickyard Mall.) Hours for public viewing are Wednesdays and Saturdays 10 a.m.–3 p.m. and Sundays 10 a.m.–4 p.m. 2701 N. Narragansett Ave., Chicago, IL 60639, 312/889-4282.

Saint George: Located in the suburbs, about 20 minutes west from downtown, Saint George's is reached via I-290. Then take the Eisenhower expressway west to Austin Ave and turn left until you reach the first stoplight, which is Roosevelt Rd. Turn right. The first street on the left is 60th. Turn left; the church is behind a car wash. Doors are usually open 11 a.m.–5 p.m. seven days a week. 1220 S. 60th Ct., Cicero, IL 60650, 708/656-2927.

✝ Mary Visits a Cemetery

Queen of Heaven Cemetery
Hillside, Illinois

How It Happened

Joseph Reinholtz has faith that can move mountains, or at the very least, a crucifix in a cemetery. On September 19, 1980, Reinholtz, a retired railroad worker in his 70s, began to experience periodic visual blurriness and blindness. Having heard of the miracles at Medjugorje, he decided to go there in 1987. He met Vicka Ivankovic, one of the six visionaries. "After Vicka prayed over Joseph, he promised he would dedicate his remaining days to working and praying for the terminally ill," explains a close friend of Reinholtz who asked to remain anonymous.

A few days after Reinholtz returned to his home in Westchester, he was saying the rosary before his statue of the Virgin Mary. "He'd purchased it some thirty years ago at a resale shop for a quarter," adds the friend. While on the fifth decade of the rosary, "he saw a burst of bright light. He then knew his eyesight would be OK, and the first thing he saw was that the statue began to weep."

According to the friend, the tears went on for three days and nights. "Joe showed the statue to a priest, who told him to take it home. Everyone else was frightened by it."

Reinholtz met with the visionary again on a 1989 trip to Medjugorje. "This time Vicka told him that he should look for a cross 12-to-15-feet high, between two trees, one of which had three branches. It was to become his place of prayer." Reinholtz soon located the spot, a fiberglass crucifix in the military section at the

Queen of Heaven Cemetery, not far from where his brothers were buried.

"For over two years, it was Joe's private place for reflection," continues the friend. "He had visions of Mary, St. Michael, and angels. He visited nursing homes and said the rosary." When the crucifix began to bleed, he took pictures. "He went to Queen of Heaven daily in all kinds of weather, even though he was close to 80 years old."

Word spread through prayer groups, and others began to join him in his daily meditation. In July 1991, a story appeared in a Chicago newspaper and the stampede was on. By August 15, the Feast of the Assumption, 10,000 people were present to witness miracles ranging from Mary hovering by the cross to halos to rosaries transforming from silver to gold. "The actual color of the crucifix was rather nondescript," observes the friend. "Sometimes it would look bronze or grey, perhaps due to weather conditions. In pictures, the bleeding Jesus might appear to be gold, white, silver, bronze, or red." Reinholtz, however, was the only one who had actual visions.

Initially neither the Catholic Church nor officials at Queen of Heaven seemed pleased. "We run a nice, quiet cemetery," spokesperson Delores Vendel told the *Chicago Tribune,* seemingly without a trace of irony. According to her, employees saw nothing unusual. The tenants, however, were unavailable for comment.

"Joe was questioned by the authorities of the Church, and while that was going on, didn't go to the cross," explains his friend. However, he was soon allowed to return, although he could not give interviews to the media. A proviso, a

The faithful claim that the hues of this crucifix at Queen of Heaven Cemetery in Hillside, Illinois, change with the light.
PHOTO COURTESY OF AT THE CROSS.

sign placed near the cross, stated that the Archdiocese of Chicago "has no evidence that an unusual or supernatural phenomenon is taking place."

Joe Reinholtz had a stroke a few months ago that severely limited his activities. "He can turn in bed and write, and still tries to come to the cemetery on Sundays and special occasions," says his friend. "He can walk with a four-pronged cane, but it's difficult." According to the friend, he still has visions and revelations.

Still, little seems to discourage the faithful from coming to Queen of Heaven. All social and economic demarcations seem to disappear: Women in tennis outfits have spiritual experiences alongside recent immigrants and the wheelchair-bound seeking hope. And since it's a Catholic cemetery, they have plenty of company.

What to Expect

The crucifix has been moved to the southeastern corner of the cemetery, where it "stands in the center of an asphalt circle, looking oddly like a basketball backboard on a parish parking lot," commented Tim Unsworth in the *National Catholic Reporter*. It's near another parking lot so pilgrims won't trample on the grounds, although the residents can hardly complain.

In the warmer months, about 75 people show up each day for prayer, except on Tuesdays when there is no service. On Sundays, several hundred may attend. Daily prayers run from about 9:00 a.m. to 10:30 a.m. The Sunday service begins at 10:30 a.m., which Joseph Reinholtz leads if he is present.

Everyone is welcome and the group is low-key and dignified. Conversions are common and some healings have supposedly occurred. Books of Reinholtz's revelations and messages from Our Lady are also available (see address below).

What They Say

Sue Maher, Downer's Grove, Illinois: After seeing the crucifix bleed twice, Maher told the *Tribune* she was "awed and moved to tears. Some people that you think of as being very religious and faithful come and see nothing. Others that you wouldn't expect to see something, do. I guess that's why it's called a gift from God."

Rev. Michael Lane, Chicago, Illinois: The pastor at St. Dominic Church, Lane went to Hillside with a member of his flock, a Bolingbrook policeman. Although he refused to comment on the veracity of the apparitions to the *Tribune,* he did remark that "such judgments require a lot of prudence. But as priests we should not just allow people to go off on their own and we should pay attention to what is happening in the lives of the people that God has sent us."

Unidentified man, Hillside, Illinois: "I live only eight minutes from here," the man said in the *National Catholic Reporter.* "I come every day. I had two sons. One died at 40 of a heart attack, and last year the other one shot himself. He was only 43 and had a wife, children, and "loads of money. I learned later that he had cancer. Couldn't face it.

"I began coming here. Not long after, while I was in bed, I heard my son just as clear as if I was listening to him on the phone. He said, 'Dad, I'm fine. Don't worry. I'm at peace.' So . . . I'm paying back. I've never seen anything, but others have."

How to Get There

From Chicago, take the Eisenhower Expressway (290W) about 20 miles. Exit Mannheim Rd. South to Roosevelt Rd. (about 1 ½ miles) and turn right on Roosevelt. Go another mile or so and turn left, as the entrance leading to the cross is off Wolf Rd. Take two more left turns, then you will see the parking lot and crucifix. For more information, contact: At the Cross, Box 5224, Long Grove, IL 60047, no phone.

Kentucky

✝ **A Woodstock for Catholics**

Our Lady of Light
Cold Spring/Falmouth, Kentucky

How It Happened

In 1992, Reverend Leroy Smith, then a pastor at St. Joseph Catholic Church in Cold Spring, Kentucky, had been planning on retiring to Florida. "I'd vacationed there for 47 years and was looking forward to helping out with a small parish," remarks the gracious, grey-haired priest.

God apparently had other designs, for Smith was contacted by a Batavia, Ohio visionary "who told me she'd been to a Marian conference in Chicago and that Our Lady had given her messages, one of which was to get in touch with me." Although the visionary didn't know him from Adam, Smith had made numerous pilgrimages to Medjugorje and led several large and successful prayer groups.

And a year earlier, a "reputed locutionist" in Arkansas "foretold that St. Joseph's would be a place of great devotion . . . where Our Lady would manifest herself . . . and there would occur healings and conversions," according to "Personal Revelations," a book published by the Our Lady of Light Foundation, the organization which grew up around Smith and the visionaries. Smith was also well-liked among parishioners, although the local diocese wouldn't exactly be thrilled by the events that would unfold in the coming months.

The visionary, who asked to remain anonymous, told Smith the Virgin Mary would appear at St. Joseph's at midnight on August 31, 1992 or would deliver a message. Located in the middle of a predominantly Catholic area, St. Joseph's has a congregation of about 1,500 in addition to a school, which is heavily attended by the children of the well-to-do parishioners. "There were a number of incidents which showed me certain events would come to pass," adds

86

Smith, citing the example of a prediction of his receiving a 14K gold cross. "Things Our Lady said would happen, did." He announced the pending visitation/message to his congregation in June.

Before you could say "Paul Harvey," who, along with the Associated Press and CNN, was instrumental in spreading the news, rumors began to fly about a stampede of Catholics in Cold Spring. With a population of 3,000 and only a handful of local gendarmes, the town leaders decided literally to call out the National Guard as well as Kentucky State Troopers. Special event ordinances ranged from a prohibition against sleeping in cars to a $300 sidewalk vendor's fee to the designation of parking areas. Buses were to shuttle the faithful from long-distance parking to the church, the alternative being forking up $10 to $20 for a closer spot.

Cold Spring police chief Gene Schweitzer estimated a cost of $50,000 in supplies, overtime, and cleanup, according to an article in the Louisville *Courier-Journal.* "I think the city and the church should negotiate a little bit," he huffed. ". . . the church should realize it's causing a tremendous amount of problems here."

The townspeople partitioned off their yards in anticipation of an onslaught. Beverly Spoonamore, proprietor of Buckskin Bev's Cattle Company, planned for a huge refrigeration truck but didn't know how much food to order. Holton "Nunnie" Garrison, owner of The Concrete Goose, supplemented his flock with statues of the Virgin Mary ($35 for small, $95 for grotto-sized). Leisure Time Sports advertised "Lady of Light" T-shirts at $8 each.

Appalled by the tumult, the Diocese of Covington released a statement distancing themselves from the event. Even Smith issued remarks emphasizing that this was "nothing more than a spiritual happening" and not to expect "something extraordinary . . . on August 31." He recommended that people stay home and pray "because of the possibility of a huge crowd descending on our little city."

The actual event, however, was almost an anticlimax. Fewer than 8,000 people showed and "were very well-behaved and respectful of each other's property," observes Gerry Ross, president of the Our Lady of Light Foundation. "The militia soon realized this wasn't a rock concert or a riot and took away the armored vehicles and troop carriers."

And there *were* reports of sightings—during the day and especially around 12:00 p.m., some saw flashes of light, visions of Mary in a tree, spinning suns. Others recognized the Golden Door on Polaroids (see page 63, "Visions by Nancy Fowler") and a few rosaries turned from silver to gold.

Perhaps the biggest wonder was the sense of peace that occurred at midnight. As Smith began to pray over the loudspeakers, a great silence descended. Thousands, according to *The Courier Journal,* "[sat] in one place . . . without there being a cough, a baby's cry, a horn blowing . . . a rustling of clothes, a shuffling of feet."

Father Smith regarded the event as a success. To the 1,500 permitted inside the church, "Mary put on quite a light show. There was a tremendous amount of activity which could not be explained by flash bulbs or cameras which weren't permitted in here anyway." He also claimed to hear thunder "although the sky was clear" and to have received messages from Mary via the Batavia visionary and visionaries in Arizona.

The diocese, while noting in a prepared statement that "nothing of a miraculous nature occurred in St. Joseph's Church" that night, avoided commenting upon the events outside and praised the devotion of the crowd. "I'm very impressed with the genuine faith of everyone," spokesman Reverend Thomas Sacksteader told *The Courier-Journal.*

And this was just the beginning. Not only was Smith contacted by another visionary from northern Kentucky known only as "Sandy," but the August 31 gathering has become an annual event. And although Smith has since left St. Joseph's ("The Parish Council wasn't too happy with me"), the Our Lady of Light Foundation purchased the old St. Mary's Seminary in Norwood, Ohio from the Archdiocese at a bargain price and made Smith its director. Although it's in need of repair, the 13-acre Our Lady of the Holy Spirit complex boasts several magnificent buildings and will be used as a residence and Marian center. (It also has a baseball field and tennis and handball courts for more worldly pursuits.)

The organization also obtained a 98-acre farm in Falmouth, Kentucky where Sandy has *her* sightings. "The visions are dissimilar from what happens at St. Joseph's," explains Smith. Mary appears as "Our Lady of the Most Holy Rosary and people experience her in a different way, such as seeing circular rainbows in the sky." Most of Sandy's visions take place on the 8th of the month.

These, too, have proven to be popular. May 8, 1994 (Mother's Day and a month in which Roman Catholics revere Mary) drew an estimated 25,000. Sandy simply reads the message—often a plea to return to Jesus and the Bible—to the crowd. She, too, is pleased with the results. "I have noticed the wonders of [Mary] working through so many people," she told *The Cincinnati Enquirer.* "She's just touching them and the feedback I'm getting is, 'I don't even know why I'm going to the farm. I just feel I need to. Or I'm supposed to. Or I have to.' So they go and when they do, they just have a different outlook on life."

Both the Cold Spring and Falmouth gatherings draw believers from all over the United States, and their numbers are increasing. So it looks like Father Smith won't be retiring any time soon.

What to Expect

Cold Spring: The prayer service at St. Joseph's begins shortly after 9 p.m. on August 31 and lasts past midnight. Recent participants have claimed to see lightning flashes around the church and smell roses.

Although thousands show up, the crowd is orderly. Those who don't make it into the church can pray and sing in the parking lot and commune with like minds from all over. You'll hear lots of stories about other places where there have been religious sightings.

Come as early as possible and bring your own cooler, blanket, umbrella, and lawn chairs. Priests will be hearing confession all day and there is an 11 a.m. Mass at the Our Lady of the Holy Spirit Center.

Falmouth: These gatherings are bare-bones: with no drinking water and no seating, visitors must bring their own food, blankets, and chairs (portable toilets are provided, however). There is neither admission nor souvenirs. Contributions are welcome but no one is pushed to donate; even the rosaries handed out to participants are gifts from individuals and organizations. A volunteer medical team is on hand to assist with any emergencies.

Prayers start at about 11 a.m. on the eighth of the month. People gather on a hillside where the Foundation has placed a statue of Mary. You can put flowers at the base of the statue and prayer requests go into a box. Sandy privately reads some requests; most are burned to protect confidentiality. Sandy usually announces the message between 1:30 and 2:00 p.m. and services conclude around 3:00 p.m.

The winding country roads can present a challenge to buses and campers. However, dozens of volunteers from the Our Lady of Light Foundation help direct traffic, and parking is plentiful.

Related Masses and prayer groups are held at other Foundation sites; contact the Foundation/Our Lady of the Holy Spirit Center for more information.

What They Say

Gerry Ross, Crestview Hills, Kentucky: Involved with Our Lady of Light from almost the beginning, Ross has visited several shrines and was especially touched by Medjugorje. "You sense a presence," he says of the experience. "It's like being tapped on the shoulder and looking around to see who's there.

"I feel blessed," he continues. "The world has lost its spiritual sense of direction and God has left so many of our lives. We need to get back to the basics and focus on what's really important, such as the love of God and of our neighbors."

Mickey Smith, Monroe, Michigan: A nurse, Smith had been at Conyers, Georgia where, she told *The Cincinnati Enquirer,* she had seen lights in the sky but no Mary. "It's a prayerful time," she observed of Falmouth. "It's a wonderful feeling of prayer. Who knows what people will see? Maybe nothing. You come to pray. I love coming to these things and seeing all these people praying. It's praying that I come for."

Jan Wuchner, Dry Ridge, Kentucky: A state trooper, Wuchner is also a believer who traveled to Medjugorje. He planned on attending the events at the farm along with his wife and mother. "It's Mother's Day, is it not?" he asked *The Enquirer.* "May is Mary's month. Mary is the mother of the church and the mother of us all. I am personally part of a Marian devotion group. That's why I'm going."

How to Get There

Cold Spring: From downtown Cincinnati, take I-471 about 6 miles to the Alexandria exit (expressway ends and runs into US 27). Follow 27S a little over a mile to St. Joseph's, which is on the left.

Falmouth: From downtown Cincinnati, take I-471 about 6 miles to the Alexandria exit (expressway ends and runs into US 27). Follow 27 south to KY 177. Go east about four miles to KY 159 and turn right.

For more information, contact the Our Lady of Light Foundation, P.O. Box 17541, Fort Mitchell, KY 41017 or call the Our Lady of the Holy Spirit Center at 513/351-9800.

✝ Visions amid the Vegetables

Our Lady of Tickfaw
Tickfaw, Louisiana

How It Happened

In 1989, Alfredo Raimondo, a native of Tunisia and pipefitter from
Chalmette, Louisiana, had a vision. The Virgin Mary told him to go
to Tickfaw, a tiny town about 45 minutes north of New Orleans,
and honor St. Joseph. Apparently Raimondo owned some property
there, a vegetable field that he also used as a weekend camp.
Raimondo erected a 12-foot wooden cross and the word began to
spread.

An outside Mass, candlelight procession, and rosary prayers were
planned for Sunday, March 12. With an expected crowd of up to
60,000, every available law enforcement auxiliary was deputized in
anticipation of the gathering of the faithful. "But since they're all
religious people, we're not expecting any real problems," Chuck
Reed, a spokesman for the local sheriff's office, told the Reuters
news service.

According to police estimates, some 20,000 did show. Loaded
with lawn chairs and coolers, families lined up to pray. Well-wishers
heaped flowers, food, and religious pictures on a makeshift altar
dedicated to St. Joseph. Women knelt amidst muddy cabbages and
onions. Some clutched floral crosses while Raimondo sequestered
himself in a mobile home at the edge of the property.

When he finally emerged, pilgrims reached out to touch him as
he wandered through the crowd. "I'm very happy," he told the
Associated Press. "We're letting Joseph show the way. There are a
lot of people here."

And, indeed, the usual assortment of miracles was reported:
visions of Jesus, Mary, and Joseph; rosaries changing color; photos
of the gates of heaven; the smell of roses; spontaneous healings.

There were also "blue light specials"—colored mist or luminescence supposedly symbolic of the Holy Family. Tickfaw had earned its spot on the visionary map, although the Catholic Church seems to have ignored it completely.

Today the field is a complex of sorts, with a sacred holly tree, a fountain, a Sanctuary of the Holy Spirit, several statues, and a shrine to Jesus, Mary, and Joseph. Our Lady of Tickfaw, as the group calls itself, consists of Raimondo, his family, and associates and seems to have been created through vision by committee. For instance, on July 16, 1989, "Mark Johnson . . . was given the exact details of how the shrine was to be built," states the organization's brochure. "He was also told the exact spot that a spring of healing water was to come up. The area has been prepared and a pool of blessed water is [there] now."

The brochure also cautions against hoping for too much. "You may find that you will be able to see something and the person next to you cannot, or . . . that the person next to you can see something and you can't. Although some have had wonderful experiences on their first

Alfredo Raimondo served as the catalyst for visions and other happenings in a former vegetable field in Tickfaw, Louisiana.
PHOTO COURTESY OF AT THE CROSS.

visit, many have waited patiently . . . before the right time for them. If you are not able to see anything, that shouldn't make you feel unworthy. . . ." Perhaps it's something in the water.

Their next big project, according to the brochure, is "a white chapel with a dome-shaped roof at the back left of the property." Several people "from different states" had visions of it, presumably down to the five confessionals (which the faithful are to approach on their knees) and the key shape of the chapel's design, signifying the key to heaven. According to all these visions, it is to be built within three years, although the brochure is dated 1990 and it is still under construction.

However, three wooden crosses (as instructed by assorted prophecies) have been positioned next to Raimondo's original. And although the site is on a former landfill, as the brochure points out, the cave at Lourdes where Bernadette had her visions was originally a garbage dump.

What to Expect

"Our Little Medjugorje," as it is also called, seems a rather humble abode. But it is peaceful, with lots of places to meditate and worship. Freshly baked bread is sometimes available, thanks to a vision by Raimondo, and reinforced by Mark Johnson. Even the man who built the oven claimed to see Mary while working on it.

There are restrooms, pop machines, and ample parking. The rosary is prayed every afternoon except Sunday, when there is a service at 11:30 a.m. Other times change according to the season. Weekend tours explain the visions and messages as do books of miraculous photos. Our Lady of Tickfaw welcomes all visitors, regardless of religious or ethnic background.

What They Say

Theresa Thibodeaux, Hammond, Louisiana: "I'm expecting a miracle," she confided to the Associated Press. "I'm blind in this eye and I have glaucoma in the other. My nephew is crippled and my uncle has cancer." She began to sob. "It may not be for me, but I believe in my heart. You have to believe for a miracle."

Kathleen Williams, Chalmette, Louisiana: The veteran of several pilgrimages, including Lubbock (see page 180), Williams told the UPI, "She's here, she's in your heart, she's in your home. Please, please, please keep praying. Mary wants to tell you, peace. . . ." Along with Jesus, Mary, and various saints, Williams and her companion Shelly Decker purportedly glimpsed two birds near the end of an apparition. "The birds were to show peace among us."

Lou Reis, Slidell, Louisiana: According to Reis, the links of her rosary transformed from silver to gold while she prayed at the site. "We watched them change," she told the UPI. "I have no idea how it happened, but I feel blessed. I believed other people when they said a miracle happened to them, but I never believed it would happen to me."

How to Get There

From New Orleans, take I-55N to Hwy 442 (exit 36). Turn left, then go to Antioch Rd. and turn right. The field is located between the Antioch Baptist Church and the Sisters of St. Benedict Monastery. Open seven days a week. Our Lady of Tickfaw, P.O. Box 97, Antioch Rd., Tickfaw, LA 70466, 504/542-7537.

✝ Another Knothole for Jesus

29 Burns Street
Fairfield, Maine

How It Happened

San Francisco had the Summer of Love; New England can boast the Summer of Jesus Trees. On June 21, 1992, Jim and Lisa Rummel of Fairfield, Maine, discovered an image of Jesus in a lopped-off limb of a maple in their front yard. Then exactly one month later in Milford, Connecticut, Claudia Voight, a single mother, looked out the window and saw the face of Jesus in an amputated section of one of *her* trees. She'd never heard of the Rummels and at the time thought Medjugorje was "something you order at an Italian restaurant," according to *Yankee* magazine.

Then in August—also almost one month to the day—a New Haven, Connecticut, tree was noticed (see page 52). No wonder author Stephen King came to visit the Fairfield site; these occurrences were stranger—and perhaps more unbelievable—than the stuff even he comes up with.

But like a summer romance, the popularity of the Voight/Rummel trees seemed ephemeral. Although tens of thousands descended upon both families, visitors trickled off as the leaves turned, especially after the face disappeared in Voight's yard. The Rummels' tree remains accessible, even though the image is fading somewhat. Yet letters addressed to "The Jesus Tree" always find their mark in the tiny burg of Fairfield (population: 6,700). And townspeople continue to provide directions to the curious and faithful.

Its beginnings seem the stuff of a situation comedy. "I was having a cookout with my wife Lisa, her brother and his girlfriend, when Lisa called me over to the tree," recalls Jim Rummel, a mason contractor. "She asked me, 'What do you see?' and I responded, 'Jesus Christ!'" He meant it as both description and reaction.

"The big question in my mind was, what was something like that doing in a Protestant's yard? We don't even go to church!" The Rummels kept the find to themselves for a week or so, then shared the news with a neighbor, who also happened to own a hair salon. By the end of the day, the media had arrived and mobs of onlookers descended. "I think the whole town showed up," says Jim. It certainly beat watching Fairfield's single traffic light change. In fact, the town's narrow streets became packed with vehicles from as far away as Alaska and Hawaii, and pilgrims from over 10 foreign countries.

The Rummels were quick to accommodate their visitors. Along with providing a guest book to sign, Jim sold pictures of the tree for $2 a pop, "just to cover expenses." Setting up lawn chairs, the family made themselves available to answer questions.

"People seemed to think because I had this tree, I had some special knowledge," chuckles Jim, who claimed to enjoy having 20,000 people in his driveway. "Heck, I was just as puzzled by it as they were." Still, they had to put up a handmade sign asking visitors not to touch the tree. "People were taking bark, leaves, even gravel from the ground."

Physical phenomenon or act of God? This image of Jesus put the town of Fairfield, Maine, out on the limb in more ways than one. PHOTO COURTESY OF JIM RUMMEL.

Along with the hoopla came the experts. Rob Lively, an associate professor of religion at the University of Maine in Farmington, became fascinated with the Jesus trees and spent a lot of time hanging around Fairfield just watching and listening to people's reactions. "What's so striking about the Fairfield image is that it looks like a famous painting of Jesus praying in the Garden of Gethsemane," he observes. "And the Fairfield and Milford trees had similarities: both were maples and the Jesus images faced towards the northeast."

He became friendly with the Rummels and in fact took them to the New Haven tree and to meet Claudia Voight in Milford. "How many people can share that kind of experience—the crowds, the questions and tears, the midnight visitation of complete strangers, the crosses and flowers left in their yards? They could have erected fences and posted warnings, yet they welcomed people with open arms."

Vance Wells, a botanist at the University of Maine, also examined the Fairfield image and found it to be a combination of moss, fungus, and/or algae. He opined that it likely formed quickly, a result of sap rising in the tree in the spring. It might also eventually glow in the dark, as certain fungi produce a fluorescent chemical reaction.

The doubters met the phenomenon with typical New England skepticism, comparing the likeness to a teddy bear, an Ewok, actor Willem Dafoe, Jeff Reardon of the Boston Red Sox, singer Kris Kristofferson, even Elvis (a definite stretch). According to *Yankee* magazine, one editor barked, "We don't do Jesus and we don't do vegetables," as in an eggplant that resembles Richard Nixon or a double tomato wrapped around a cucumber that's more suited to an X-rated publication. Professor Lively observed that males in particular had a difficult time getting out of their cars and/or accepting the image.

But those who believed derived great comfort. "Many were Roman Catholics who brought mats to kneel on the drive," comments Lively. "Lots were repeat visitors; some even came for daily prayers." There were also reports of healings, although none were substantiated.

"People felt an affinity for the image, because it's a sign of hope in a world where lots of nasty things happen," he adds. "In fact, I heard the best sermons just standing beside that tree." No wonder he found the local Roman Catholic and Protestant clergy "not particularly sympathetic."

Jim Rummel even exchanged a few words with a priest. "He said it was totally wrong for these people to be here, that they should be praying in church. But what church is unlocked at 3 a.m. when someone feels the need to seek God?"

What to Expect

The Fairfield knothole is about 4½-inches-by-3¼-inches wide, about 7 feet from the ground. The image is your typical WASP Jesus, with white flesh and light brown hair, clad in a red cloak. Encircling it are what appear to be two serpents: "A good analogy for modern life, in that we seem to be surrounded by evil," points out Lively. Some say Jesus seems to be holding a lamb or a little child, while others profess to also see the Virgin Mary, the Sacred Heart, and Moses with the Ten Commandments.

The house at 29 Burns Street is currently for sale. The Rummels have moved to Connecticut with their young son. "Lisa prefers a larger city," explains Jim. He's a little disappointed that no one has snapped it up: How many properties can claim their very own religious shrine?

What They Say

Claudia Voight, Milford, Connecticut: Voight was going through a nasty divorce when she discovered the Jesus face in her yard. Her first reaction to the pilgrims was to draw the drapes, lock her doors and flee town. "I was scared to death of it," she told *Yankee* magazine.

However, she gradually warmed to her visitors, who continued even after the image was gone. She became known as the Lady with the Tree and pulled herself back together emotionally and began to make a success of her home business. "I know it's something with the tree," she stated to *Yankee.* "It's changed me. I feel that no matter what happens, things are going to be fine.

"People ask me why Jesus would come in a tree. That's easy. A tree gives us so much . . . shade and fruit and it reaches way up into the sky . . . [and] material to make our houses and our furniture. We can burn it for heat. There's nothing a tree can't give us, so I think a tree is just right."

Rob Lively, Wilton, Maine: Lively noticed a similarity in the reaction to the various Jesuses. "Pilgrims have acted this way for thousands of years, whether it's towards shrines in Jerusalem or an image in a tree. They come from great distances, consider it a sacred space, leave offerings, and express the desire to take away a relic. There are apparent miracles. . . ."

The most affecting comments came from children: A 10-year-old boy said, 'This means Jesus is the tree and we are the branches,' and an 8-year-old girl, after being held up to the image, said, 'Jesus spoke to me and he was crying.'"

As for himself? "Personally, I think it's a fluke of nature. I still had an affinity for it. I liked the way it looked and it gave me a world view of what was going on with people spiritually."

Rev. Samuel Najar, Waterville, Maine: As pastor of St. Joseph's Maronite Church, Najar went to see the Fairfield tree for himself. "There is an image there," he said in the central-Maine *Morning Sentinel.* "But I can't say that it's Jesus. I think it's great that people believe and want to believe, but I just can't authenticate it." Besides, "we don't have any idea what Jesus looked like."

How to Get There

Take 95N to exit 37 (Fairfield), then turn right on High St. and take it to the end (just before it merges with Main St). Burns St. is the last road on the right. Turn right and No. 29 is the eighth house on the left, a small white Cape Cod with red trim. The tree sits at the front of the drive.

✝ "Vision Night" at St. Joseph's Catholic Church

St. Joseph's Catholic Church
Emmitsburg, Maryland

How It Happened

"I've never seen anyone so beautiful in my life." Visionary Gianna Talone-Sullivan was speaking of Mary in a 1994 interview with *The Catholic Review*. "She has wavy dark hair, steel-blue eyes, a very fair complexion, a round face and very soft skin, rosy cheeks and lips, a long neck and long, slender fingers. She wears no jewelry—not even a tennis bracelet."

Fresh from her visions at Scottsdale (see page 15), Talone-Sullivan, a pharmacologist, and her soon-to-be second husband, internist Michael Sullivan, stopped at the Grotto of Lourdes in Emmitsburg on their way back from a pre-marriage class in January 1993. At the Grotto "Gianna had a vision in which Our Lady invited her to come here after her marriage," explains Father Alfred Pehrsson, senior priest at St. Joseph's Catholic Church there. "She told Gianna she had good work for her to do, if she chose to move here after her marriage."

The vision also instructed her to introduce herself to the pastor of the Catholic church in the town of Emmitsburg. Although Father Pehrsson has admitted to being initially skeptical, he maintained "an open mind about the possibility of extraordinary gifts from the Lord. Gianna asked me if I was prepared to hear all the confessions Our Lord and Lady would be sending me. I said 'Yes' to what was to become a prophecy."

The Sullivans attended their first prayer group meeting on Thursday, November 3, 1993. At that time, it consisted of a little over a dozen people. "During the service [Gianna] bolted up from her seat and her face just electrified," Pehrsson told *Frederick* magazine. "She became just beautiful. She appeared to be in a state of ecstasy."

The appearance of visionary Gianna Talone-Sullivan transformed the picturesque St. Joseph's Catholic Church in Emmitsburg, Maryland, into a major religious and media attraction. PHOTO COURTESY OF ST. JOSEPH'S.

Since then, Talone-Sullivan has been packing them in on Thursday nights. On August 11, 1994, a statue of Mary cried in front of 200 people in the parish hall. A scientist on the scene could not give an explanation for the phenomenon, which lasted for over an hour. And rosaries seemed to take on a golden hue. Thousands of the faithful flooded the tiny (population about 2,000) town of Emmitsburg. And Father Pehrsson and the other priests at St. Joseph's found themselves spelling each other in the confessional booth.

"A tree is known by its fruits and what is happening here is good fruit," he enthuses. "People are returning to the church after decades-long absences. And they come from all walks of life—admirals, ambassadors, doctors, nurses—as well as ordinary citizens" from as far away as Japan and Venezuela and as near as the suburb of Bethesda.

But the sudden surge of spirituality was not without its problems. Pilgrims parked in driveways, picnicked in the cemetery on the graves of locals' ancestors, and in general overran the place and annoyed the townspeople. And with seats for only about 400 and attendance easily doubling that, parishioners who wanted to see what all the uproar was about were shut out. The faithful began arriving early in the morning, so most seats were taken by 1 p.m.

Still, a generous distribution of parking violations, the organization of bus tours, and the utilization of nearby lots alleviated many traffic snafus. And people needing food and lodging have brought in welcome tourist dollars. Reserved seating for registered parishioners helps control overcrowding. St. Joseph's also put in loudspeakers and a large-screen TV with a camcorder in the parish hall for those who don't make it into the chapel.

Since Talone-Sullivan was among the Scottsdale visionaries whose revelations were not defined as miraculous, no investigation from the local diocese has yet taken place. But she went through several rounds of psychological and medical tests. "The tests revealed nothing unusual about her," Father Pehrsson said in *Frederick* magazine. Talone-Sullivan also claims to have had her brain waves analyzed at the University of California at San Francisco, where she was shown to be "in a state of ecstasy at the time of her visions," continues the article. That's hardly a startling revelation.

Still, the Sullivans have founded the Mission of Mercy. A medical center in the form of a 32-foot Pace Arrow van, it traverses the county, offering free help ranging from cardiovascular treatment to diagnostic studies to basic assistance. Volunteer doctors and nurses provide care to the homeless, uninsured, or otherwise indigent. "We want to reach out to the people who have been falling through the cracks," Michael Sullivan told the *Emmitsburg Regional Dispatch*.

Talone-Sullivan was expecting a baby in early 1996. "During the early part of her pregnancy, Gianna experienced nausea," recalls Father Pehrsson. "On two evenings, she wasn't sure she was going to make it through the service without getting ill. But during the third decade of the rosary she went into an ecstatic state. She was completely out of herself, and as any woman knows, you can't turn off morning sickness." A small feat for someone who's been intimately acquainted with two members of the Holy Family since 1988.

With her detailed descriptions of the Holy Family and dramatic transformations into a state of ecstasy, visionary Gianna Talone-Sullivan drew believers first at the St. Maria Goretti Church in Scottsdale, Arizona, and then at St. Joseph's Catholic Church in Emmitsburg, Maryland. PHOTO COURTESY OF ST. JOSEPH'S.

What to Expect

Emmitsburg has a long and distinguished Catholic history. Along with being home and national shrine of the first American-born saint, Elizabeth Ann Seton, it has the oldest parochial school in the U.S., Mount Saint Mary's College and Seminary, and the Grotto of

Lourdes, where Talone-Sullivan heard the call. In fact, centuries before Samuel Emmit lent his name to the town, Chief Ottawanta, a Piscataway Indian and converted Catholic, moved to the area to escape religious persecution. He, too, supposedly had visions of the Virgin Mary.

A 150-year-old grey stucco church beautifully decorated with stained glass and paintings, St. Joseph's is a friendly place. Pillars, arches, and high ceilings add a touch of grandeur to the already dramatic weekly events. It's best to arrive early; seating is limited and available on a first-come-first-served basis.

Services start every Thursday at 7 p.m. and last around three hours. Talone-Sullivan's visions usually occur about 7:30 p.m. during the third recitation of the rosary and last approximately seven minutes. "Her eyes alive, she stares upward, facing the altar, fixated on something only she can see," Pehrsson explains. This goes on "for five to six minutes. Many evenings she does not blink. Her lips move, but no sound comes forth."

Talone-Sullivan writes down the message (which she claims to have no long-term memory of), passing it to the church secretary. It is read later in the service and copies are passed on to those attending (booklets of the missives are also available). Most messages focus on love, mercy, and devotion to Jesus and Mary.

What They Say

Reverend Frederick Jelly, Emmitsburg, Maryland: A professor of theology at Mount Saint Mary's College, Jelly holds Talone-Sullivan in high regard. She "is a very normal . . . very down-to-earth person," he told the *The Baltimore Sun.* "People who are inclined to have visions are often considered to be spacey. There's nothing like that about her. From a psychological view, there doesn't seem to be unrealistic behavior or hallucinations or anything like that."

Allen Harris, Buckeyestown, Maryland: After attending the Thursday night services, "people who have had some faith have . . . it magnified about 100 times," Harris, a member and volunteer youth minister at St. Joseph's parish, said in *The Catholic Review.* He works on Saturdays so he can be present on Thursday. "The business has to wait. What I've experienced means so much to me.

"God's grace is everywhere, but for some reason, it's as though he's concentrating more of it here."

Maureen O'Brien, Rochester, New York: O'Brien and her mother drove six hours to reach Emmitsburg. "I feel [the Virgin Mary] is trying to call us back to God," she told *The Catholic Review.* "There's so much godlessness in this nation.

"You can pray in your own church, but this is like a morale booster. It gives you hope to see so many people praying."

Jerry Horner, Emmitsburg, Maryland: "I'm not Catholic, but when I'm out there directing traffic, I feel a presence . . ." the Frederick County deputy sheriff admitted to *The Washington Post.* "It's not going to hurt to believe. . . . And if this brings that many people together to pray and be close to God, then whether it's true or not, it's worth it."

How to Get There

From Washington, D.C., take 495N to 270N to Frederick, Maryland. Follow the signs that say 15N towards Gettysburg. Go about 25 miles to Emmitsburg and take the South Seton Ave. exit (to the left). Pass the National Shrine of St. Elizabeth Ann Seton and go right into town, past the traffic light. St. Joseph's is half a block on the right on the corner. 47 DePaul St., Emmitsburg, VA 21727, 301/447-2326. Hours vary. Please obey all parking and traffic laws.

Massachusetts

✝ Rock of Jesus

Proposed Bethany Community and Spiritual Life Center
Medway, Massachusetts

How It Happened

Like a newborn baby, the 6-inch, 4-pound stone didn't weigh much, but it certainly created havoc. On April 26, 1993, a prayer group, led by Venezuelan mystic Maria Esperanza de Bianchini and Sister Margaret Catherine Sims, were touring a site for a proposed Catholic retreat center and residential development near Medway, Massachusetts. Before Sims even set eyes on the property, de Bianchini had allegedly seen it in a vision, recounting it in detail to Sims. A few days later while running errands, Sims spotted a green house and other particulars described in the mystic's revelation.

So de Bianchini, Sims, and about 70 followers trooped over to inspect the 109-acre former summer camp, which had been abandoned for decades. They were about to get back on the bus when the mystic suddenly broke away from the group and dashed over to a spot a few feet away from the road. She drew a cross in the dirt with a stick and began to dig, hitting a rock about 5 inches below the surface. She wiped it off, uttering, "Lips, nose, eyes . . . Jesus." An added bonus to the miracle was that she'd never been to the area before and didn't speak a word of English.

The crowd began to sing and pray, lining up to kiss the stone, which was still in the ground. According to *The Boston Sunday Globe,* "It is not difficult to make out the rough outline of . . . a man's face in the rock's surface. Something appears to be on the head," which was interpreted by the visionary and her followers as a crown of thorns. Sims removed the rock and placed it in a velvet-lined case.

Sims, a native of Medway who taught school during most of her 40 years in the Bethany convent in Framingham, tried to downplay its magnitude. "The rock had no significance in us buying the property," she told the Franklin *Country Gazette*. "We had already selected the property. But it's a sign from the Lord that we selected the right property. It's not a miracle rock, but it is a miracle how it was found."

After making several pilgrimages of her own, Sims had begun organizing trips to Medjugorje and Betania, Venezuela. In 1989, she and others formed a nonprofit organization now called Marian Messenger (formerly Medjugorje Messenger), later establishing a nonprofit fund-raising arm for the proposed center.

Still, the stone gathered no moss in attracting attention. The group obtained the $750,000 for the property plus $49,000 in back taxes from an anonymous benefactor. And they had big plans for the $4 million project: The Bethany Community and Spiritual Life Center would consist of about 65 homes in addition to a residence for clergy. Not only would there be single-family dwellings, but smaller congregate homes would also be available.

Although the setup was geared towards adults, children would be included in various outreach activities. The corporation's promotional brochure also called for a spiritual center with a computer room, bookstore, exercise room, and chapel. The stone would supposedly have a special place of honor in the latter. Donate money, and you might have a piece of the rock.

"This wouldn't be a retirement community," Sims told the *Country Gazette*. "The majority of people would still be working but . . . would [also] be studying theology and scripture. It would be for people in the local area who want to lead a life of prayer, service, and sacrifice." She envisioned it as a community for the 21st century: ". . . lay people would work more closely together with nuns and priests for the service of the church."

But the town of Medway cast some stones of its own. Some citizens reportedly feared a cult mentality, similar to the situation in Waco. A few rumors linked the group to various fringe organizations, although it's difficult to imagine a Catholic sister stocking up on firearms and plastic explosives.

And there were zoning ordinances and wetlands rules to deal with. When the Medway Zoning Board of Appeals expressed reservations about the project, John Boczanowski, a local builder and Sims supporter who was chairman of the ZBA at the time, brought a snapshot of the rock to a meeting in hopes of allaying concerns. "It's just weird," board member Stephen Reding told the *Globe*. "It sends chills through the old backbone."

Questions were also raised about the methods of obtaining donations, which included active solicitations such as displaying the rock at the local Dunkin' Donuts. "The group was trying to promote the Center," observes selectman Lee Henry. "And anything embraced with the fervor of zealots is looked upon with doubt in New England."

By summer 1994, Sims and the others met with the Archdiocese of Boston and abruptly stopped talking to the media. They put fundraising efforts on hold and got rid of the brochures, although Boczanowski and his construction crew had demolished several old buildings and cleared some of the land. The idea was to get the Roman Catholic Church's sanction for the project. "Sister Margaret has always gone by the Church's rules," states Father William Mackenzie of St. Joseph's Church in Medway. "She's kept everyone informed of what she's doing."

Despite the controversy, the faithful swarmed to the property from Maine, Florida, and other points. They claimed to see a rainbow-colored sun, butterflies signaling Mary's presence, and a brook with healing powers, although it was near a toxic waste site and the water had been deemed unfit for human consumption. The butterfly "was just flapping its wings and talking to us," Betty Harlow from Cranston, Rhode Island remarked to the *Middlesex News*. Well, OK.

"This will be a second Lourdes," Joseph Grenier, a Florida resident vacationing in Connecticut, added. "I believe in this very strongly . . . things are going to be changed—they are getting worse and worse. You can't even stay in your own home and feel safe anymore."

Along with flowers and crosses made from twigs and wooden planks, visitors left handwritten prayers, pictures, rosary beads, and paper angels. Makeshift memorials honored loved ones, such as a family who died in a Memorial Day weekend car crash, and a young person killed while setting off fireworks.

As of this writing, progress towards the Bethany Community and Spiritual Life Center is as stagnant as the water on the property. According to an official in the Medway Town Hall, "No Trespassing" signs have been posted and all religious artifacts were removed. "But even though the building permits have been turned down so far, people still keep coming," adds the official.

An investigation of the rock by the church remains pending. "Sometimes these things take years," comments Mackenzie. Currently it's in Sister Margaret Sims's possession. Although the project's stonewalled for now, no doubt the faithful will keep chipping away.

What to Expect

The property, previously known as Breezy Meadows, has a fascinating if checkered history. According to legend, Indians believed part of it was sacred ground. And in the late 1800s, authoress and local eccentric Kate Sanborn entertained writers, actors, politicians, and even a Middle Eastern guru there, scandalizing the townspeople. The site of a large Prohibition raid that netted 1,000 gallons of moonshine, Breezy Meadows was also a camp for black children from Boston in the '40s.

But by the time Sister Margaret and her entourage arrived, the manicured lawns, exquisitely tended gardens, and Japanese-style buildings were eroded and uprooted by neglect. Chicken Brook, which bisects the property, had become polluted with the runoff from upstream chemical companies. In the summer months, mosquitoes abound.

Nothing seems to deter the faithful, who cart away the yellow liquid by the gallons. "This is very powerful," 12-year-old Paul Balentine told the *Milford Daily News*. "This will cleanse your soul. It will keep the devil away." It also might send you to your reward sooner than planned.

The folks in Medway just roll their eyes in exasperation. "Those poor misguided people," remarks one citizen who went to the site in 1994 and asked that her name not be used. "They come in their wheelchairs, praying for a miracle. Every week, the cars line up. It's downright bizarre." Kate Sanborn would have loved it.

What They Say

Lillian Almeida, Cumberland, Rhode Island: Almeida also visited the property in 1994, and recounted the following to the *Middlesex News*: "All of the sudden the sun came through the black clouds and it was turquoise in color, really turquoise, and all around the sun the sky was pink. All the leaves of all these trees turned gold and shiny and glittery, and they were really glistening, it was beautiful to see. . . . I believe in miracles, don't you?"

Father "X," Holliston, Massachusetts: This pastor requested anonymity because "I live in the community and hope someday these people will take a more rational approach to religion.

"Although I have nothing against Sister Margaret and her followers, they have taken a sensationalistic approach, presenting God in a distorted way," he continues. "They are manipulating people's minds, and in doing so make Catholics look bad."

He is also disturbed by actions of the pilgrims. "They can ruin their eyes by looking directly at the sun . . . God can't help them then. You have to be in charge of your own self. Otherwise, religion becomes a kind of drug."

David Dunne, Medway, Massachusetts: "The real thing here is that people are sensing peace, Our Lady's presence . . . in the world," Dunne, who works on the Bethany steering committee, said in the *News.* "She really is not calling people here to see the sun spinning or rosaries turning to gold. She is calling people to prayer, to change our lives . . . and if they don't respond to that they become tourists rather than pilgrims."

How to Get There

Located about 20 miles west of Boston off I-90, Medway can be found by taking 495S to route 109 Medway/Milford and turning left. Go 4 miles to route 126, an intersection with a fire station and other businesses, then turn left. The site has a gate with a sign "Bethania" on the front; if you pass the Fatima shrine you've gone too far. Take the dirt road and cross a bridge. For more information (should they decide to return your call or respond to your letter), contact Marian Messengers, 265 Hollis St., Framingham, MA 01701, 508/879-9318.

✝ Mary Cries at Christmas

St. Mary's Church
Ware, Massachusetts

How It Happened

In December 1988, a group of waywards trashed the Sears-issue nativity set that graced the lawn of St. Mary's rectory. "Some kids hoisted Baby Jesus up on the flagpole and smashed a wise man," recalls Reverend Charles Kuzmeski. When he investigated the possibility of a replacement display, he found the cost prohibitive.

Jean Ciukaj and her husband Stan were concerned as well. Both active in the parish, Jean is a hairdresser and owner of Marlene's Beauty Salon in nearby Palmer. After a discussion with Father Kuzmeski, she decided to try her hand at a nativity scene. After the initial approval of a scale model, Jean went to work with plywood and non–water-soluble house paint. Her creation was to include a 28-foot-long stable and 18 larger-than-life figures.

Having never attempted a project of this magnitude she was understandably nervous. "After I went to her house to check on her progress, her first words were, 'You don't like it,'" comments Kuzmeski. "Of course I did. It was beautiful."

Stan, who used a jigsaw to cut the figures from ¼-inch plywood sheets, suggested that Jean paint Mary's gaze straight ahead, rather than downcast. "I had her glancing at Baby Jesus because it was easier," explains Jean. Unsure of her ability, she prayed for inspiration and found the courage to make the change. "I must admit Mary looked a lot better."

Completed in late 1989, the tableau had Mary and Baby Jesus, Joseph, three kings, two shepherds, three camels, six sheep, a donkey, and assorted other animals surrounded by a barnlike manger built by parishioners. It took several days to install in the subzero weather; on December 8, the Feast of the Immaculate Conception, it was finally complete. "We were just finishing up when we noticed what looked like tears coming down Mary's face," comments Kuzmeski.

Other eyewitnesses also observed the gray streaks in the pale skin beneath her pupils. Two perfect tears flowed and stopped in the middle of her cheeks. "It was only on Mary," he goes on. "The figures had been indoors next to a stove for two months, so the paint was completely dry."

When Stan called Jean at the shop to tell her, "I couldn't understand what he was talking about," states Jean. "I thought someone had vandalized my work."

When tears were spotted on her nativity scene at St. Mary's Church in Ware, Massachusetts, no one was more surprised than amateur artist Jean Ciukaj. PHOTO COURTESY OF ST. MARY'S.

"Everyone who saw it thought it was a sign," remarks Kuzmeski, who made no attempt to seek the verification of the local diocese. Even though the incident was kept basically quiet, word spread quickly in the close, tightly knit religious community. Townspeople, nuns, and parochial school children came to marvel at the sight.

The tears only lasted a few weeks; a New Year's Eve rainstorm washed the Virgin's face clean. But someone took a picture, providing a permanent record of a streak under Mary's left eye.

Then in 1991, a reporter from a Springfield newspaper got an earful about the amazing orbs. An article appeared on Christmas Day and soon the Associated Press and the local TV affiliate came calling, along with several hundred visitors. Pilgrims knelt by the stable, touching the figures and taking pieces of straw. "People want to believe. They're hungry for some kind of faith experience," adds Kuzmeski.

Although those at St. Mary's are reluctant to label the happening a miracle, it fits right in with a couple of other incidents. According to Jean Ciukaj, the sun always shines on the parish carnival. In fact, one year a toxic gas cloud from nearby Springfield executed a providential 45-degree turn, avoiding imminent evacuation of the carnival. "Father went somewhere and prayed," Jean told the *Springfield Union-News*. His invocations have also been known to hold off downpours on a float of Mary during the town's anniversary parade. No vandals in their right minds would want to mess with *those* kinds of connections.

What to Expect

Located on ten rolling acres in a mill town of 9,800, St. Mary's consists of a rectory, school, church, and convent. The parish of about 950 families was mostly of Polish immigrants and their descendants.

The nativity scene is displayed from around the first of December until shortly after New Year's. Mary is the only figure covered with Plexiglas: "People were taking the hay and touching her," explains Father Kuzmeski. "We want to prevent the painting from being scratched." A picture of the crying Mary hangs behind the figure of Joseph.

The nativity draws several hundred visitors a season. You may not find spinning suns, changing rosaries, or miracle cures, but "sometimes we have caroling on the front lawn and it's a beautiful sight," he says.

What They Say

Jean Ciukaj, Ware, Massachusetts: Jean described her experiences in a letter that was part of a scrapbook presented to Pope John Paul II in March 1995. "I stood trembling in front of my Mary," she wrote. "What did this mean? Mary had answered my prayer. She really heard me ask her for help with her eyes. The tears were her way of autographing this attempt at a painting of her."

Sister Mary Claire Milewski, Ware, Massachusetts: Sister Mary Claire works at the parish school. She felt the incident provided a good lesson for children. "It made them more aware of their religion and showed them anything is possible with God." But she was just as surprised by the tears as everyone else: "Jean has used the same paint for *every* one of those figures and they were all exposed to the same elements. God used this particular event to bring us closer to Mary."

Reverend Charles Kuzmeski, Ware, Massachusetts: The liquid on Mary's face "followed the natural flow of teardrops," Kuzmeski said in the *Union-News.* "I thought that Mary was telling me something, that it was her way of expressing joy for what we were doing—or sorrow for what was going on in the world. At that time, Communism was starting to go out in Poland, the Russian government was crumbling, the Berlin Wall had just come down."

How to Get There

From Springfield, take the Massachusetts Turnpike towards Boston and follow it to the Ware-Palmer exit. After you get off the exit, turn left at Rt. 32 and go into Ware. Make a right-hand turn onto Main St. ware, er, where it dead-ends. At the second light make another right; you'll come to South St. St. Mary's Church, 60 South Street, Ware, MA 01082, 413/967-5913.

New Jersey

✝ Rough Riding on the Marian Trail

Home of Joseph Januszkiewicz
Marlboro, New Jersey

How It Happened

In 1988, Joseph Januszkiewicz, a middle-aged draftsman who lives and works in New Jersey, visited Medjugorje. At first, he claimed to be healed of an old back injury and hearing loss. Then six months later, the Virgin Mary allegedly came to call.

According to *The New York Times,* she appeared to him as he sat on a plastic bucket in his yard. She was bathed in a golden light: "She told me: 'My son, I have chosen you to do our work,'" he said. "She just told me to pray, pray, pray. Pray for the conversion of sinners." The visions usually took place around 9:30 in the evening on the first Sunday of the month.

Per Mary's instructions, Januszkiewicz built a shrine at the edge of his patio in his backyard. Word of his sightings began to spread through prayer groups and other religious networks, and people began showing up on his doorstep. They prayed at the blue-and-white statue of Mary, re-created in the form that Januszkiewicz said she appeared to him. They sat on blankets under trees or in lawn chairs or benches, and left flowers and notes.

Januszkiewicz posted signs requesting prayerful silence, to watch out for children, and to keep off the deck. He ignored the grumbling of his neighbors, who complained of blocked street access and loud slamming of doors and conversations throughout the night. They began to set out their own "No Trespassing" warnings.

By the first Sunday in August 1992, 8,000 of the faithful appeared in the normally quiet town of Marlboro. With its gently rolling hills, farms, and sporadic clusters of homes, the 29,000+ burg prided itself on a pleasant, if gentrified, community. The police set up barricades and directed traffic. Farmers sold parking spots for $5 each, along with cold sodas and watermelon slices. A special phone number provided recorded directions to the site. Emergency trucks and ambulances waited nearby, as did porta-potties. By 9:30 a.m., the county sheriff closed off all approaches to Januszkiewicz's street, 12 hours *before* the vision was scheduled to appear.

Since this looked as if it wasn't going to die down any time soon, city officials began to worry. Eight thousand people could easily become 20,000, then upwards of 100,000. They had already been contacted by out-of-state tour bus companies and vendors asking for permission to set up stands selling food and religious items. "We don't allow that sort of thing in Marlboro, particularly on a Sunday," city manager Robert Albertson told *The New York Times*.

The State Police Emergency Management Team, which offers assistance during natural disasters, was called in and the Town Council passed a temporary ordinance prohibiting parking in Januszkiewicz's neighborhood. Paid parking would help replenish the $21,000 spent on overtime and for extra services.

Several angry residents organized a petition calling for traffic limitations and protection of neighbors' privacy. Although many felt sympathy for the lame and infirm who arrived in wheelchairs and on crutches seeking a miracle, "people here have their own rights and lives to lead," township clerk Evelyn Piccolini told the *Times*.

Even the local Catholic church grew edgy, rejecting an offer of a donation of parking proceeds and suggesting that monies be used to reimburse the town of Marlboro. The diocese of Trenton "needed to investigate the matter and determine its validity," explains Joseph M. Donadieu, director of communications for the diocese. "The bishop asked people to stay away until a commission studied the event and everything surrounding it."

Marlboro mayor Matthew Scannapieco also put in a cease-and-desist request to the curious and faithful. "This is beyond the ability of the township to deal with," he said in the *Times*. "This has gone outside the boundaries of the town, the county, and the state. And it could eventually go outside the boundaries of the country." And indeed by the close of 1992, 10,000 were showing up on the first Sunday.

Finally the town asked Januszkiewicz to install "No Trespassing" signs. He reportedly refused, so officials amended a local zoning ordinance to include a definition of a place of worship, requiring him to apply for a permit. Whether he actually complied remains unclear.

Meanwhile, a group of four priests visited the site several times. They interviewed Januszkiewicz and his wife Veronica, members of the local community and parish, over 50 people who came forward with their experiences, and even township officials. "Because of the evident faith of so many people, there have been reports of conversions, reconciliations, spiritual renewals, and healings," stated Bishop John Reiss in diocese findings. Rosaries also allegedly changed colors, and "unexplained figures" appeared in photographs.

Despite this, "the commission was unable to document even one truly miraculous event . . . that would require suspension of the laws of nature and could not be accounted for by natural causes." Plus, the messages for the people were "for the most part repetitious" while those meant for priests had a "tone of chiding, exasperation, and judgment," not a particularly tactful approach when the latter are determining the validity of an event.

"Mr. Januszkiewicz stated to the press that Mary would not agree to moving the site of the claimed apparitions anywhere else. In view of the hardship that had already been caused to many people in the township, grave doubts arise that such a response would come from the Virgin Mary," he continued. Although Januszkiewicz professed not to encourage the gatherings, "at the same time he maintains a shrine, grants interviews, and speaks to groups in connection with his claims. . . . Others have arranged buses, printed flyers, and otherwise promoted the attendance of thousands. . . ."

So the diocese ordered Januszkiewicz to put an end to his activities and cooperate with the town of Marlboro "to alleviate the inconvenience, burden, and danger that remains." Any future divine messages were to be cleared through the diocese.

Today Joseph Januszkiewicz is mum. He has an unlisted number and, according to Donadieu, finally did put up those "No Trespassing" signs. "He announced there would be no more visions after January 1, 1995." Apparently his option with Mary wasn't renewed.

But he and his followers won't soon be forgotten. "It ruined my life," says one neighbor, who asked that his name not be used. "They overran the town and disrupted everything and it's made me bitter." Mr. Rogers' neighborhood this isn't.

What to Expect

Visitors are taking a chance of not seeing anything at all. Januszkiewicz lives on one acre in a heavily wooded area; his house has no identifying markings. Minimal street lights and narrow roads surrounded by ditches can make driving hazardous, particularly at night.

Still, it's a pleasant community and people willingly provide directions and advice. Just don't go knocking on any neighbors' doors or wander into their back yards (see below).

What They Say

Robert Albertson, Marlboro, New Jersey: Although he's been in city government for nearly four decades and has handled political hot potatoes ranging from desegregation to abortion clinic shutdowns, Albertson found the Januszkiewicz situation his toughest challenge. "There were no firm answers and no one to negotiate with.

"The community was really torn apart by this," he goes on. "We have a high percentage of Jewish people and they are very sensitive to issues of persecution, especially when religion is involved. The Catholics also were upset because people didn't listen when the bishop said to stay away."

The town also had to deal with health and safety concerns. "People were going behind bushes and defecating" in neighborhood yards. "It was very disturbing, but yet you felt sorry for them because they were looking for help."

Cal Fussman, reporting from Marlboro, New Jersey: "As he did on the first Sunday of each month, Januszkiewicz stepped out of his back door and walked across his patio to the statue of the Virgin," Fussman wrote in *Harper's Bazaar.* "When he finished praying, photoflashes lit the darkness, a cross appeared in the sky, and the crowd gasped. I saw a television antenna or a crisscross of power lines. . . .

"'I smell roses!' exclaimed one woman, nearly fainting. Others wept and embraced. At that moment it didn't matter whether Januszkiewicz was hallucinating, seeing God's Mother, or simply making it all up. The woman in the wheelchair was smiling."

Various bystanders, Marlboro: The bishop was only telling people to stay away, "until he proves it," Kathy Kirkland of Fort Washington, Pennsylvania, told the *Times.* "We can believe without proof. That's what faith is."

"I feel very peaceful," Adeline Fahy of Oceanport, New Jersey, added. "It feels joyous when you're with all these people who believe. They're like family."

A former mayor of Sparta, New Jersey, Andy Massey suffered a recurrence of cancer after several months of remission. "I came down here not to ask for a cure but for strength for my battle coming up. As I prayed today, it felt like my heartbeat went down and I felt a sense of ease . . . I haven't had in a long time."

A woman who wished to remain anonymous remarked, "I asked my family priest about it and he said, 'Do what's in your heart— you'll have inner peace.'"

How to Get There

From New York City (about two hours), take Routes 1 and 9 South, then follow 9S to Route 18 South. Then turn left on SR 520 and take 79S for about five blocks. Turn left on East Schoolhouse Rd., which runs into Buckley Rd., Januszkiewicz's street. The house is on the left-hand side, but it's unmarked. For more information, contact the Marlboro Township Hall, 1979 Township Dr., Marlboro, NJ 07749, 908/536-0200.

✝ A Chameleon of a Statue

Our Lady of Pompeii Church
Paterson, New Jersey

How It Happened

This is the stuff of cloak-and-dagger novels: a cover-up, a secret manuscript, people seemingly afraid to talk. And all because a small replica of an Our Lady of Fatima statue apparently transformed itself into a rainbow of hues.

The Diocese of Paterson and the priests involved claim that the statue was one of a batch that was defective. Yet both priests refuse to speak about what transpired. And the Chancellor's office treats inquiries as if they're being asked to convert to Buddhism.

But scratch a cluster of the faithful from Our Lady of Pompeii, and you'll get another story. Although the parish forbids them from discussing it directly, one of their number, Mary Jo Kalchthaler, has written a book—actually several manuscripts—about her spiritual experiences. According to her tome "If It Didn't Happen to Me," a Vatican icon, the International Pilgrim Statue of Our Lady of Fatima, had made the rounds of several churches. She and others in the parish purchased a reproduction of it "so there would be a remembrance of her [the Vatican statue] in our little statue . . . and this [small] statue would tour different homes in the parish and people could pray" to it.

On January 8, 1992, a group was saying the rosary at the St. James Church in Totowa, New Jersey. Kalchthaler asked for a sign and "as soon as I completed those words, the statue, which was white in color, began to glow blue . . . there was an aura about her." Everyone there noticed "the statue was a different color and it was glowing." As they approached it, it "started to change colors before our eyes . . . red, blue, green, yellow, and pinkish. . . . One of the women was so overcome she ran out of the church."

Although the two pastors at Our Lady of Pompeii were contacted, the transformations were kept quiet for several months. But finally someone told the diocesan paper, and the local media picked it up. Soon the Associated Press, TV stations, and the *National Examiner* stopped by and pilgrims from all over crammed into the 400-seat church. "People were coming in wheelchairs, on crutches," says Kalchthaler in her book. "Those who suffered from spiritual . . . [and] mental problems were there in reverence and in prayer." The church increased special and regular services to accommodate the faithful.

Reports of healings ranged from recovery from an aneurysm to the mysterious clearing up of a brain tumor. There were also several conversions: Souls as well as marriages were saved. And Father Martin D'Auria of the church praised the statue's "good effect" in *The Beacon,* the diocesan paper.

Still, one might say this statue represented a litmus test of belief: Some saw it change colors, while others did not. More than a few left disappointed and angry, feeling as if they'd been hoodwinked. But those who witnessed the transformation were from all walks of life, from professionals to street people. Many were educated, Reverend Frank O'Grady of the church told the Associated Press. "They're cops. They're secretaries. They're not just a crowd of people who are poor and easily led." Like the other priest at the church, Father Martin D'Auria, he also claimed to observe parts of the statue glow in various shades.

"There was a such a sense of community, love, caring . . ." reports Kalchthaler in her manuscript. "You could walk into that church feeling a little tired . . . and down with whatever happened . . . that day, but you would never leave [feeling] that way. You were filled with joy, encouragement, hope, and a promise that you could go on."

Then the local bishop forbade the prayer group from speaking about the statue. Yet he didn't rule "if he felt what really happened at Our Lady of Pompeii was true or not."

Although the statue, during its glory days encased in glass and displayed near the altar for all to see, has been moved to the back of the church "in a more appropriate spot" according to a church official, the faithful believe it still works its magic.

"[It] changes [its] color like a rainbow shining alongside the presence of God," asserts Kalchthaler's manuscript. "Now, the scene of Our Lady of Pompeii is mocked as Jesus was mocked so long ago, and as Jesus was left alone to die on the cross," so the statue is "now left alone in the tabernacle."

The statue could be made from the same stuff as mood rings or it could be waiting for the Second Coming. And, like many a mystery, there's a sequel (see the next chapter).

What to Expect

Located in a working-class neighborhood, Our Lady of Pompeii is a rather unassuming church, with only a few statues and wooden pews. Situated in the back of the church, the Our Lady of Fatima statue is a pale plaster reproduction about 2½-feet tall.

The church is open most days, although evenings may be problematic. With a graffiti-covered school building and clotheslines in the back yard, this is not a yuppiefied area. Paterson is a typical New Jersey manufacturing town and the people seem friendly and helpful.

What They Say

Mary Jo Kalchthaler, Wayne, New Jersey: In her unpublished manuscript, "If It Didn't Happen to Me," Kalchthaler stated: "[The statue] would start out dull-looking and then there would be a vitality to the color. . . . It would grow deeper and it would form, in the folds of the [clothing] . . . and then it would disappear and form in another area. . . . This continued . . . [it] was alive with color, changing before our eyes."

Kalchthaler and others also claimed to notice a change in Our Lady's facial appearance as well. "There was a strong sense of peace, joy, and love . . . a total feeling of being euphoric."

Larry Spagnola, Paterson, New Jersey: "I'm not what you call a regular churchgoer," Spagnola, a police inspector in Paterson, told the Associated Press. "The way things are, when you see something like this, it makes you feel good and . . . wonderful. This is the best stress management you could ever have."

How to Get There

Located about 25 miles from New York City, Paterson is best reached via I-80W. Take exit 56, Squirrel Wood Rd., and follow the signs to Paterson (*not* West Paterson). The road will automatically lead to Nagle St.; circle around and go about six blocks to Caldwell, then turn right. The church is on the corner of Caldwell and Dayton. Mailing address: Our Lady of Pompeii Church, 70 Murray Ave., Paterson, NJ 075021, 201/742-1969.

✝ God Finds a Loophole

St. Ann Melkite Catholic Church
West Paterson, New Jersey

How It Happened

Located just down the road from Our Lady of Pompeii (see previous chapter), the St. Ann Melkite church seems to have had a rather charmed existence. In the early '70s, the church refused to sell its land for what eventually became Route 80 and was levelled by a mysterious fire. Still, the Byzantine Catholic congregation, mostly descendants of Syrian immigrants and Italians, constructed an even nicer complex on 21 gently rolling acres in West Paterson obtained from the Roman Catholic diocese.

Then there was the missing icon. Commissioned in 1976 to honor the Bicentennial, the priceless, bejeweled Queen of the Americas was stolen a few years later. Although the thieves attempted to remove the diamonds, rubies, sapphires, and emeralds, "the parishioners prayed the icon would somehow come back to them," states author Mary Jo Kalchthaler. It was found intact, in a field. The thieves, however, may not have been so lucky. According to local legend, the Mafia was instrumental in its safe return. Today the icon is encased under glass and protected by a burglar alarm, although that hardly seems necessary if rumor is to be believed.

But perhaps the strangest coincidence happened on May 25, 1995. Near the end of the service on that Ascension Thursday, "we noticed a liquid seemed to be coming off of the dome," states Father Philip, the senior priest at St. Ann's. Located over the central altar of this ornate church, the elaborately decorated dome is the centerpiece of religious activity.

Even more curious, "only the walls and not the paintings around the dome were sweating," adds Kalchthaler, who visited the site a few weeks later. "It was phenomenal. The entire interior part was oozing. Nothing was dripping, although the church had put plastic on the rugs just in case."

At first, Philip thought the moisture might be water, "but my assistant got up on a ladder and discovered it was oil." He then called in the bishop, the police, and a paint expert, "but no one could explain it." Although an untouched sample could not be obtained—the oil has to actually drip into a container and cannot be analyzed from a cloth or cotton ball—the paint was latex-based anyway.

Even though word spread quickly among the parishioners, the church has kept a relatively low profile. Some anointed with the oil claimed to have been healed. "The sugar of a severe diabetic dropped to 150 from around 400, avoiding amputation of a leg," Father Philip continues, citing several examples. "A woman who had a cesarean with her first baby had an easy delivery with her second, and another lady whom the doctors said could not become pregnant" suddenly became fertile.

According to Philip, the seeping appears more active during Holy Communion. And the oil seems to have unique properties: "It evaporates quickly and doesn't leave the cotton matted or dirty. It dries with no residue."

Kalchthaler believes the dome is a continuation of the happenings at Our Lady of Pompeii. "Because of the rule of obedience set forth by the bishop, I was not allowed to talk about the events there. But my spiritual director told me God would find a way to get the message through." And the Byzantine bishop "saw and immediately approved the miracle. So Pompeii's loss was St. Ann's gift."

What to Expect

Father Philip is friendly and open. Those wishing to be anointed with oil need only contact someone in the church.

Thus far, the daily business of the church seems unaffected by the sweating blue-and-gold gilded dome. That may change as the oil greases the wheels of more miracle cures and conversions. But with its spacious gardens and exquisitely rendered paintings and icons, St. Ann's can be a respite for the spiritually weary regardless of whether anything extraordinary occurs.

What They Say

Mary Jo Kalchthaler, Wayne, New Jersey: "My first reaction was to roll my eyes and think, 'Oh, no, not another one,'" states Kalchthaler. But curiosity and a traffic jam got the better of her: "It was closer than the other shrine I pray at."

As soon as she went inside St. Ann's, she noticed a spiritual quickening. "I hadn't felt that way in a long time, not since the incidents at Our Lady of Pompeii." She became convinced of the site's veracity when the priest seemed to intuitively know what she wanted. "I asked God for three signs and they all came to pass.

"It's incredible that God would suspend natural laws for one place and outstanding that he would do it for two."

Father Philip, West Paterson, New Jersey: A pastor at St. Ann's since 1989, Father Philip regards the seeping dome with cautious elation. "This is happening in the Middle East with other icons," he observes. "God doesn't send telegrams, but he's showing his love and mercy and trying to strengthen people's faith by giving healing and encouragement."

Still, he's concerned that the church may be overrun with thrill-seekers and tourists. "We don't want a bunch of people coming in and gawking. But those with a prayerful attitude are always welcome."

How to Get There

Located about 25 miles from New York City, Paterson is best reached via I-80W. Take exit 56, Squirrel Wood Rd., and follow the signs to West Paterson (*not* Paterson). Go to a stop sign and turn left at Rifle Camp Rd. The church is about three miles up on the right-hand side. Open Monday to Friday and Sunday, 8 a.m.–1 p.m.; Saturday 5–7 p.m. Mailing address: St. Ann Melkite Catholic Church, 802 Rifle Camp Rd., West Paterson, NJ 07424, 201/785-4144.

New Mexico

✚ A "Pit" Stop on the High Road to Taos

El Santuario
Chimayo, New Mexico

How It Happened

The Tewa Indians recognized a good thing when they saw it. Even before the Spaniards came to conquer in the 16th century, they believed that the dirt in the general area known today as Chimayo had magical powers. According to their legends, in the time of the Ancient Ones, fire and scalding water produced a sacred pool, which became a mud puddle, which turned into dust. Eating the dirt seemed to cure many ailments, including that of iron-poor blood.

Then in the early 1800s, a Hispanic farmer by the name of Don Bernardo Abeyta saw a light coming from the ground near where he had been praying. He dug a hole with his bare hands and found a large crucifix in the same spot that had once been so venerated by the Tewas. The area had a long and bloody history of conflict among the Church, Indians, and Spaniards, so a piece of cloth belonging to two priests killed during an uprising was also present.

Although the local clergyman took the crucifix to the parish church and placed it on the main altar, by the next morning it had disappeared, only to turn up in the original location. After this happened a few times, people got the message and in 1816 a small shrine was completed around the hole where the statue had been found.

Today it is a full-fledged church, with a prayer room, nave, and picturesque and colorful reredos (sacred paintings). Called El Santuario de Nuestro Senor de Esquipulas after the crucifix, and better known as El Santuario, it draws tens of thousands of visitors a year. People take handfuls of dirt from "El Pocito" (the little well) and swear by its healing powers, "although we make no secret of the fact that it comes from a bigger pile of dirt outside," states

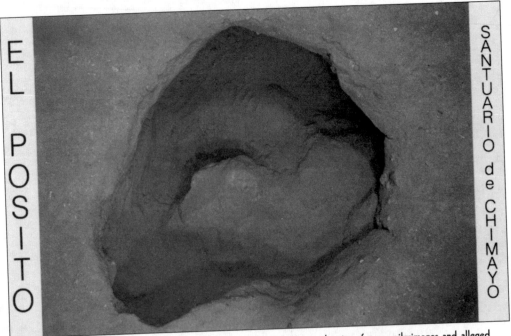

EL POSITO

SANTUARIO de CHIMAYO

El Santuario, this humble hole in the ground at Chimayo, New Mexico, is the site of many pilgrimages and alleged miracles. PHOTO COURTESY OF EL SANTUARIO.

Father Miguel Mateo, the parish priest. "It does not automatically regenerate" even though it *is* blessed by the clergy.

Although no one admits to eating the dust, they will take handfuls and rub it on themselves or put it in jars for their loved ones at home. The Catholic Church has expressed no interest in confirming or denying the phenomenon, despite a roomful of abandoned orthopedia and dozens of offers of medical records documenting alleged cures.

"The dirt itself doesn't have magical properties," insists Father Miguel. "It's the faith of the person, their wish to be healed. The dirt is only a symbol." "Cures" range from the cessation of physical ailments to emotional healings.

And people don't just come to dish up the dirt, so to speak. "This is a very peaceful place," he continues. "There's a sense of art and history here, as well as a feeling of spiritual renewal. Many non-Catholics respond to it as well."

El Santuario has been called "The Lourdes of America," albeit a dusty one.

What to Expect

One of the most visited shrines in America, El Santuario is rather unimposing from the outside. But its smallness serves it well; not only are the main attractions (the cross and El Pocito) easy to find, but it's a comfortable church that makes most visitors feel at home. Located in a tiny cubicle outside the nave where the cross sits, El Pocito is surrounded by offerings from grateful supplicants.

What They Say

Ida P., Chicago, Illinois: "He was to have six more radium treatments," she wrote about a family member who had cancer. "[We] rubbed it on his neck Sunday and on Monday they examined his throat and found nothing there. In six months they will know for sure if it has come back. With all our hearts, we know it was the healing dirt. . . ."

Father Miguel Mateo, Chimayo, New Mexico: The shrine is on what is known as the High Road to Taos. "Winters and summers are mild here, even though we're in the middle of the mountains," observes the priest, who serves 700 families in several surrounding towns. He marvels at the fact that miracles can occur in such an out-of-the-way place. "Coming here allows you to become in touch with creation. Its simplicity is its beauty."

*Melissa Phillips, Columbus, Ohio: "I'm not a believer, but El Pocito really blew me away," Phillips remarks. "It's this tiny little place, just a pile of dirt, but it gives off a powerful aura. It's humbling that something so simple can have such a strong influence on people's lives. I came away with a greater respect for spirituality."

How to Get There

From Santa Fe, take 84/285N to just past Pojoaque. Turn right to Hwy 503, go 12 miles, then turn left on County Rd. 98. Hours: 9 a.m.–5 p.m., seven days a week. Mailing address: El Santuario, P.O. Box 235, Chimayo, NM 87522, 505/351-4889.

*Name changed by request.

✝ Jesus Up against the Wall

Sacred Heart of Mary Chapel
Holman, New Mexico

How It Happened

Consider it a Rorschach test of faith. The image on a concrete wall of a school building next to the Sacred Heart of Mary Chapel in Holman, New Mexico, has been likened to everything from Satan to cloud formations to the series of inkblots that probe for underlying psychological disturbances.

Many, however, claimed to see Jesus when after May 25, 1975, two teenaged boys noticed an odd "shadow" on the wall. "It was graduation night and there was a total eclipse of the moon," recalls Father Leonard Bayer, who at the time was pastor at nearby St. Gertrude parish in Mora. The Sacred Heart was one of 18 missions serviced by St. Gertrude's.

As the youths drew closer, they glimpsed what appeared to be a head-and-shoulders drawing of Christ. But rather than being an actual sketch, it seemed to have formed within the wall itself. They fled in terror, but soon hundreds of pilgrims and the media were making the long and dusty trek to the isolated town on the edge of the Santa Fe National Forest.

Most residents won't soon forget that summer and the one that came after. "No one had ever observed anything before," states Bayer. The wall had been last painted and plastered in the early '60s and the lone street lamp had been around for years.

With only a post office and a store, Holman had suddenly become a destination spot, with visitors arriving by bus and carloads. "We really had no place for them," remarks Bayer. "We couldn't provide lodging or food, so they'd come in campers and trailers and stay for several days."

Still, the townspeople managed quite well. Four concession stands popped up, featuring menu items from candy to hamburgers to tacos. Flourescent orange and black bumper stickers proclaiming "I Have Seen the Wall" and commemorative posters also became available. None of the profits went to the church; concessionaires claimed that on a good night they could take in $150, which went a long way back in 1975. Artists also cashed in by selling drawings and paintings of the wall. "Some portraits were wonderful," adds Bayer. Framed color composite photos were also popular; you could choose from either Jesus or Mary superimposed over the likeness.

Still, even the hawkers were respectful, utilizing flashlights and keeping their distance so as not to interfere with the image. "Although police officers had to direct traffic, everyone was very orderly, devotional, and reverent," he continues. "People came from all over; we had inquiries from as far away as Europe. And the archbishop of the United States preached about the image at his cathedral."

As darkness enfolded the little plaza, the curious and faithful waited in front of the chapel for the shadowy figure to materialize. A small shrine at the base of the wall held rosaries, candles, pictures, and other prayer offerings.

And viewers weren't disappointed: "It appeared every night," recalls Bayer. Still, the image provoked its share of arguments. One woman reportedly slapped her husband when he called it a hoax, and another told her little boy to be quiet when he said he didn't see anything. When a few objectors threatened to paint over the likeness, one of the older townsfolk sat guard in front of it all night with his rifle.

Although the archbishop of Santa Fe visited the wall himself, he claimed to see no evidence of a miracle there. So after a couple of years, the crowds died down. But believers who visit the Sacred Heart of Mary Chapel may be in for a spiritual jolt.

What to Expect

Although the threat of vandalism prompted the removal of the street light several years ago, the image still remains. According to the people at St. Gertrude's, it is now mostly visible during the day, although dusk is still the ideal time for viewing.

The likeness measures 4-feet-by-2-feet and is on on the wall 7 feet above the ground. To many, it resembles your basic portrait of Jesus with a crown of thorns, long hair, and a beard and appears to be caused by a combination of lighting and tones of plaster and paint. Tar-like spots around the image have also been interpreted as hawks, doves, Moses, etc. In order to gain overall perspective, it is best seen from a distance.

The small chapel was built decades ago and was basically abandoned when the parish consolidated, "mostly due to poverty," explains Father Bayer. Still, it's usually open and the locals are friendly and those who were around during the '70s are full of lore about the image.

What They Say

Unidentified onlookers, Holman, New Mexico: "People want something to bolster their belief [sic], and this reaffirms their faith," one man told the Santa Fe *New Mexican.* "They see what is already in their minds."

Another couple disagreed about what the image represented. "I saw the Devil better than anything else," the husband observed. "Does that make me a Satanist?"

"You're a sinner," his wife retorted. "You haven't been to church in three months."

When asked by him for her interpretation, she replied, "It's sort of like watching clouds . . . I could see a sort of face, but no crown of thorns and the face was sort of like modern art. . . ."

Father Leonard Bayer, Rio Rancho, New Mexico: Father Bayer was only assigned to the Sacred Heart of Mary for a few years, then was transferred to a new parish. But this is not his first experience with visions, although "they were on a much smaller scale" and he prefers not to go into detail. "These things seem to be following me," he half-jokes.

Although he acknowledges that the image resembles a Christ-like figure, he has no clue as to what caused it. "God didn't need my permission. It wasn't there before, so how did it get there? I had no indication that such a thing would happen." So he let events play themselves out. "We just let people come."

How to Get There

Holman is about 150 miles northeast of Albuquerque. Take 1-25/84 north and east to Las Vegas, New Mexico, then go north on highway 518 to Mora. The church is about seven miles down on the left side, just before you get to Holman. It's best to come in daylight as there are no street lights. For more information, contact St. Gertrude's Parish, PO Box 599, Mora, NM 87732, 505/387-2336.

✝ Heaven on a Burnt Tortilla

Home of Mrs. Maria Rubio
Lake Arthur, New Mexico

How It Happened

Before you read further, take note of this fact: the Rubio family of Lake Arthur, New Mexico appear rational and quite ordinary.

Originally from Mexico, Maria and Eduardo Rubio met while picking cotton near Artesia, New Mexico. Both Catholics, they married and had six children. Life wasn't always easy: Eduardo struggled with dark moods and a drinking problem and Maria suffered from nervousness and panic attacks. For several years, the entire family had to pick cotton and ferry to Kansas to clean sugar beets just to pay the bills.

So at 6:20 a.m. on the morning of October 5, 1977, when Maria found a burnt image of Jesus Christ on a burrito she was cooking for her husband's breakfast, the family took it seriously. "I felt something deep inside, and I noticed it was God's face," Maria, who speaks mostly Spanish, said through an interpreter. The dark brown image on the tortilla, which was to be filled with cheese and chiles to make a burrito, resembled a long-haired man looking to the right and wearing a crown of thorns.

Maria called in her daughter Rosy and Eduardo, who stared at his breakfast tortilla and exclaimed, "This is really crazy. What are we doing wrong?" After Rosy and the other children went to school, Maria told a neighbor, who informed another friend, who called the press. By the time the Rubio children returned, the media and dozens of onlookers had swarmed outside the family's modest three-bedroom home.

Meanwhile, since the insides of the fateful tortilla had been filled before Maria noticed the likeness, she snipped a 3-inch-by-3-inch square which had remained dry. Those who viewed the image cried, fell to their knees, and crossed themselves. One lady reportedly crawled in homage across the railroad tracks to the Rubio home to pay her respects, then crawled back. When Eduardo came home from work and saw the crowd, his mood changed from pessimism to elation. He piled his family—tortilla and all—into their 1968 Chevy and went to see the local priest.

The Reverend Joyce Finnigan examined it and pronounced it a coincidence, not a miracle. "But she told us it would mold and the image would fade away in two or three days," recalls Rosy, who works as an administrator for an agency for the developmentally disabled in Roswell. That was in 1977—today the tortilla remains relatively intact, although the likeness is a bit harder to discern. "Mom never did anything to preserve it, either. It's really amazing, because most tortillas will disintegrate," especially one with as much mileage as this.

The initial excitement was such that hundreds of people a day flocked to the Rubios. "People walked in and out of the house at all hours," recalls Rosy. "We never locked the doors, yet nothing was taken." However, when Rosy and her sister Edubina tried to come home from school and shopping, "people got mad at us because we tried to cut in front of the line" that snaked all the way across the street. "We told them, 'Hey, we live here!'" They finally resorted to sneaking through a window.

Initially the tortilla was kept in a place of honor under a glass-topped altar in the dining room. But in 1986, Maria and her sister Margarita Porras built a little shrine, or *capilla*, for it in front of the house so people could visit the tortilla without disturbing the family. Still, Maria patiently answered the same questions over and over, stating her belief that God's message had been delivered in a humble piece of food so all could understand and relate to it.

More than 11,000 people (the family has kept count) have passed through the Rubio home since then. "They mostly come around Christmas and Easter," states Rosy. Some have made the pilgrimage from as far away as England. Syndicated columnists, the *National Geographic*, "Phil Donahue," and "Oprah" were surprisingly respectful in their coverage, although one reporter remarked that the image more closely resembled prizefighter Leon Spinks. And although Maria agreed to appear on "Donahue," between rapid-fire questions from the audience and her first airplane ride ever, "she got pretty freaked out," observes Rosy. "There are a lot of skeptics and my Mom is basically a simple person."

This petrified piece of unleavened bread has had an even more profound impact on the family. "My Dad stopped drinking about 12 years ago and has become more religious and my Mom is a lot calmer these days," continues Rosy. "She works and drives a car and takes care of a teenager," Angelica, Rosy's youngest sister, born several years after the tortilla came into their lives.

The Rubio children half-jokingly refer to themselves as the Tortilla Kids. Although they've had to endure comments about the image being painted on by their parents and otherwise being a hoax, "it really has made us a lot more religious," confides Rosy. "I remember Mom dragging us out of bed every Sunday morning, making us attend Mass . . . but we still go, even though we don't live at home." Although many of the kids have degrees and all are gainfully employed, they still like to party, much to Maria's chagrin. "It's like we have an image to uphold.

"It may not be a miracle to anyone else but it is to us," adds Rosy. So whenever they sit down to their mother's tortillas, they *always* check for another kind of image.

What to Expect

Don't even think about biting into this one. Not only is the tortilla rock hard and enclosed in a 10-inch deep altar, but it's surrounded by a 2-foot-by-3-foot glass-enclosed shed with indoor/outdoor carpeting. Inside is a guest book, a bulletin board, flowers, candles, and a light bulb for late-night visitors. Around the altar, you may also find *milagros*—small metallic emblems symbolizing legs, arms, hearts, and other parts of the body believers hope the tortilla will help heal.

A few years ago, the family moved the shrine into the back yard where it's more shaded. "We think exposure to the sunlight faded the image somewhat," explains Rosy. Visitors are welcome, but don't go knocking on the Rubios' door at odd hours.

Located about 10 miles north of Artesia, the sunny farming community of Lake Arthur has about 400 souls and no actual body of water. Visitors looking for lodging and food will find only Ray's cafe, a combination grocery, gas station, and pawn shop. But everybody in town knows where to find the tortilla. So it's virtually impossible to get lost. And, as a side trip, you can stop at one of the few remaining Ozark Trail Markers in the U.S., a sphere-shaped sign a block away from the Rubios' house. (All but four were run over or otherwise destroyed.)

What They Say

Maria Rubio, Lake Arthur, New Mexico: Although the initial hoopla over the image made Maria anxious, it greatly increased her faith. She does not worship it as an idol but regards it as a mystery and feels blessed by the good it has done. "A lady [of] about 55 came in here a couple of years ago in a wheelchair," she told United Press International. "She was paralyzed and promised to walk here all the way from Artesia once a year if she was cured . . . She was, and she made her first walk last year. . . . Just yesterday, a neighbor's son pulled out of a coma and she came by to offer thanks."

Clifford Nelson, Lake Arthur, New Mexico: As longtime mayor of Lake Arthur, Nelson is impressed by the tortilla's effect on the family and the town. "Mrs. Rubio has been very generous about sharing it with the community."

Although the tide of visitors has ebbed over the years, the likeness "has given people hope. It unified the family and increased the morale of the Catholic community in general. People come here thinking it's a joke or someone's imagination and leave realizing that the image is real."

How to Get There

Lake Arthur is about a 3 ½-hour drive from Albuquerque. Take U.S. 285S through Vaughn; load up on gas because there's nothing for 100 miles until Roswell, the nearest large (for New Mexico) town. From 285, turn west (left) on Pueblo Rd. and go about 5 miles to Lake Arthur. Turn right on the Old Dexter Highway and go to the third street, Broadway. Turn left and over the railroad tracks is the Rubios' yellow clapboard home, the second on the left. For more information, contact Rosy Rubio, 303 S. Sycamore, Roswell, NM 88201, 505/625-2265.

✝ This Old Madonna

Chapel of La Conquistadora, St. Francis Cathedral
Santa Fe, New Mexico

How It Happened

In 1625, Fray Alonso Benavidez, a Franciscan priest, brought a carved wooden statue of Mary from Spain to Santa Fe. He placed the icon in the parish church, which had been built in 1610.

Today that statue still exists, enthroned in a special chapel at St. Francis Cathedral. Not only does this make both statue and church the oldest of their kind in the U.S., but for over 360 years "La Conquistadora" has been the focus of an annual procession and prayer held in Santa Fe each June. And in 1960, as part of the 350th anniversary of Santa Fe's founding, the statue received a papal coronation, making it the only one of its kind in the United States.

La Conquistadora even has a fan club of sorts, a confraternity started in 1626, which, although its membership has waxed and waned over the centuries, is still going strong. And membership dues are a bargain at only $2 a year, although you do have to pay $2 to join (additional donations are always welcome).

Now La Conquistadora has her own visionary. On June 8, 1986, as Vangie Gonzales Peterson prayed quietly at the chapel, "a bright powerful light emerged from . . . La Conquistadora . . . and made

La Conquistadora at St. Francis Cathedral in Santa Fe, New Mexico, is the only Virgin Mary statue in the United States to have received a papal coronation. And this Madonna's fan club dates back to 1626. PHOTO COURTESY OF MARIA VICTORIA ARCHULETA.

a verbal salutation," according to *Our Lady of Light in Santa Fe,* by Maria Victoria Archuleta. A seemingly normal married homemaker with two children, Peterson had made a habit of attending the 6:00 a.m. Mass since her mother had died two years before. "She had been praying for a strong faith and an understanding of who Mary is as understood by her own mother."

"[Mary] kept changing from La Conquistadora to the Lady of Fatima to the Virgin of Guadalupe," an astounded Peterson said in the book. Vangie also "felt as if something held her in a stationary position [and she was] unable to move forward or backward."

Although she was fairly upset, she vowed not to tell anyone. But "her husband noticed a change in her behavior and questioned her," according to the book. She finally broke down and confessed. "He reacted with excitement and belief."

In fact, Peterson received the love and support of the immediate Gonzales family, all forty-five of them. Her visions continued and they went to Mass *en masse.* The messages involved fasting and prayer and Vangie vowed to give up smoking. Mary even pointed out a priest in whom Vangie could confide.

Soon Peterson was seeing Jesus, Mother Cabrini, and St. Michael. "Her mystical experiences have included visions of Heaven, Purgatory, and Hell," explains the book. "She has received messages from Our Lady praising Jesus in Hebrew and several other languages." Even her brother Gerard got into the act, although he has heard locutions rather than actually seeing the Blessed Mother. Vangie kept it "all in the family" for about three months, when Mary "told" her she could "opened [sic] up the rosary to the public in other Santa Fe homes."

Per Mary's instruction, a pilgrim statue of Our Lady of Fatima travelled to various residences. "This was the first public formal

Homemaker Vangie Gonzales Peterson had her first visions at St. Francis Cathedral in Santa Fe, New Mexico, the oldest church of its kind in the United States. PHOTO COURTESY OF MARIA VICTORIA ARCHULETA.

procession organized by the Blessed Mother," continues the book. A rosary group was formed at Cristo Rey Catholic Church for services. It ". . . followed [Mary's] directives . . . filling the church to capacity with approximately 300 people. . . ." They continue to meet there to this day. A second rosary group was also organized and gathers at St. Anne's Church in Santa Fe.

Most of Peterson's messages—the public ones at least—revolve around prayer, the sign of the cross, opening one's heart, saying the rosary, family unity, fasting, and many other aspects of belief. "Mary saw young people losing their faith and not practicing religion," remarks Archuleta. "At first we kept the groups low-key, because we wanted to focus on practicing Mary's tenets." Now, however, they're a bit more anxious to spread the word, especially since Peterson's messages have been going on for several years.

As is common with many visionaries, Vangie "ceased to see and hear what surrounded her after the start of the apparition . . . ," observes the book. "She experienced the Blessed Mother as real, living, and touchable. She felt her motherly love, tenderness, and warmth. . . ." Those kneeling close to her in the prayer group "experienced a sweet aroma of roses and a loving, powerful presence. . . ." A spinning and pulsating sun, assorted "vapors" and multiple rainbows as well as rosaries changing to a gold color have also been reported.

Peterson is currently being investigated by the Catholic church. If her messages have one fourth the mileage of La Conquistadora, she's doing very well.

What to Expect

As befits the oldest Catholic church in the U.S., the Cathedral of St. Francis of Assisi has a beautiful interior and exterior and is immaculately maintained. La Conquistadora has also held up incredibly for someone who's pushing 400. An exquisitely painted statue no more than 3 feet high, the Madonna has dark hair and eyes and often carries a Christ child. Depending upon the date on the Marian calendar, her outfits change frequently, and, unlike the singer with the same name, are always in good taste.

Vangie Peterson's visions have transpired in various places: the Cathedral, Cristo Rey Church, in homes around Santa Fe, and in her father's house, among others. Many occur in the first rosary group, however. This group meets most evenings at the Cristo Rey Church; call or write (see below) for more information.

What They Say

Maria Victoria Archuleta, Santa Cruz, New Mexico: The Gonzales family asked Archuleta to write the book detailing the events, messages, and locutions surrounding Vangie and her brother Gerard. "It's a very exciting time for the groups," she says. "A lot of people are just beginning to find out about the apparitions. Mary predicted that many rosary groups would be forming in parishes throughout the Church. This has come to pass, and not just here in Santa Fe."

Father Godfrey Blank, Santa Fe, New Mexico: "I was impressed with the group's sincerity," remarks Father Godfrey, who works part-time at the cathedral. He finds Vangie Peterson to have not only integrity but humility. "I believe in the divine revelation and private revelations as long as they are in harmony, as they are here. Mary can appear to anybody she wants."

He is also pleased with the group's emphasis on what he calls the basics. "They are all for getting back to prayer, the rosary, and the blessed sacraments." And it's paying off: the parishioners are "mostly supportive" and Mass attendance has increased. "The growth has been slow but sure. I tell the group not to hurry things; Mary will let them know when it's time."

How to Get There

To the cathedral: From Albuquerque, take I-25N to the intersection of St. Francis and Cerrillos. Go straight and follow Cerrillos, come to a "V" and bear to the right. Stay in the right-hand lane and take the next "V" to Galisteo, then turn right on Alameda. Come to Cathedral Place and turn left; the church is in the approximate area, although you'll likely have to park in a city lot. Open seven days a week; hours vary. 131 Cathedral Pl., Santa Fe, NM 87504, 505/282-7545.

For more information on the Our Lady of Light Prayer Group, write or call. P.O. Box 600, Santa Cruz, NM 87567, 505/753-3684.

✞ Call 1-800-882-MARY

Our Lady of the Roses, Mary Help of Mothers Shrine
Bayside (Queens), New York

How It Happened

Until June 5, 1968, the day Robert F. Kennedy was assassinated, Veronica Leuken, mother of five grown children and wife of a construction worker, "lived the life of an ordinary New York housewife," states the literature of her organization, Our Lady of the Roses, Mary Help of Mothers Shrine.

But things changed drastically when she smelled roses in her car as she prayed for the dying senator. Shortly afterwards, the apparition of St. Theresa, the Little Flower, visited Veronica and her 10-year-old son (who was killed years later in a hunting accident). St. Theresa's most famous quote was "After my death, I will let fall a shower of roses from heaven." The stage was set.

Soon Veronica was experiencing visions and conversations with Jesus and Mary. She saw a huge cross in the sky that dissolved into the thorn-crowned head of Jesus. In 1970, the Blessed Virgin appeared to her at her church, St. Robert Bellarmine's in Bayside Hills, Queens, instructing her to hold rosary vigils outside on the eves of the Catholic feast days. Veronica was to establish a shrine there so Mary could channel "heavenly messages of worldwide importance." Neither weather conditions nor disturbances would deter the communiques, as long as the faithful, who came to be known as Baysiders (not to be confused with "Baywatchers"), continued to say the Holy Rosary during the vigil.

The more than 300 messages since include warnings of a Great Chastisement—a "Ball of Redemption" consisting of comets, earthquakes, World War III, and other disasters which would destroy three-quarters of humankind—unless people "pay universal penance and return to God." The end is also near if the former Soviet Union is not consecrated by the pope.

Through Veronica, who is also known as the "voice box of Jesus and Mary" by Baysiders, Mary also counsels against rock and roll, Communism, and abortion as well as women in slacks, television, and New York City. She calls for the return to Latin in services, kneeling before the Eucharist, communion given by mouth and not hand, and taking nuns and priests out of street clothes and putting them back in the habit and collar. This more traditional form of Catholicism also eliminates the participation of lay people, especially women, during services.

Baysiders believe Satan has corrupted the Catholic church and infiltrated Vatican II. "Satan . . . listened with careful ears in the Great Council," Veronica cautioned in '74. "You are on the wrong road! Turn about now, or you will sow the seeds of your own destruction!" In addition, Lucifer has taken over millions of children through a variety of modern influences.

Not surprisingly, the church has accused Veronica of having an overly active imagination. "No credit can be given to the so-called 'apparitions' reported by Veronica Leuken and her followers," intoned Bishop Francis John Mugavero of the Diocese of Brooklyn, after investigating the matter. "Because of my concern for their spiritual welfare, [the faithful] are hereby directed to refrain from participating in the 'vigils' and from disseminating any propaganda related to the 'Bayside apparitions.'"

But not all are vague prophecies. During the August 5, 1975, assemblage, Veronica warned of a "great challenge to science in . . . Philadelphia, but . . . your men of science shall not find the answer or the cause." A few months later, an outbreak of Legionnaire's disease occurred in a hotel there, claiming lives and mystifying doctors. On the other hand, her prediction of the attempted assassination of Pope John Paul II in 1993 in Denver never came to pass.

Despite (or perhaps because of) the church's admonitions, thousands of believers soon clogged the highways and bathrooms of this quiet New York City suburb, annoying the neighbors. The police were called and their chief offered the use of the Vatican Pavilion at the old World's Fair Grounds in Flushing Meadows-Corona Park as an alternative.

It was accepted by Our Lady through Veronica and was doubly blessed: Michelangelo's "Pieta" had been exhibited there during the 1964–65 World's Fair, and Pope Paul VI stopped by and said a prayer over the site during his visit to New York. Although the move occurred in 1975, Veronica believes it is only temporary and she will soon be allowed to return to St. Robert's.

A few years ago, city and park officials questioned the constitutionality of regular religious services in a city park. But according to *New York Newsday,* former Mayor Edward I. Koch refused to get involved. "The day I say, 'Oh no, not here,' the Virgin Mary will appear," he reportedly observed. If the prayers stopped, Baysiders believe, chastisement would come immediately. And there would be hell to pay.

What to Expect

Baysiders describe Veronica as a "victim soul"—one who suffers many illnesses for the sake of others. Now in her 70s, she has a heart condition and other ailments and makes few personal appearances, avoiding publicity and contact with the outside world. When she does show up, she guarantees a vision.

She's usually surrounded by over a dozen guards, among them single men between 18 and 55 who constitute her "workshop," an organization responsible for printing and disseminating her messages around the world. "There are evil people out there who have tried to assassinate her in the past," explains James Donohue, a former Manhattan doorman who has worked closely with the group for many years. "We must be very careful."

Located on top of an old city landfill, amidst the rumble of planes taking off and landing at nearby LaGuardia Airport, the site can host a few hundred "regulars" from New York, New Jersey, Pennsylvania, and Connecticut to the thousands who converge from around the world during summertime and for the major Catholic feast days. The most well-attended of the latter include June 18, the "anniversary" in which St. Theresa appeared to Veronica, and October 2, St. Theresa's feast day. They also meet every Sunday morning, rain or shine.

Many are white, middle-aged, and older women who have become disillusioned with the "new" Catholic faith. They wear skirts, as per the Virgin Mary's directive, and often sport lace mantillas. Some claim to have visions of their own. Most skeptics stay at home and the crowd is devoutly respectful.

The group's publication "Rose Notes" and tapes of Veronica's messages are distributed to an estimated 60,000 Catholics worldwide. Those who can't make it in person can mail in petitions for help, which will be placed at the foot of the statue during the next vigil. Along with religious revelations, believers have also claimed miracle cures for diseases. Many major cities have local directors who help organize pilgrimages and recruit newcomers. But there are no direct appeals for funds.

However, along with unsolicited contributions, devotees can donate their best Polaroids to the shrine, which sells them separately in books and videos. "Miraculous photographs" of squiggly lines and odd silhouettes are interpreted as shadowy Marys and skybound saints; doves or rats; a man wearing a white St. Michael beret ascending a stairway to heaven; a reflection of someone's dead aunt on the statue of the Blessed Virgin.

And videotapes, radio, and television shows featuring Veronica are also disseminated; there have even been advertisements on billboards and on the subway. Although Baysiders may object to the effects of modern technology, they are willing to utilize it to save souls.

What They Say

Robert F., Providence, Rhode Island: "Our first visit was on June 18, 1988, at the Anniversary of the Shrine. Before our arrival, I thought that this was no more than a group of religious people gathering, hoping to see God. And also, myself, being a police officer and seeing so many phonies and crooks, I was very doubtful. After taking [a] Polaroid shot and seeing the white dove, I knew that Our Lady of the Roses was telling me that this Shrine was and is real, and that she appears there with Jesus. Being a Providence police officer, my mission also must be to tell all the other police officers about Bayside. . . . Tell the world that a Providence police officer has found God at Bayside."

Patricia S., South Beach, New York: "I started smoking at 18 years old. I always loved the smell of smoke.

"By age 62, I smoked three to four packs a day. I even woke up at night from sleep desiring a cigarette. I was addicted. I had a terrible temper which I would unleash on anyone who would dare to take it away. I'd tell my friends to leave me to my one bad poison. I even went to be hypnotized; it didn't work.

"[Then] one day I fell down in the street, twice. I was having a stroke—I prayed so hard to our Blessed Mother in the hospital, to help me not to smoke. I couldn't do it on my own. I . . . closed my eyes, took a deep breath, kissed the holy rose, and prayed—I could hardly believe I had no desire.

*Name changed by request.

"I never had withdrawals or any bad day. All my friends and relatives can't believe it.

"It's two years and my health is fine, and I tell everyone about my miracle and blessing from Our Lady of the Roses."

Peter Z., Charlestown, New Hampshire: "I am not given to imagination, having been a chemist. Having been raised in an Orthodox Jewish home, I never was interested in Christianity.

"Even though I married a Protestant girl, who later on became a Catholic, and our children were raised Catholic, I never considered changing my religion.

"My wife had flyers from Bayside, and we decided to go down to the apparition grounds to get more insight. I said, 'If God wants me to become a Catholic—something has to happen to me—this is Your sign.'

"We drove down to New York on the Feast of the Holy Rosary. Many people had given us their rosaries. I had checked every rosary to assure no false claims could be made. I had put all rosaries into an open compartment of my car; we were a half an hour from home when I noticed something shiny.

"Among the rosaries I could see our son's rosary turning in front of our eyes. The Hail Mary beads turned into a gold color while the Our Father beads turned into a copper color. There was no logical explanation for this. Having studied chemistry, I could not find an argument to disprove what had happened. Finally I realized that I had to follow God's call."

How to Get There

Flushing Meadows-Corona Park is about a 20-minute ride from New York City. It is located off the Grand Central Parkway (exit 9), near Shea Stadium. Once you get there, look for the Unisphere—the Vatican Pavilion's not far.

Services are held every Sunday morning from 10:30 a.m.–12 noon and on the evenings of major Catholic feast days from 8:30 p.m.–11:30 p.m. Those wishing to receive literature and leave messages should call 800/882-MARY (6279) or 718/961-8865. The mailing address is Our Lady of the Roses, Mary Help of Mothers Shrine, P.O. Box 52, Bayside, NY 11361.

*Name changed by request.

✝ A Divine Wedding Gift

St. Paul's Greek Orthodox Church
Hempstead, New York

How It Happened

When Pagona and Banagiotis Catsounis left their native Greece to come to America, a maiden lady friend of Pagona's gave them a small portrait of the Virgin Mary as a wedding present. "She was a very religious woman, always in church," recalls Pagona. "She said, 'Please Pagona, take this because I can't afford anything else.'"

The lithograph became part of a mini-shrine in a bedroom alcove in the newlyweds' Island Park home. "As a young girl, I always loved to pray to the icons and light the candles," says Pagona, who was only 22 at the time. "On March 16, 1960, I was finishing up my devotions when I saw a tear coming from the eye of the picture. It was shining like a diamond. . . . I was totally shocked! I then called my husband, who rushed over" and verified the phenomenon.

"We were totally speechless and a little afraid," she continues. "So we decided to say nothing." For two days, the couple kept their silence. "But people at work noticed something was wrong. They thought I was sick or that something bad had happened." Finally she decided to confide in her fellow employees: "All the Catholics rushed over to pray and we contacted our pastor," Father George Papadeas at St. Paul's Cathedral in nearby Hempstead.

"When I arrived, a tear was drying beneath the left eye," Papadeas told *Newsday*. "Then just before the devotions ended, I saw another tear well in her eye. It started as a small, round globule of moisture in the corner . . . and it slowly trickled down her face." The tears fell onto the frame and disappeared.

Papadeas blessed the icon and then called in the heavy artillery, His Eminence Archbishop Iakaavos, head of the North and South American Greek Orthodox Church. According to Pagona, the archbishop held a special service and declared the weeping portrait a miracle. Shortly afterwards, the tears ceased.

The secular world also stepped in. After taking apart the picture and examining it, scientists found no evidence of tampering. "The moisture was not that of human tears; they couldn't figure how or why the lithograph was weeping," observes Reverend Nicholas Magoluias, who has been pastor at St. Paul's for over 30 years. *Life* magazine stopped by and took photographs, exposure equivalent to being on "Oprah," "Entertainment Tonight," and the "Tonight Show" all rolled into one.

Suddenly the Catsounis apartment was filled with thousands of visitors. "People were coming at all hours and we couldn't accommodate them all," says Pagona. "They would travel great distances to view the icon and we hated to disappoint them. . . . So we decided to donate it to St. Paul's so everyone could enjoy it."

Then on May 23, the day the lithograph was transported, "three beautiful white doves followed the procession from my house to the church," she continues. "When we reached St. Paul's, we waited outside to see what the doves would do. They circled around the church and disappeared into the sky." Perhaps they were carrier pigeons to heaven.

Pagona has never regretted her decision about donating the lithograph to the church. "I go there and see people lighting candles and praying. Every time they go near the icon, they tell me they feel good."

It seems to have charmed her own life—she and her husband own a home in Oceanside, New York and have three children and two grandchildren. Even a serious auto accident in 1992 turned out okay. "It was raining very hard and my husband lost control of his car and ran into a pole. I couldn't walk for four months and almost lost an eye. I'm sure the Virgin Mary was watching over me, because now I'm fine."

Although the icon stopped weeping decades ago, its effects continue to reverberate. "This occurred before my kids were born, so they grew up with it. And we sometimes wonder why this happened in our house. But I figure God and the Virgin Mary must have their reasons."

What to Expect

Built in the late '50s, St. Paul's consists of a basilica with a dome in the shape of a cross. It is decorated with 13th century Byzantine mosaics and has cushioned pews. All visitors are welcome.

The icon is under glass in a place of honor to the left of the altar. There's a sign leading to it, so you can't miss it. It may be joined shortly by a relative, so to speak. A few weeks after the Catsounis icon wept, the late Antonia Koulis, an aunt of Pagona's, reported a crying portrait of her own (she also claimed to have a third portrait, which is in the possession of her daughter). However, the Koulis icon has remained with the archbishop for several years. "We really don't know where we're going to put it when it finally does arrive," admits Father Magoluias.

The Catsounis lithograph consists of a 6-inch-by-8-inch tinted Byzantine portrait of Mary. This Madonna has a gentle expression with two painted-on teardrops near her eyes. "Sometimes when people go near it, they say they see the eye move a bit," states Pagona.

Flowers, notes, and mementos usually surround the icon, but "traffic isn't what it was when we had all-night vigils and lines a quarter of a mile around the street," remarks Magoluias. Still, a steady core of the faithful "continue to venerate it and derive spiritual comfort from it."

What They Say

Reverend Nicholas Magoluias, Hempstead, New York: According to him, tearing icons are quite common in Greece and Istanbul and "they're usually a bad sign, often the precursor of tragedies to come." In 1960, when the Catsounis picture came to light, "things were pretty quiet. Then we had the assassinations of John F. Kennedy, Robert F. Kennedy, Martin Luther King, and the situation in Vietnam.

"Today's world is not a savory place," he continues. "So the sudden onset of Marian visions seems to be the natural course. They are a reaction to what's happening around us."

Mrs. Tally Angelone, Island Park, New York: After viewing the icon at the Catsounis home, Angelone told *Newsday,* "I will never forget it as long as I live. I looked once and came back a second time. . . and [the weeping] happened again."

Her neighbor, identified as Mrs. Charles Luisi, also saw the picture cry twice. "You hear about things like this," she remarked. But when you actually witness it, the sensation is tremendous."

How to Get There

Coming from New York City, take the Long Island Expressway and go east (about 20 miles) to 34S. Exit at Hyde Park Rd., then take a right to Stewart Ave. in Garden City. Turn left. Stay on Stewart Ave., which turns into Cathedral Ave., and go over the railroad tracks. The church is down about ¼ mile on the left-hand side and is usually open. St. Paul's Greek Orthodox Church, 110 Cathedral Ave., Hempstead, NY 11550, 516/483-5700.

✝ A Jewel in the Bronx

St. Lucy's Catholic Church
Williamsbridge (Bronx), New York

How It Happened

In 1939, Monsignor Pasquale Lombardo had a vision. Not the kind where he saw angels and heard voices, but one in which he viewed the church he founded, St. Lucy's, as a mini-Lourdes. Throughout the replica of the Scala Sancta, based on the holy steps in Rome, and nook-filled caves with statues and mosaics depicting the different saints, cool and clear water flows. Although local legend says it once came from a natural spring beneath the shrine, the water's origin has no mystique today: It is the same H_2O every New Yorker bathes in and imbibes.

Yet for nearly three generations, thousands of the faithful have come to St. Lucy's seeking healing, comfort, and deliverance. "I personally know of a woman who was cured of stomach cancer," recounts Nick Gravina, who sells candles for the shrine and acts as a general caretaker. "She drinks only our water and has done so for the past four or five years."

Some wash their cars in it, thinking it will make for safe motoring, while others take it home by the gallonful for family and loved ones. Clad in burlap shirts, the repentant approach the shrine on their knees, hoping for salvation and answered prayers. Groups or individuals sit on the wooden benches outside, watching, meditating, or reading.

This is one place in the Big Apple where you can linger as long as you want without fear of being harassed for loitering. "A fellow who was terminal came from California last year and prayed here 12 to 14 hours a day," comments Anthony DelGaudio, the parish business manager and a lifelong area resident. "I got a letter from his family—there seems to be a marked improvement in his condition."

On Sundays and holidays, when the church and shrine are most crowded, "people stand outside and compare notes about what has happened to them," he continues. Even those who don't speak the same dialect somehow manage to communicate. "They tell their stories through gestures and tone of voice." Of the initial church, which was built in 1927, and peaceful grotto, he observes with a half-grin, "When you're here, you ask yourself, 'Am I in the Bronx?'"

Pilgrims come from all over the country to partake of the healing water at St. Lucy's Catholic Church in the Bronx.
PHOTO BY SANDRA GURVIS.

The Roman Catholic Church seems to have turned the other cheek on this particular miracle factory. "[The healings] have been occurring since the '20s and there has been no movement to verify any of this." In fact, many prominent members of the clergy visit and speak at St. Lucy's.

The north side neighborhood has transformed from mostly Italians to Hispanic, Black, and Albanian families. Although some streets are desolate with boarded-up businesses, "everybody makes an effort to get along," observes DelGaudio. Church services are held in several languages and "we get people of all faiths—Buddhists, Jews, Protestants —as well as from all over the world. Someone will come and say, 'My father told me about this place. I have a problem and this is where he told me to get help.'"

However, not all is always heavenly at St. Lucy's. "We do have some vandalism," admits Gravina. "In the past, there has been evidence of black magic and desecration." Teenagers find the dark corners and crevices of the catacombs especially appealing, leaving litter from their visits. Several of the statues and mosaics are crumbling and in need of repair.

But according to shrine personnel, plans for renovation are under way and although attendance dropped off for several years, recent times have produced an upsurge in visitors. "We get between two and three thousand people on the weekends and even more during holidays," states DelGaudio. "The regular Sunday line for water extends 100 feet around the block."

DelGaudio doesn't necessarily think the water itself causes the miracles. "Faith can work wonders." And the shrine has nary a statue that moves or cries.

What to Expect

St. Lucy's started out as a storefront church but has spread out over a city block. The rectory is separate from the Scala Sancta and the caves. The main attraction, however, is the grotto: Along with featuring a white statue of the Virgin Mary, it is also the main source of holy water. People come and say their devotions, nestling flowers and notes in the rocks. When visitors leave canes or crutches behind, caretakers remove them. Although this may be the Lourdes of the Bronx, the stated purpose is for devotion.

The Scala Sancta and catacombs are also replete with statues. Candles are available and Gravina supplies stories of faith and hope along with directions to your favorite saint.

The neighborhood is fairly safe during the day (when the church is usually open), but it's not advisable to travel there alone at night. Unlike the water, it may be hazardous to your health.

What They Say

Anthony DelGaudio, Bronx: DelGaudio worked on Wall Street before coming to St. Lucy's, and his stock in skepticism has plummeted: "I can tell you dozens of stories of those who have experienced miracles. I no longer question these things. I truly believe they are occurring.

"A lot of these people are in desperate need; some have no hope medically. Even if they aren't cured they usually leave with a greater peace of mind."

Sylvia, New York City: A regular visitor at St. Lucy's, Sylvia would not give her last name. "Aileen had a sore on her foot, it never got better until I brought her here," she told *The Reuter Library Report*. "Then there was that girl, I forget her name, but she was real nervous until she came here and now she's better and has a job." As for herself, the water cured her stomach ailment, ". . . but you have to have faith."

Rosa, New York City: Rosa also refused to give her last name. "My husband doesn't want me anymore," she confided to *The New York Times*. "I want to get together with him again. I don't want to stay by myself. . . . He got a new girlfriend." She lost custody of her three children and her husband called the police on her, so she comes to the grotto for prayer. "I come and drink the water."

How to Get There

St. Lucy's is most easily reached by public transportation. From Manhattan, take a bus or subway to Allerton Ave. and go west for six blocks until you reach Bronxwood; turn right. The complex is located at the corner of Bronxwood and Mace. The grotto is open seven days a week, 9 a.m.–5 p.m. Scala Sancta is only open in good weather—seven days, from 11 a.m.–4 p.m. from May through October and during the other months only on weekends, 11 a.m.–4 p.m. Mailing address: 833 Mace Ave., Bronx, NY 10467, 718/882-0710.

✝ From Magic City to Miracleville

Shrine of St. Jude
Barberton, Ohio

How It Happened

Although the Shrine of St. Jude, a.k.a. the St. Jude Orthodox Church, in Barberton, Ohio, can only accommodate a handful of people, visitors have seen an icon weep, had rosaries turn from silver to gold, smelled roses, experienced miracle cures, and watched the sun spin and dance over the church. Who says good things don't come in small packages?

On March 10, 1992, Anthony "Tony" Fernwalt was cleaning the 24-seat church, a former barber shop nestled between railroad tracks and a factory. Little more than a decade old, the church was in the throes of renovation. Money was tight, so improvements were mostly done by volunteers.

In the chapel, Fernwalt allegedly came across a strange woman dressed in red, who told him Jesus Christ was her son. Fernwalt, who has a police record and a history of mental illness, offered to get the priest, Father Roman Bernard. By the time Father Roman arrived 20 minutes later, the visitor, who supposedly had a glowing aura and robes so stiff they wouldn't move, had (not surprisingly) disappeared.

Whether or not this encounter was real, the tears rolling down the canvas painting of the Virgin Mary were definitely verifiable and immediately noticed by the two men. Titled "Our Lady of the Holy Protection," the portrait hung to the left of the altar near several statues and other religious art. Completed in 1980 by Cleveland artist Elias Hasigan, the 2-foot-by-3-foot icon was mounted on inexpensive plywood and cost $800.

Father Roman and some parishioners examined the painting carefully, checking the wall behind it to make sure no trickery was involved. There seemed to be no physical cause for the tears, so they contacted the news media. Not only might this marvel give their struggling church a much-needed boost, but "we wanted to share it with others," adds Father Roman.

Regardless of their origin, the tears were visible to everyone, appearing about once a day for a period of several weeks. According to an account in the Akron *Beacon Journal*, ". . . from the side, two very narrow glistening streaks can be seen extending from the inner portion of each eye to the . . . painting's lower edge." The tears made tracks in the oil paint, ruining Our Lady's makeup.

"My first thought was, 'Why here?'" admits Father Roman, a bishop in the Orthodox Catholic Church of North and South America, which has about 4,000 followers in the United States. But "when Jesus was born, he was born in a stable," he told the Barberton *Herald*. "When God was deciding about this, he saw this little church. [So] . . . why not here?"

Word spread quickly. Thousands of people flooded the dead-end street, causing traffic jams and fender-benders. Father Roman's phone rang constantly with requests for newspaper and TV interviews. But the mood of the crowd was congenial and orderly, with people squeezing past each other in the Lilliputian church to get a glimpse of the icon. And Father Roman kept the church open night and day to accommodate visitors.

Accounts of other wonders began to trickle in. Some reported their rosaries changing from silver to gold. Others experienced an overwhelming smell of roses, a sensation lasting only a couple of minutes. One morning, a group of people in the parking lot stared at the sky, claiming to see the sun vibrate and pulsate over the church.

And a little over three months later, on June 28, a 14-inch-by-18-inch icon print of Our Lady of the Perpetual Help reportedly wept during an outdoor procession. Witnessed by nearly 50 people, it occurred on the fifth anniversary of the death of Father Roman's grandmother, who was the original owner.

Then there were so-called miracle cures, the most documented of which involved 85-year-old Irma Sutton. Sutton's gangrenous, ulcerated left leg was scheduled for amputation. But when her niece Barbara Phillips took her to view the painting, the leg inexplicably improved. Circulation returned and the pain stopped; today, Sutton remains symptom-free.

Sutton's physician, Dr. Carlos Saavedra, a vascular specialist trained at the Cleveland Clinic, was amazed. "From a religious standpoint, it could be a miracle," he acknowledged in the *Beacon Journal*. However, he preferred to call it an "unexplained improvement," noting the power of the mind in healing. Still, Sutton, who is Protestant, and Phillips remained convinced the icon did the trick.

However, skeptics cited causes for the tears that ranged from condensation to freak atmospheric conditions. "There's [sic] several different reasons that the icon could have weeped [sic]," Veronica Brown, who lived next door to the shrine, told the TV show "48 Hours." ". . . they might have a leaky . . . ceiling. . . ."

Added Chris Brown, "I believe you can see the stains underneath the soffit . . . where the water runs down the side instead of running to the gutter." Mistrustful of Father Roman and the church, the Browns have since moved.

Father Roman and Tony Fernwalt also parted ways. "I had asked Tony and his followers to comply with certain rules, and they didn't," explains the former, who at one time had legal custody of Fernwalt. Fernwalt and his group have set up "some sort of cult" near Steubenville, Ohio. "The sheriff got involved down there and compared it to a potential Jonestown."

Although the icon has stopped weeping, visitors still flow in regularly, coming alone or as part of religious tours. And declarations of various "miracles" continue with amazing regularity. "So much has happened—and still happens—that I can't keep track of it all," remarks Father Roman. "I believe the message from God is that people need to come back to church and rededicate their lives."

The teeny shrine has garnered enough donations to pave the parking lot and for capital improvements, such a new altar and carpeting. Father Roman wants to enlarge it a bit, but not so much as to detract from its snug ambiance.

At the turn of the century, Barberton was locally known as the Magic City because the match industry helped spark an economic renewal. Now the faithful have their own smorgasbord of miracles. That's especially good news for the followers of St. Jude, the patron saint of lost causes.

What to Expect

This church always welcomes visitors and is even listed with the Ohio Department of Tourism. But Father Roman wants people to call first, "in case we've stepped out for a few minutes." Large groups and out-of-towners should make advance arrangements, so he can be available to answer questions.

Although it's now glassed in, the icon still supposedly turns rosaries and religious medals colors; visitors simply touch the edge of the frame with the object. Others leave pictures of loved ones who are sick and/or troubled. "It all boils down to whether or not you have faith," observes one volunteer.

The fact that the painting might weep again adds suspense to the visit. "People are always asking, 'when?'" comments Father Roman. "Their guess is as good as mine. It could happen tomorrow, a hundred years from now, or not at all."

Services are still held at the chapel, presumably scheduled during times when trains don't rumble by. Those who come unprepared can purchase rosaries and crosses at the church. Postcards, pictures, and even paperweights of the icon are also available. They don't sell T-shirts, however.

What They Say

Ted Sherman, Portage Lakes, Ohio: A member of St. Francis Church in Akron, Ted Sherman has visited Medjugorje several times, according to the Barberton *Herald*. While outside, he took a videotape of the sun "dancing" above the church. "On film, [the sun] appeared to flash or pump like a heart beating," stated the article.

One of the first people to witness the weeping portrait, Sherman described the tears "to be wide, like your thumb. Since I've been to Yugoslavia, I've been close to God."

Eve Riblet, Barberton, Ohio: Shrine volunteer Eve Riblet attends weekend Mass at a Roman Catholic church. But she also goes to St. Jude's and enjoys day-to-day contact with what she describes as "the awesome. Just being there is very inspiring, and many visitors feel the same, although there are some who are matter-of-fact." Along with talking to tourists, Riblet tends the dozens of candles that are lit in the Virgin Mary's honor.

Even the priests who examined the icon were impressed: "They found no moisture anywhere, just on the eyes. I didn't come here until the Madonna started weeping," she continues. "And it was simply astonishing, like if you went outside and saw something totally unexpected. It makes you feel humble."

Linda Kobyluc, Akron, Ohio: "About two weeks ago, I was empty," Kobyluc confided to the *Beacon Journal*. "I had tried the New Age thing. Everything. Then, suddenly, I felt at peace. God came into my heart. My lights flashed on and off. I said that I would not ask God for some goofy miracle. Just something. Then I read about [the icon]."

How to Get There

Just south of Akron, Barberton can be reached from I-76. Take 619S to State St., turn left and then turn right on 5th St. The shrine is located at 594 Fifth Ave., 216/753-1155.

✝ Conspicuous Communion

Our Lady of Consolation
Carey, Ohio

How It Happened

To understand the origins of this alleged miracle worker, you need to go back to the second century, when St. Ignatius of Antioch bestowed the title Mary, the Consoler of the Afflicted, upon the Blessed Virgin. Then, in the 1600s, while the bubonic plague ravaged Luxembourg, a group of people got together to pray to Mary the Consoler, building and enshrining her image on the outskirts of their community. Legend has it that many of the faithful were cured; the area became a magnet for those seeking Mary's special favors.

Descendants of this group wanted to carry on the creed when they came to the United States. So a reliquary (a small portion of the original statue) and an icon from the Luxembourg basilica were brought to Frenchtown, Ohio, in 1875 to be ensconced in a Roman Catholic church built for Our Lady. In spite of a raging thunderstorm, the priest of record stated that the sun shone exclusively on the procession carrying the statue to its new home in nearby Carey. No one in the statue's presence got wet and a phenomenon was born.

Since then, a steady stream of recuperations and other divine interventions have supposedly occurred. Still, "we don't put people through the church's examination of a verified cure," explains Brother Joseph Candel, a Franciscan friar who lives on the grounds of the shrine. "We're not magical or New Age mystical."

One of about sixty minor basilicas in North America and located on several dozen acres, the shrine has grown to include a rectory/friary, retreat house, lodging for pilgrims, cafeteria, gift shop, Franciscan mission home, school, gardens, and park. And regardless of whether the statue really works, Our Lady of Consolation, U.S. is a testimony to the power of religious art.

Grateful visitors left these reminders of their former ailments at Our Lady of Consolation in Carey, Ohio. PHOTO BY SANDRA GURVIS.

Despite a rather modest brick exterior, the main basilica/shrine consists of a remarkable mélange of Byzantine and Romanesque designs. Murals, sculptures, and marble saturate the first floor, which is partially paved in individually crafted, glazed tiles.

The arched ceiling and dome above the main altar boast gold-etched, jewel-encrusted paintings that include depictions of Jesus, Mary, saints, and Conventual Franciscans who rose to pope. Exquisite marbles make up the high altar: Its panels contain gold mosaic inlays and tile and bronze inserts, with Venetian ornamental glass patterns on the canopy. All sculpture work is Italianate, down to the ornately carved choir stalls.

And we haven't even gotten to the statue—a genial, sandy-haired depiction of Mary and Baby Jesus located to the right of the altar. Surrounded by various marbles, mosaics, and vigil lights, Our Lady is made of oak, encased in Plexiglas and elevated so high even Shaquille O'Neal couldn't touch her toes. In 1991, the icon's jeweled ornaments and crown were stolen, and there had been attempts to take other things as well. Now, "we're hooked up to the county and everything is videotaped," states Brother Joe, as he likes to be called. "The police can be here in 15 seconds."

Our Lady's wardrobe is located in the basement or lower church. Made from bridal dresses, baptismal robes, jewels, and other luxury items donated by grateful supplicants, the selection of over 200 frocks rivals the Miss America evening gown competition. "The statue is clothed according to the liturgical season," explains Brother Joe of the glassed-in, two-tiered case holding the outfits. "The custom of dressing a statue goes back to the Middle Ages when people sacrificed precious fabrics as a form of offering."

Within sneezing distance of the wardrobe is a mind-boggling collection of spontaneously discarded braces, wheelchairs, and corrective shoes, the last of which are painful reminders of polio. Pleas for divine intervention are scrawled across bibs and diapers; crutches stacked against a wall resemble an orthopedic bicycle rack. A wicker body litter bears a laminated note dated February 22, 1916: "I walked home and to this day I can see perfectly and am enjoying full health. Thanks to almighty God and the Virgin Mary. P.J. Columbus, Lima [Ohio]."

Many are several decades old. "The signs of today's diseases aren't as visible," observes Brother Joe. "Someone may recover from a heart condition or an infertile woman may become pregnant, and we don't hear about it until much later. We have no way of tracking exactly how many people have been helped."

Not all the crutches overcome at Our Lady of Consolation in Carey, Ohio, are as visible as this grouping. PHOTO BY SANDRA GURVIS.

But "this is not just about miracle cures. People come here to pray for loved ones, a job, to renew their lapsed faith, anything." Empty and crumpled beer cans, pill containers, and cigarette packs attest to renunciation of vices as well.

The less palatial chapels in the lower church are dedicated to various saints, including St. Therese, the Patron Saint of Daily Living. The Chapel of the Holy Relics includes artifacts from over 500 saints and according to shrine literature, an altar of St. Ann instructing the child Mary and a depiction of Jesus in the tomb are perennial favorites.

PHOTO BY SANDRA GURVIS.

Believers can find total acceptance and faith at Our Lady of Consolation. "I can't explain why a 78-year-old man with terminal cancer is cured while a baby with the same condition dies," reflects Brother Joe, who is often mistaken for a priest and has to locate one to hear spur-of-the-moment confessions. Regardless of the outcome of their prayers, "if people can leave their worries here and find peace of mind, then the visit has done them good."

What to Expect

The shrine gears up for its busy season in May through September. In August, during the anniversary of the procession of the statue and the Feast of the Assumption of Mary, visitors arrive in droves. So along with beefed-up service schedules, a candlelight procession on August 14 goes to Shrine Park where pilgrims celebrate a special Mass.

Unless you plan ahead, you may find yourself sleeping on park benches or in the church or driving several miles to Findlay to find a hotel. The town of Carey offers very little, although Shrine Park is a great place for a picnic on a nice day. And for about $5 you get a choice of an entree, salad, vegetable, and potato at the Shrine Cafeteria, which provides lunch during the summer months. It's closed Mondays and only open during the winter by special arrangement.

Still, there's plenty of parking and holy water from a large concrete tank outside the shrine. People bathe in it and take it home by the gallonful for their afflicted ones. "They can use as much as they want, because a little drop of holy water purifies the entire tank," says Brother Joe.

Lest you forget to bring a container, the gift shop sells bottles for a minimal fee. Like decals, pencils, iron-on transfers, and other memorabilia, they are embossed with a picture of the statue. Touted by the shrine as the largest religious article store in Ohio, the shop also has an astounding selection of rosaries, books, kitchen items, and other things, including holy trading cards.

The church itself is open 24 hours a day, seven days a week; you have your choice of the sprawling upper basilica (with the statue) or the cozier individual chapels downstairs in which to say private devotions. Every Sunday at 2:30 an afternoon Mass is held; from May through October, Our Lady is carried aloft in an outdoor rosary procession (during the winter, there is an indoor litany). Special masses can be organized during the week at 2:30 p.m. for groups. Regular Masses are also held daily.

Visitors during the colder months need to arrange for food and lodging. "We can accommodate groups or individuals who contact us in advance," says Brother Joe.

Those can't make the trip can have a candle lit in their honor, where it will join the hundreds of votive lights and other offerings around the shrine altar. Requests can be sent through the mail to the shrine (see below for address).

What They Say

Paul and Kay Chester, Findlay, Ohio: The Chesters were impressed by their first visit. "We read about the shrine in the paper, so we thought we'd bring our kids, who are approaching confirmation age," says Paul, a United Methodist. "We wanted to expose them to other religions."

Still, "I prayed for my brother-in-law, who was in a serious auto accident, and my dad, who died recently," remarks Kay. "I felt better afterwards, although I'm not sure what actual good it will do." The children, who requested anonymity, found the Basilica spooky.

Deb Hussey, Carey, Ohio: As the manager of the Shrine gift store, Hussey has encountered all types of pilgrims, from the devout to the cynical to those who had lapsed for 50 years. "People who linger are often struggling with themselves. They're reluctant to cross the street" to the shrine and face whatever problem they've been wrestling with. Hussey makes a point of being available to talk. "Sometimes they just need someone to listen." And then there are those who come strictly to shop.

She feels the approach of the millennium has a lot to do with the recent increase in Marian activity. "When the country is down, the number of visitors is up." Yet even during fallow times, "I've never had anyone come here and say they were disappointed with or upset by the shrine.

"After a while, you form relationships. People come back to tell you how things came out or to express their gratitude. Or they call and ask you to light a candle for a loved one."

How to Get There

Take the Ohio Turnpike (I-80/90) to 75N (Toledo), then 15E to Carey. Follow the signs; you can't miss it. Mailing address: Our Lady of Consolation, 315 Clay St., Carey, OH 43316, 419/396-7107 or 396-3355.

✝ Rust Stains on Tank or Sacred Image?

Archer Daniels Midland Company
Fostoria, Ohio

How It Happened

One summer night in 1986, Rita Rachen, who owned a drapery business in Fostoria, Ohio, was driving back from a client's. As she motored down Route 12 towards her home in the quaint Ohio city of about 17,500, she glanced at a dimly lit soybean oil storage tank

. . . and saw a large likeness of Jesus Christ. "It seemed like he was walking on water," she recalls.

At the time, she was so shocked she nearly ran her new Ford Taurus off the road. "But I didn't go back out that night to look at it," she says. She did visit the next evening, however. "The more I studied it, the more it came out. I could see a small child next to Jesus." She kept the discovery to herself for the next few days, slipping out after dark when the view became prominent.

Finally, her desire to share the experience overcame her fear of ridicule and possible internment in the local mental health facility. One Sunday night she took Dorothy Droll, her best friend of 35 years. Without prompting, Dorothy immediately recognized the image, as it came to be known. And then Rita told another friend and word began to spread through Fostoria faster than a soybean oil fire.

Although it initially dismissed the story as nonsense, the local paper, the *Review Times,* took things more seriously after some of its own employees weighed in with their observations. On August 19, it ran the headline "Image of Christ Reported West of Town." The story was picked up by the media and the stampede was on. Photographers, amateur and professional, attempted to take clear photos; because of the strange lighting and shadows and the fact that it appeared to wax and wane at odd hours of the night, few succeeded.

Soon it took nearly two hours to drive from the local Putt 'N' Pond to the tank, which was less than two miles away. The clearest view was from the Hi-Lo gas station looking at the tank itself, going towards Fostoria.

By September, thousands of people had flocked from Ohio and elsewhere, tying up roads and frustrating the truck drivers who frequently fly along that less-patrolled route. According to an account in *Time* magazine, one fellow behind an 18-wheeler demanded to know what the holdup was and was given the answer "Jesus."

"That's what I say," he replied. "What's causing it?"

"Jesus Christ."

"Are you trying to be funny, or what?" he retorted before pulling away.

But the faithful weren't the only ones who rejoiced. One man invested $1,800 in "I Saw the Image" T-shirts and hoped to realize a profit of $2,000, while another sold 1,000 coffee cups with the same slogan. Still another peddled photographs—some 700 sets of two shots of the image as well as his other pictures—while an ice cream vendor arrived from Sandusky to cash in on the crowds.

Officials at the Archer Daniels Midland Co., which had purchased the tank, and the Toledo diocese were less impressed. Installed in early July, the tank had rust and paint stains from being primed and was surrounded by sodium vapor security lights. The combination of these things accounted for the image, according to the company, which nevertheless postponed a repainting project after the public organized a "Save the Tank" movement. The diocese refused to investigate the phenomenon as a legitimate miracle, although spokesman James Richards conceded that it might be a natural occurrence.

Rita Rachen states some people interpreted the image as other than Jesus. "Jews thought it looked like Moses and teenagers [believed] it was their favorite rock star. But many claimed it changed their lives, that they'd start going to church more."

Yet she too feels that the image is not a miracle, "but rather a picture, not the Lord himself up there in that soybean oil tank." Although her then three-year-old grandson expressed concern that Jesus and his young companion might smother inside.

What to Expect

In late September 1986, a Findley firefighter with what locals describe as a fondness for alcohol threw paint-filled balloons on the image, partially obscuring it. He was arrested and charged with criminal damaging, a second-degree misdemeanor. "Basically, he was sick of the traffic and the disruption," stated a neighbor, who asked that his name not be used. The Archer Daniels Midland Co. went ahead with their plan to repaint the tank.

Today the 40-foot-tall-by-95-feet-wide tank still stands at the westernmost point on the property and is indistinguishable from its neighbors. But in October 1994, some believers again claimed to see a face there. Yet the excitement generated by the mini-rejuvenation was but a drop in the tank compared to the original.

What They Say

Dorothy Best, Toledo, Ohio: "Oh my God, they're beautiful," Best commented to *The Columbus Dispatch* about the depictions on the tank. "I see Christ's head and maybe a beard. And then there's a child. I can't see the body, only a head or maybe it's Christ's heart. It's where his heart would be.

"I think sometimes the Lord gives us a little glimpse, just to keep our faith alive."

Paul Feasal, Fostoria, Ohio: "I was a laborer at the Autolite plant and wanted to make a career change. When my father first informed me he saw something on that soybean oil tank, I was skeptical. But after he took me out there, I decided to get a photo, despite the fact that I hadn't done much with a camera.

"I was determined to do this right and finally got a fairly decent color picture, even though we had to go all the way to Columbus to get it developed. But [the picture] was eventually picked up by *Time* magazine and other publications and the experience gave me the idea to start my own photo developing lab. The guys at work thought I'd made a pile from that picture, but the truth was, my wife Linda and I got a bank loan. After eight years, our business, Image Photo, is still going strong.

"To believe in it required a leap of faith; it gave me the courage to start a new life."

Donna and Anthony Wade, Fostoria, Ohio: Anthony Wade was a pastor at the Overcomers Teaching Center Church, which purchased a building next to the Archer Daniels Midland plant. "One of the things we have been praying for is that we want Jesus to become famous to the people of Fostoria and then this image appeared," his wife Donna told the *Dispatch.* "My husband really felt that the Lord had spoken to him about this particular location and building—and this happened.

"We're just so excited about this opportunity to bring people to the Lord . . . Sometimes people don't stop and think because their [lives are] so busy. But then something like this happens [and] some people stop and think, 'There is a God.'"

How to Get There

Fostoria is located at the intersection of Routes 18, 12, 199, and 23 and is approximately 30 miles south of Toledo. The tank is on the west edge of town off Route 12, but no visit would be complete without a stop into town to get an earful of lore. And the company doesn't usually turn on the spotlights, so you need either really good night vision or lots of faith to make anything out.

✝ A "Contagious" Icon

St. Nicholas Greek Orthodox Church
Lorain, Ohio

How It Happened

In July 1988, 14-year-old Sam Boumis was at a Greek Orthodox Church camp in Mercer, Pennsylvania. He and dozens of children from Ohio, West Virginia, and Pennsylvania were winding up a week-long retreat. Sam decided to stop by the camp's gift shop and purchase a 9-foot-by-11-foot wooden laminated icon for his parents for $14. The portrait of Mary holding Baby Jesus had been blessed by the camp chaplain and anointed with a mixture of holy water and tears from an icon at St. Nicholas Albanian Orthodox Church in Chicago (see page 77).

Sam brought his icon back to the cabin, placing it on his top bunk. He reached for a pair of socks, glanced down and saw tears streaking down Mary's red cloak. "I freaked out," he told the Associated Press. "I got scared. The tears soaked part of the sheets." He feared people might think he was crazy. "Why me? There were fifty kids at that camp. Why me?"

Even stranger, eighteen other icons at Camp Nazareth were discovered to be weeping as well. When Bishop Maximos, head of the Pittsburgh diocese of the Greek Orthodox Church, went to investigate, he learned that some had been produced at monasteries while others came from private homes. All were similar versions of a Greek Orthodox–style tableau of Jesus and Mary.

Along with the plywood icons, "some were paper prints and some were paperback book covers [from] books about the Chicago phenomenon," Father Michael Gulgas told the Associated Press. Pastor of St. Nicholas Greek Orthodox Church in Lorain, Ohio where the Boumis family worshipped, he hurried to the camp as soon as he heard about the occurrence.

Rather than running straight down as might be expected on a flat surface, the tears followed the contours of Mary's face, as if it were three-dimensional. When Gulgas wiped one of the icons with a cotton ball, he claimed the oily substance had the distinct fragrance of myrrh, which is commonly used in religious services. "There was no indication that anyone had messed with the icons," he adds.

"That's a sign given to these children," Maximos remarked to the Associated Press. "Not everyone can see. . . . [And] for them, the supernatural does not exist and they will dismiss it. . . . [But] that's always the case for any miracle. It only has meaning to the eyes of the faithful."

The notoriety of the eighteen other icons faded with their tears; most stopped crying within 24 hours. But Sam Boumis's was brought back to St. Nicholas in Lorain. It continued to weep and for a few weeks drew onlookers from around the U.S. and Canada.

It was given a place of honor on the lectern at the front of the altar. Candles, roses, and carnations surrounded it; taped hymns played in the background. People of all ages, religions, and walks of life filed by, hoping to glimpse a tear or two, or at least streaks made by the moisture. One woman "jumped up and down like a game show contestant" according to an Associated Press account, pro- claiming, "I saw the tears! I saw the tears! It's a miracle!"

Most, however, were orderly and subdued, claiming to feel a great sense of peace and gratitude at witnessing a mystery firsthand. Gulgas turned down all offers to dismantle and examine the icon for the source of the tears. "It would serve no purpose," he told the Associated Press. "The faithful don't need authentication to believe it and those who don't want to believe don't have to." The bishop had declared all nineteen icons to be a miraculous occurrence and that was good enough for him.

By the summer's end, the icon had stopped weeping, the only physical reminder being faint stains on Mary's face. In the ensuing years, Sam Boumis graduated high school and is now in college; the icon remains in his possession.

But he still brings it to St. Nicholas for special occasions, such as the beginning of Lent and in August when the church honors the Repose (death) of Mary. "I don't know why a miracle happened at this place and time and I really don't know what it means," observes Gulgas. "But it shows that God is still alive. And it helped build our spirits and faith, as well as drawing our attention back to God." Anyone up for a reunion of the Camp Nazareth icons?

What to Expect

Located in downtown Lorain, a steel industry town of about 80,000, St. Nicholas is a medium-sized Greek Orthodox church. When the icon is present, it is placed in the front of the altar. Worshippers can then file past and venerate it.

A print copied from a painting, the icon depicts a Semitic-look- ing Mary holding infant Jesus in the crook of her arm, reaching out towards him with her other hand. It's not much larger than a piece of paper and is housed in an ornate frame in the shape of a Byzantine temple.

What They Say

Helen Sack, Bay Village, Ohio: Helen Sack stopped by St. Nicholas to pay her respects and say thanks. "[Mary] already helped me," she told the Associated Press. Upon discovering a lump in her breast, "I couldn't stop crying. I was hysterical . . . and didn't know what to do—so I called the convent." A sister there told her to repeat a prayer to the Virgin Mary over and over until ". . . suddenly I realized I was smiling. I wasn't crying anymore. And the growth turned out to be a cyst . . . So I wouldn't have missed [the icon] for anything."

Elsa Alicea and Enrique Rusa, Lorain, Ohio: Alicea, who is wheelchair-bound, was taken by Rusa to see the icon. "[Mary's] crying for the pain being caused by other people," she told the Lorain *Morning Journal.* "I didn't expect a miracle . . . to stand up and walk. I am a miracle. I survived 36 hours of surgery" that left her a hemiplegic. "I expected inner peace. And I found it."

Added Rusa: "God wants to tell us to prepare . . . it's a warning that something may happen soon, good or bad."

Sam Boumis, Cincinnati, Ohio: "I feel like I've been lucky," Boumis, a college student majoring in political science and pre-law, remarks. After he gets his degree, "I plan on either working for or doing something with the church and the poor."

Looking back on his experience, "I think the reason I might have been chosen was because when you're young, your soul is pure. . . . And my mother is very religious. I think she has some big connection upstairs," he half-jokes.

How to Get There

From Cleveland, take I-80W to Exit 8. Follow the signs to Toledo/Sandusky, then take Rt. 2 heading west. Exit at Rt. 58 and make a right. Go down four stoplights and turn right on Tower Blvd. Call or write to find out when the icon's next appearance will be. St. Nicholas Greek Orthodox Church, 2000 Tower Blvd., Lorain, OH 44053, 216/960-2992.

Pennsylvania —

✝ Did He Blink?

Holy Trinity Church
Ambridge, Pennsylvania

How It Happened

On Good Friday 1989, Thomas Cvitkovic, his two brothers, and Joseph Rozman were acting as altar servers at the Holy Trinity Catholic Church. "As he received communion, my brother Jim looked up at the crucifix and noticed the eyes were closed," recalls Tom, now in his thirties. "He pointed it out to me, and I saw it, too."

Previously the life-sized statue had been placed in a small, candlelit side room in the church. Refurbished a few months prior by local artist Dominic Leo, it was then hung several feet above the altar in January. And the eyelids had been one-third *open*. Now all comers to the church perceived them to be tightly shut. When Leo was called in to explain, he was spooked also, voicing shock at the alteration in expression.

Other changes were observed as well. Tom's uncle and the pastor at the time, the Reverend Vincent Cvitkovic, commented that the statue transformed from vivid hues on that fateful Friday to dull ones afterward, and that it seemed to develop "a sheen, as if it was perspiring, and also appeared bloody," reports Tom. In the ensuing weeks, "sometimes the eyes would be open and at other times they would shut."

When the "Unsolved Mysteries" TV program came to film a re-enactment, "one crew member actually saw the eyes open and close. Although the camera was running, no movement showed on film, even though it had been trained on the crucifix's face the whole time." Apparently God hadn't signed a release form.

Soon the small church became the focal point of a controversy. On one side were the curious, the faithful, and the media, who flocked to the small Ohio River town just 15 miles northwest of

Pittsburgh. Father Vincent kept the doors unlocked fifteen hours a day to accommodate the thousands of visitors. Holy Trinity was also made more accessible to the handicapped. He sent videotapes of the statue with its eyes open and shut to the diocese of Pittsburgh.

"If this is of God, it's bigger than me, the diocese, and Rome," Father Vincent told *USA Today.* He was convinced of the statue's veracity. "I'm not that smart to even think of a hoax."

On the other side was a committee appointed by the diocese. Consisting of theologians who interviewed the altar servers, Father Vincent, and artist Leo, it reviewed pictures taken by church members as well as those from an independent agency. By the first week of July, the verdict was in: In a formal statement, the committee could find "no convincing evidence" that the statue had closed its eyes.

"The eyes of the figure of Jesus, as seen in the photograph taken [on] March 24 [Good Friday] do not differ in appearance from the eyes in the photograph . . . taken on January 28, when the crucifix was raised to its position over the altar," the statement continued. Any discrepancy was chalked up to "a variety of visual perceptions and from the unique features of the crucifix."

In addition, there had been reports of locutions and revelations among the Holy Trinity youth organization. "Since we are a Croatian church, we had been aware of Medjugorje for many years, and had an active prayer group," explains Tom Cvitkovic. "I mean, guys were crying when they saw the statue."

Yet the commission found no indication of private revelations relating to the events. Rather the locutions "appear to arise from a normal Christian life of prayer and fidelity to the church." Wink, wink.

Although the commission praised the devoutness and sincerity of all parties involved, within a few months of the investigation, "the diocese asked my uncle to resign as pastor," states Tom. "He was attracting big crowds, many of who believed in the statue and Medjugorje."

Tom maintains that his uncle was caught in a theological crossfire. "The diocese consolidated five churches—most of which were ethnic—and basically kicked out the Franciscans, replacing them with their own priests. The bishop tried to quash everything."

Yet the statue remains in its place at the altar and the prayer group stays active. Tom still claims the eyes open and close at various intervals. "This is an ongoing phenomenon. Our beliefs are stronger than ever." No one's pulling the wool over *their* eyes.

What to Expect

A simple white concrete church, Holy Trinity holds about 250 people. The interior, however, is rather statue-intensive, with many depictions of Jesus and Mary. Restored with acrylic paint, the crucifix in question is located in front of a stained glass window. Whether or not the play of light has anything to do with its seeming change of expression is anybody's guess.

Visitors are welcome at Holy Trinity, although it may only be open at certain times. Contact the Diocese of Pittsburgh (see below) for information on hours of operation.

What They Say

Thomas Cvitkovic, Ambridge, Pennsylvania: "God gave us a sign to change our lives," Cvitkovic asserts. The statue "is just one of many signs throughout the world, telling people to convert before the chastisement comes." In that respect, the statue was a success: "According to the priests, there were many conversions, people coming back to the church after 20 to 30 years. And others said they were helped spiritually, physically, and emotionally. Those are the real miracles."

Reverend Richard Delillo and Dr. William Dinges, Washington, D.C.: A pastoral counselor at Catholic University, Delillo expressed skepticism about the statue. "People have a basic need for meaning and happiness in their lives," he told *USA Today,* explaining that many find the lure of sensational claims irresistible. "When something like this comes along, it's the way of easy surrender."

"The human capacity for self-deception is incredible," added Dinges, who teaches religion at the University. His own view was "cautious, guarded."

How to Get There

From Pittsburgh, take 65N until the Ambridge exit. Get off at 4th St., turn right, and go up one stoplight; the church sits off on the left. Address: Holy Trinity Church, 415 Melrose Ave., Ambridge, PA 15003, 412/266-4049. For information on hours of operation, contact the Diocese of Pittsburgh, 111 Boulevard of the Allies, Pittsburgh, PA 15222, 412/456-3000.

✚ Parochial Vision during the Eisenhower Years

Fairmont Park
Philadelphia, Pennsylvania

How It Happened

On a warm September night in 1953, five young girls watched a group of boys play football at the edge of Fairmont Park. Students at St. Gregory's Parochial School, the girls suddenly lost interest in the game when they saw an outline of a woman in a nearby privet hedge. "It was all lit up," Roseanne Pinto, then 14, told the *Philadelphia Daily News*. The other girls glimpsed something too, then fled in fear. Nevertheless, they came back the next evening and brought two friends, along with several rosaries.

Again, they experienced a vision. "As we knelt, the Blessed Mother came right at us," Pinto continued. "She was beautiful. She had on a white gown and a blue veil. She was life-sized. She had her hand out as if she was trying to give us something. . . . We couldn't move. . . . We smelled roses." According to Pinto's account, the bush was enveloped by a haze of light smoke. Then the likeness disappeared as quickly as it had arrived.

"The moon had not yet come out," Pinto told the *Sunday Bulletin*. "The bush had not yet begun to shed," eliminating the possibility of a silhouette of leaves on the tree. And fragrant blooms were nonexistent in Fairmont Park that time of year.

Priests and nuns comforted the frightened girls, but word about the visitations began to spread. Soon thousands showed up at Fairmont Park, kneeling and praying, leaving flowers, rosaries, candles, and money on the humble shrub. Its branches also became laden with photographs, bracelets, handkerchiefs, handbags, a bath towel, even a caged canary, which was turned over to the local animal shelter. Miniature shrines were built atop a nearby table and chairs. People gathered around nightly, and abandoned orthopedic shoes and crutches lent credence to reports of healings. An enterprising photographer sold snapshots of a nearby tree where a white shadow resembling a robed figure seemed elevated amidst the greenery. Although newspaper accounts explained it as a trick of light and shadow, it only added to the mystique.

The uproar confounded park officials. They neither knew what to do with the thousands of dollars which had begun to accrue nor how to handle the faithful, who, although they were orderly, had begun to trample the grounds. So the park erected a fence around the overgrown hedge and left the issue of the money to be decided by a city judge.

But things only got more intense. On October 25th, it was rumored, another vision would occur. Three miracles would be performed on that day and one of the girls would ascend into heaven. Nearly 50,000 people showed up, and a line stretched 500 feet across the field. The barricades leading to and protecting the tree threatened to collapse under the weight of the crowd. Local merchants ran out of food and had to shut down temporarily. Ephren J. Stevens, known as "King of the Gypsies," collapsed and died while he and the members of his tribe camped under trees or in their cars. Gypsy clans had come from as far away as Ohio and Florida to view the event.

Or non-event, as it turned out. The only concrete happening was that the multitude got rained on, forcing many to scatter for cover. Although a few people claimed to see a figure when the moon briefly appeared, most went away disappointed. According to *Philadelphia Magazine,* some blamed it on "too many disbelievers," while others attributed any likeness to "just the way the branches looked against the sky."

Although the devout continued to pay their respects, their numbers gradually dwindled. And the Catholic church truly hedged the issue and never made any official statement. By the following spring, the overburdened branches and base of the plant threatened to collapse under the weight of so many objects. A self-appointed committee claimed the bush would die without proper care, and many of the objects were removed. By then, the city had decided to use its $6,500 windfall to help build a stone and wood shelter near the site.

But the urban legend of the "vision bush" lives on. Follow-up articles 10, 15, and even 20 years later traced the lives of the girls, most of whom married and moved away from the area. Catherine Perchick, a housekeeper at nearby Holy Spirit Roman Catholic Church, claimed to pay her devotions there every day for nearly two decades. "I'd like to see thousands praying the rosary in the park the way they did [back then]," she said in a 1973 *Philadelphia Daily News* article. "Not so many people pray the rosary any more. Some say it's old-fashioned. Some say the bush isn't holy. But I know."

What to Expect

Today the bush still stands, as does the shelter, although the latter is in disrepair and covered with graffiti. Yet many Philadelphians remember the story behind it and a few may even still have post-cards of the supposed apparition that materialized in a large tree near the bush.

Although this hedge looks no different from dozens of others in Fairmont Park, you just might find a cross or two hanging from it. And if you're really lucky, you'll encounter one of the five former parochial school girls who stop by now and then for an occasional nostalgic visit.

What They Say

The former Rose Pinto of Philadelphia: By the late '50s, Pinto had left Philadelphia to get away from the attention, moving to an unspecified area of the country. Of her girlhood experience, she remarked in the *Sunday Bulletin:* "Looking back . . . I suppose the church and the religious just assumed we were a group of girls at an impressionable age using our . . . imaginations to attract attention to ourselves. This was not the case." Although some labeled the events in the park miracles, "we never said that. We said we saw two visions of the Blessed Virgin."

Margaret Kelville, Florida: Married twice and a mother of five, Kelville, another of the original group, moved to Florida. "I can assure you . . . it was the Blessed Mother I saw," she told the *Philadelphia Daily News.* "It's had a tremendous effect on my life.

"The Virgin Mary has helped me get through a lot of hard times. I've had trouble and I've prayed to the Virgin and, most of the time, she's answered my prayers. . . . [Mary] is my friend." But "I still think about what I saw and I always wonder why—why me?"

Roberta Held, Philadelphia: "I knew all the girls," she remarked to the *Daily News.* "Roseanne Pinto was one of my best friends. . . . Sure, sure I believed about the vision. My mother used to take my crippled brother to the bush . . . no, it didn't do him any good, but I still believed.

"You'll believe anything when you're a kid."

How to Get There

From I-76, take the City Line Ave. exit, then follow the signs to Belmont Ave. Turn left on Belmont and go to N. Concourse Dr. and turn right. The bush and shelter are near 51st and Parkside, across the street from Mann Music Center, an outdoor facility. For more information, contact the Philadelphia Park Commission, Memorial Hall, P.O. Box 21601, Philadelphia, PA 19131-0901, 215/685-0000.

✝ Seeping Beauty

Office of John Demetrius
Pittsburgh, Pennsylvania

How It Happened

Although this statue was neither of Jesus nor Mary, her tears seemed genuine nonetheless. On August 6, 1945, the day a nuclear bomb was dropped on the Japanese city of Hiroshima, the late Allen Demetrius saw his bronze bust of a Japanese maiden cry. "I remember that I had read the headlines, . . ." he told the *Pittsburgh Press*. "That night I looked at the statue [and] the teardrops ran down the cheeks. I was astonished. I can't explain how it happened." The bombing, it has been said, was so inhumane that even the stones of Hiroshima wept.

Almost 25 years later, in July 1969, Demetrius's daughter Annabelle Sollon was dusting the statue in her home. Demetrius, a clock and antique dealer, had given it to her as a gift. Overnight, it seems, the bronze features were suddenly marred by green streaks around the eyes. "I don't know how they got there—I never polished the bust—my Dad wouldn't let me," she said in the *Press*. She called her father and he immediately rushed over.

"I realized what . . . they were," he remarked. "The stains were in the exact spot the tears were. So it had to be the oxidation occurring where the tears had streamed down the statue's cheeks."

Thus continues the long, strange saga of what has come to be known as the Weeping Bronze of Hiroshima. Although the Demetrius family has been told the statue should be considered a sort of Oriental Virgin Mary, the current owner, Allen's son John, disagrees. "For one thing, the inspiration for the statue was a Japanese princess. Her tears are for all of humankind."

According to his father's research, this die was cast in 1877 at the Raingo Foundry in France by one Emile Truffant. "We think the Japanese royal family was visiting, ordered a sculpture of the princess, and for some reason never picked it up," continues John. Allen believed that Emperor Hirohito, the leader of Japan during the Second World War, was a direct descendant of the young woman.

"My father acquired the statue in the '40s," he goes on. "Pittsburgh had become a mecca for millionaires, so there was a great call for antiques." The maiden came from the estate of a salt manufacturer's daughter, and, until the time it distinguished itself by producing moisture, was one of many art objects in the Demetrius

When his statue of a Japanese maiden wept on the day the atomic bomb was dropped on Hiroshima, the late Allen Demetrius of Pittsburgh devoted his life to eradicating nuclear destruction. The tears permanently stained the statue. PHOTO COURTESY OF JOHN DEMETRIUS.

home. "My father wasn't a religious man; we were brought up Protestant."

Still, the seeping beauty inspired the elder Demetrius to write a poem about it ("In nineteen forty-five from an awesome glare/eyeballs melted as birds cindered in the air/ and as cooked human flesh sizzled off the bone/ashes that were people into the sky were blown. . . .") as well as dedicate much of the rest of his life to promoting knowledge about the statue. He asserted that the maiden could change her expression from smiling to indifferent to sad and that she even spooked him once by looking him straight in the eye. After that, he kept a covering over it, as does his son today.

In 1969, when the green streaks were discovered, there was a flurry of publicity, but the real coincidence occurred a decade later, during the Three Mile Island incident. A reporter who stopped by to purchase a grandfather clock ended up writing about the statue a week before the accident at the nuclear power plant, once again thrusting the bronze maiden into the limelight. "Dad claimed she was trying to intervene and warn us again about atomic destruction," says John.

Over the past five decades, the maiden has been featured in newspapers and magazines and on television around the world. Since the family was beleaguered by strangers showing up at their door at all hours, the elder Demetrius periodically put it on display in Pittsburgh shops, banks, and even a department store where Nikita Khrushchev was reportedly invited to see it.

"Dad wanted it to end up at the United Nations or at a memorabilia museum in Hiroshima," observes John.

Allen Demetrius passed away in 1994 at the age of 87. "Dad believed the statue would take care of itself, that it would generate its own publicity." The maiden also depicted more than just one race or people. "She has the kind of angelic beauty anyone can appreciate. What better way to express a concern for humanity than through a work of art?"

What to Expect

Like his father, John Demetrius deals in clocks and antiques. The life-sized statue remains cloaked by a black silk scarf at his shop in Pittsburgh. Basically a detailed rendering from the waist up of a young woman in a kimono and traditional headdress, it is mounted on a pedestal.

Although the bronze seems unmarred by time, the streakage around the eyes is very evident, making her appear as if she's permanently crying. And based on various photos, the statue does seem to change expression, although the word "depressed" comes frequently to mind in describing her.

Demetrius will allow visitors, but only if they contact him first. Like his dad, he hopes the maiden will become a part of a permanent exhibition. "Right now we're trying to arrange something with the museum in Hiroshima."

What They Say

The late Allen Demetrius, Pittsburgh, Pennsylvania: Demetrius welcomed all visitors, even the gentleman who arrived at 2 a.m. who claimed to have never seen anything supernatural. Still, he never wandered far from his platform: "The whole world is someday going to be destroyed by the atomic bomb," he told the *Pittsburgh Press*. "We'll end up just like Mars, Jupiter, and the lifeless planets in our solar system."

John Demetrius, Pittsburgh, Pennsylvania: According to John, there is no physical explanation for the maiden's tears. "The statue is solid bronze, so there's no place to put in holes or place wax over it. Besides, how can you coax matter from an inanimate object?

"People have offered to buy it, but it's not for sale. It needs to be in a place where it can remind us that when you deal in nuclear devastation, you're imperiling the whole world."

How to Get There

For more information, contact John Demetrius, 1420 W. Liberty Ave., Pittsburgh, PA 15226, 412/341-9768.

✝ Stampede at the Ayob Home

St. Mark's Coptic Church
Bellaire, Texas

How It Happened

Although Tharwat and Nahed Ayob had all the material things—excellent jobs as a veterinarian and co-owner of a restaurant respectively, and a nice home in a suburb of Houston—in 1989 their son Isaac was stricken with leukemia. By November 1991, Isaac, then 12, was given less than three months to live. On Sunday, November 10, Nahed went to their church, St. Mark's Coptic Orthodox, and wrote a note to God saying He was their only hope for a cure. She asked the priest, Father Isaac Soliman, to place it in the altar under the chalice.

An answer wasn't long in coming. The next day, the boy felt very ill and lay down on his parents' bed. He prayed to a portrait of Jesus hanging on the wall. Then suddenly, according to a church pamphlet, Isaac looked up and "saw the eyes in the picture moving and the figure of Jesus protruding out." He screamed, calling for his mother. Nahed came running and verified that indeed the portrait of Jesus, one that has been reproduced millions of times in its normal state, was weeping.

"We saw the picture flooded with oil," Nahed told *The Houston Post.* "I did not believe but I put my hand up and my forearm was covered with oil." Father Soliman was called; all felt a miracle might be pending for Isaac.

On Tuesday, November 12, the pamphlet states, "Isaac was checked by Dr. Atef Rizkala, a family physician . . . and was diagnosed as having no sign of leukemia." Two weeks later, his regular doctor in Houston corroborated the same results. Isaac appeared to be cured and today is a high school student in Houston.

Isaac Ayob of Bellaire, Texas, was given only a few months to live when this picture of Jesus began to weep at his home. Isaac, then 12 years old, was cured. PHOTO COURTESY OF ST. MARK'S COPTIC CHURCH.

But the icon was only getting started. Not only did it continue to weep and sweat profusely, but every picture that was placed on the wall did the same thing. Soon bedroom furniture was replaced with dozens of crosses and portraits of saints, Mary, and Coptic Church leaders, forcing Nahed and her husband to sleep elsewhere in the house. Votive candles and incense burned continuously.

An Egyptian bishop stopped by, inspected the instigating portrait and Isaac's medical records, and called it a miracle. Even after the original icon was brought to St. Mark's on January 6 (the Coptic Christmas Eve), the remaining pictures of Jesus and Mary shed oil on the stucco wall of the Ayob bedroom.

Naturally this attracted a great deal of attention. Not only did the Ayobs have an estimated 20,000 visitors in a two-month period, but many, hoping for cures, brought their own icons. Although Nahed kept their address out of the papers, pilgrims honed in on them anyway. Still, "the family never complained from having such a big crowd in their home," said the pamphlet. "[They] feel the miracle was a great blessing from the Lord."

Eventually, however, the crowds at the Ayob home dissipated, although the icon at St. Mark's continued to weep for a year-and-a-half afterwards, drawing tens of thousands. "Although we mostly get Catholics, Orthodox Christians, and Hispanics, there have been Protestants and Baptists as well," observes Father Soliman.

The church covered the weeping icon with clear plastic for cotton ball damage control; people kept wiping the picture to get oil, harming the surface. However, a flaw that appeared on the plastic was explained "as Jesus opening his mouth and his breath forming a human heart," volunteer Sami Zachary told *The Post*. "I view it as Jesus saying, 'Come to a new heart and I will comfort you.'"

Other icons placed near the crying portrait of Jesus in Bellaire started to weep as well. The tears consisted of fragrant oils, and thousands came to witness the miracle. PHOTO COURTESY OF ST. MARK'S COPTIC CHURCH.

Supplicants arrive hoping to be healed, and indeed the church willingly provides signed letters of testimony. But many also want to repent. "They're looking for a cure for their spirit," adds Soliman. "And in a way, that's better than the cure for the body." But as Isaac Ayob knows, the latter is much more easily quantified.

What to Expect

The tiny (about 250 families) church, the only one of its kind in Houston, consists of members of mostly Egyptian origin. But they welcome all visitors and have established a small gift shop featuring icons, informational booklets, and copies of the weeping picture.

The actual picture, which looks to be about 2-feet-by-3-feet, has a place of honor on the main altar. People are allowed to touch it, and although it's rather smeared-looking and stopped weeping a few years ago, those ubiquitous cotton balls with oil are still available.

Although St. Mark's doesn't get as many pilgrims these days, the Ayobs are still members. So you might get a firsthand glimpse of the recipient of a miracle.

What They Say

Martha Riess, Robstown, Texas: "A miracle happened on February 29, 1992," she wrote to St. Mark's. " A blood vessel in [her brother] Pete's eyes had bursted [sic] and the doctor had said he was going to be blind. We had brought him to the church and rubbed the tears from God on his eyes. . . . He can see now."

175

Christina and George Mourad, Houston, Texas: "He looked at me," Christina Mourad told *The Post* of the original icon in the Ayob home. "He opened his mouth. It was dark red. . . . He blew incense at me. I got scared and made the sign of the cross."

Her father George also claimed to see the picture move. "It is a message from the Lord, Jesus Christ. Everybody is busy making a living but the Lord is moving his eyes and lips to tell us to watch and listen."

Nancie Levey, Houston, Texas: "My cousin in Los Angeles was diagnosed with acute lymphoma and was in need of a bone marrow transfusion," she stated to the church. "I flew to Los Angeles . . . and I took her the cotton ball that I had received from the Holy Father at St. Mark's. . . . I told her that I had witnessed the miracle of the crying Jesus and that she should carry the cotton with her at all times. She then went . . . for her monthly blood checkup and two days later her doctor . . . told her that her blood count was normal and he couldn't explain it. . . . The whole family is very happy."

How to Get There

In Houston, take 610 to Bellaire St. and go east. Turn left on Mulberry; the church is on the right-hand side. Hours: 11 a.m.– 7 p.m. daily. St. Mark's Coptic Church, 424 Mulberry Lane, Bellaire, TX 77401, 713/669-0311.

✝ Tears in a Trailer

Christ of the Hills Monastery/New Sarov
Blanco, Texas

How It Happened

On May 7, 1985, an Eastern Orthodox monk named Father Pangratios was cleaning the trailer that housed the main chapel for the then-minuscule Christ of the Hills Monastery. "We moved here in 1981, after a fire destroyed our monastery and furniture-making factory in Smithson Valley," he says. He regards the near-tragedy (which took no lives) as a blessing: "We were too busy fulfilling orders to conform to monastic life. So God took control of things."

Left with only three monks and no running water or electricity, they truly had to start over. Which was why on that fateful May day, Pangratios thought the moisture from a Vladimir icon of Theotokos

(The Mother of God and Ever-Virgin Mary) was simply spilled oil. But when he wiped it off, he smelled fragrance. "That was my first indication of something extraordinary. But I thought it was a one-time occurrence. So I said a quick prayer and continued on with my work."

But curiosity nudged his return a few hours later. And indeed the icon, which was "written" (painted) in 1983 by a monk in an Orthodox monastery in California, was weeping again. So Pangratios brought another monk, who confirmed that the moisture was myrrh, the fragrant, oily resin presented to Baby Jesus by the Three Wise Men.

The tears from this portrait at the Christ of the Hills Monastery in Blanco, Texas, seem to have brought good fortune to this previously struggling religious outpost. PHOTO COURTESY OF CHRIST OF THE HILLS MONASTERY.

The tears continued and when Father Benedict, the monastery's founder, saw the icon, "he fell prostrate," recalls Pangratios, who felt bad about his own response to the weeping. "My reaction had been intellectual whereas his was one of complete faith."

Officials of the Russian Orthodox church sent an archbishop and bishop to investigate. After examining the underside of the icon for pipes and camping out in the trailer overnight to make sure of no human intervention, they blessed the icon and permitted the public to come and pray. Because their faith considers it sacrilegious, "we don't subject [the icon] to any type of scientific experiments," Bishop Hilarion, one of the original investigators, told *"D," The Magazine of Dallas.* "But we see there's nothing wrong with it, nothing suspicious. We believe it's from God."

Still, the weeping was not cause for celebration. "This is a call to repentance," observes Pangratios. "Mary is saddened by our sins. She wants us to change our lives to fasting and prayer, love of God and neighbor, and nonjudgment."

Yet the tears resulted in happiness for some. Blind twins allegedly left the monastery with sight. A woman with uterine cancer spontaneously recovered. A man due for brain surgery found it unnecessary. And cases of mental illness and depression disappeared.

But Christ of the Hills did not become an overnight phenomenon, although an estimated 100,000 visitors annually make the odyssey from all over the world. "We slowly began to build up," observes Pangratios. "At first, only a few people came." Although the icon produced myrrh steadily for six months after the initial discovery, the stream of tears has become intermittent. "It happens about once a day. There's no liturgical pattern or fixed time."

Today Christ of the Hills is a thriving enterprise, with 32 buildings and trailers, over a dozen monks and nuns, an incense factory, and a gift shop that does a land-office business in icon knick-knacks and religious articles, including Jesus pens. There is also a place for those who wish to go on retreat, although the guest cells, as they are known, are reserved months in advance. "We're revving up to start a candle-making industry," adds Pangratios.

But this time, they haven't lost sight of their priorities. The icon remains in its original trailer and the monks maintain a strenuous schedule, rising at 3:30 a.m. for a day of prayer, fasting, and hard labor. "We know that we are not worthy to have the spiritual treasure that has been entrusted to our care," Father Benedict has said. "However, we are profoundly aware of our deep responsibility to share it with all who come in faith."

What to Expect

Modern women might have a tough time at Christ of the Hills/New Sarov. Shorts and miniskirts are not allowed. Women are expected to wear dresses or long skirts and cover their heads in the presence of the icon. And everyone is asked to talk softly "as monasteries are quiet places," according to the descriptive brochure.

A wood and stucco main trailer/chapel houses the 13-foot-by-15-foot icon, the original of which is said to have been painted on Jesus's kitchen table by St. Luke in the first century. Surrounded by a bed of rosaries, the acrylic-on-wood portrait has yellowed streaks beneath the eyes, although it doesn't always weep from them. A box of cotton balls is propped underneath to anoint the faithful. Although constant tours and refreshments are available, there may be long lines.

What They Say

Mary Louise Cantu, address unknown: A visitor to Christ of the Hills, Cantu took her niece and nephew and their young daughter, Anna Patricia, who had spina bifida. "[Anna Patricia] had been having a lot of bladder infections," Cantu said in a written statement; ". . . she [had] to have [an] operation.

"We came here on Saturday of Memorial Day weekend. The following Tuesday, she went to the doctor to get the results and to set . . . the date. . . . When the doctor examined her again, he came back beaming and he said, 'I don't know what you've done for this little girl, but whatever . . . keep on doing it, because she doesn't need the operation any more.'"

Ryan Trimble, Blanco, Texas: As mayor of the small town (population about 1,400) of Blanco, Trimble is fully aware of controversy generated by a monastery plunged amidst suspicious locals. According to *The Dallas Morning News,* rumors have ranged from general rumblings about illegal activity to tales of bodies being buried in the churchyard. "Sure, I was concerned about it a little bit," he said. "I wondered if it was really miracles happening or . . . an isolated incident."

But a visit to the monastery allayed his fears. "Basically, they are good people. And they're bringing a lot of money into the town's restaurants and shops. It's a very spiritual place."

Does he believe in the icon's magic? "Although it could be moisture from the humidity and material used in the painting, no one really knows," he adds in classical political style.

How to Get There

Getting to the 105-acre monastery is a feat in itself. From Austin, take U.S. 290W to U.S. 281S to Blanco (about 60 miles). Once you pass through Blanco, turn right on SR 102 just past the self-service laundry. Now things get tricky: bear immediately to your right, so as not to enter the state park. (The monastery brochure has a detailed map, prompted in part by complaints from rangers.) Cross the Blanco River, then you'll come to a gate marked "Clear Spring Ranch." Turn right. Go 2½ miles past several cattle guards and the monastery is on the left.

Visiting hours are 10 a.m.–6 p.m. seven days a week from June through August. The monastery is closed on Tuesdays and

Wednesdays from September through May. Mailing address: Christ of the Hills Monastery/New Sarov, Blanco, TX 78606-1049, 210/833-5363.

✚ Lone Star Lourdes

St. John Neumann Church
Lubbock, Texas

How It Happened

There are two ways of looking at the events at St. John Neumann Church in 1988—through the eyes of a spectator or from the perspective of John Hein.

In February of that year, Mary Constancio claimed to hear the voice of Mary during her Monday night prayer group. "The feeling that came over me was a very deep sense of holiness," she told the *Chicago Tribune*. Yet the former respiratory therapist also wondered if she might be losing her mind. "I wanted to make sure it was not myself making this up, but that it was from the Lord. But after I wrote the messages down and read them, I knew they cannot be from me."

About a month after Constancio got the word, two others in the small prayer group, Theresa Warner, a homemaker, and Mike Slate, a retired Air Force officer, also began hearing from Mary.

"Basically, they were messages of encouragement—to come to the church and pray the sacraments," relates Slate. "More people started showing up at the prayer group." The word spread and attendance jumped from 6 to 600. When parishioners wrote letters to the newspapers claiming to be healed, participation escalated into the thousands.

Mary supposedly encouraged publicity "throughout radio, throughout television, throughout the newspaper, throughout the pulpit, throughout the world," according to Constancio's revelation. So by August 15, the Feast of Assumption, excitement at this, the smallest of Lubbock's six Catholic churches, had reached a feverish pitch. "Bring your lame, your crippled, your souls which have no hope, for I will be merciful to them," Mary, sounding suspiciously like the motto of the Statue of Liberty, told the visionaries.

But the town was ready. "We're prepared for anywhere from 0 to 50,000," Police Chief Thomas Nichols remarked to the *Tribune*. The local hotels and restaurants geared up for sellouts and the parish even commissioned an official St. John T-shirt and planned on distributing a pamphlet with an order form for a $10, 200-page book on the rosary messages.

"It's like Christmas every day here," Monsignor Joseph James, the pastor, enthused in the *Tribune*. "This has taught me that Mary is for real. She's not a plaster statue. She's not a theological construct." He, too, has had his own healing experience—a recent trip to Medjugorje had supposedly rid him of hypoglycemia (low blood sugar).

And the 15th was a spectacle indeed. Between 10,000 and 15,000 of the faithful showed up for the evening Mass, spilling into the parking lot, the lawn, and the street in front of the charismatic Roman Catholic church. A cornucopia of marvels occurred: changing rosaries, the smell of roses, spontaneous cures, a spinning crown on a statue, and formations of doves. "Then in the middle of mass, shortly before dusk, the sun broke dramatically through a gathering curtain of clouds," reports *The New York Times*. "Shrieks went up on the lawn, and many of those assembled cried, prayed and pointed toward the sky. Some said they saw Jesus . . . the Virgin Mary . . . the gates of heaven. Others, including a number of priests stood by, craning their necks but seeing nothing at all."

Monsignor James, no doubt sensing a prime opportunity, broke into a rendition of "Amazing Grace" while church deacons recorded testimonials from the faithful and gathered up film, purportedly to be used to prove the veracity of the events to the Vatican.

Although a diocesan visitation committee allowed for continuation of the messages, it stopped short of calling the happening a miracle. "Something like that has to suspend all natural laws," explains Slate.

John Hein might take issue with the latter. On October 8, 1988, Hein, who was in his early 60s, went to Lubbock to make his final peace with Mary and Jesus. Diagnosed by several doctors in Wichita, Kansas, as terminal, he had been exposed to a poison gas in the workplace that had nearly destroyed his lungs. "There were four of us who'd inhaled the gas, and three were already dead," he recalls. As an independent contractor and owner of machine shops, hospital visits and medical bills drained his life savings. "Once I lost my business, I lost my insurance." Along with breathing problems, he suffered from strokes and brain damage and was on oxygen 24 hours a day.

Hein arrived at St. John Neumann with his oxygen tank set at the highest level. "I was praying, asking Mary to help me, when she appeared to the side of me. I thought my brain had finally went.

Then I felt her hand on my shoulder. . . . She was beside me, I could see her gown." When he turned, he passed out. "The next thing I knew, Monsignor James was standing over me in the courtyard, praying and anointing me with holy water."

At first, he didn't realize that anything was different. "But then I wanted to get something to eat, and started walking across the courtyard and climbing stairs without my oxygen bottle." He hasn't used it since that fateful day and his lungs are completely clear. He now travels the country talking to prayer groups and churches.

"Somebody is keeping us alive," he says. "I found out who it is. I was cured in less than five minutes."

What to Expect

With about 400 mostly Hispanic families, this charismatic Catholic church believes in the immediate presence of God's spirit in worship. It can manifest itself in the laying on of the hands and speaking in tongues.

Although Monsignor James has since been transferred to the Our Lady of Mercy Retreat Center in Slaton, Texas, the prayer group still meets at St. John Neumann every Monday night. According to Mike Slate, Mary Constancio is the only visionary who still receives messages. All visitors are welcome and there's a rosary service at noon and on Marian feast days. The church is usually open seven days a week; hours vary.

What They Say

Mike Slate, Lubbock, Texas: Although he's in his mid-40s, Slate only has use of 20 percent of his heart. "I am a shy person," he admits. "But having contact with Mary has enabled me to talk to all kinds of people. They would ask me questions and I could get them answers." He was bereft when the messages stopped. "It was like she died. . . . I had come to love her and know her as a mother."

Although he says the events at St. John Neumann brought him closer to God, "There are still times when I struggle with my faith."

Archie Bottoms, Vice-Chancellor of the Diocese of Lubbock, Texas: "I'm deeply concerned that this whole thing has snowballed . . . into the realm of auto-suggestion and emotional hysteria," he admitted to the *Tribune*. "I'm embarrassed by the whole thing. I've had Pro-testant friends call up and say, 'Are you hearing any voices?' And my standard reply is, 'Yeah, one voice: yours, and I don't like it.'"

How to Get There

From Amarillo, take 27S to Lubbock. Go west on Hwy. 62 to Frankford Rd. Turn left on Frankford; the church is on the corner. St. John Neumann Church, 5802 22nd St., Lubbock, TX 79407, 806/799-2649.

✝ Mary Appears in an Automotive Context

Progreso Auto Supply/Home of Santiago Quintero
Progreso/Elsa, Texas

How It Happened

Ray Trevino had finished cleaning up the restroom in the back of his auto parts store in Progreso. Shortly after the job was done—December 3, 1990, to be exact—he beheld a 2½-foot-long image of Our Lady of Guadalupe on the concrete floor by the shower stall. "I closed my eyes, I was so shocked," he recalls. "I couldn't believe it. I thought I was seeing things."

In fact, he was so confounded by this turn of events that he got down on his hands and knees and tried to rub out the image. Despite his best efforts it remained, "so I told myself that I would take the first person who walked in the store back there and ask them what *they* thought."

It happened to be his mother. "When she came out, she had a look of amazement on her face and said, 'That's the Virgin of Guadalupe!'"

Recently, however, things had not been going well for the Trevino family. "About nine months before, my wife had an accident at home and was paralyzed from the waist down," explains Ray. "Plus the business for my auto parts store was slow. I was debating whether to close and work for someone else or continue there."

Yet despite these trials, he kept his faith. "I always thought God was with me. . . . My wife coped well with being confined to a wheelchair and I had other jobs lined up."

But commerce was about to escalate in a manner he couldn't possibly have imagined. After only a few trips to the shower stall, the world seemed to land at his door. "People started coming from everywhere—I got radio interview requests from New Mexico, San Francisco, London."

Visitors to the Holy Camaro in Elsa, Texas, will find the car housed in this mini-shrine. PHOTO COURTESY OF THE QUINTERO FAMILY.

During the height of the brouhaha, an estimated 14,000 a week wended their way past fan belts and spark plugs, leaving candles and flowers on the floor between the shower stall and toilet. "Parking became impossible and I couldn't get any work done."

Part of this may have been instigated by Trevino himself, who discouraged visitors from taking photos, thus providing incentive for more to stop by and see the phenomenon for themselves. "I want them to take the image home with them in their hearts," he has said.

Although some were skeptics, others were deeply moved. "I let them believe what they want," remarks Trevino. "One lady was real angry because her husband made her wait in line. When she came out, she was crying. 'I've wanted to go home all afternoon,' she told me. 'But when I saw the Virgin Mary, I felt at peace and forgot all about my back pain.'" However, by the end of the month, Trevino decided to shut down Progreso Auto Supply for good. "It got to be too much."

Then in September 1993, in Elsa, Santiago Quintero was repairing the bumper of a Camaro when *he* noticed an image of Our Lady of Guadalupe there.

Some may see black spots and dents while others might glimpse Our Lady of Guadalupe on the bumper of this Camaro in Elsa, Texas. PHOTO COURTESY OF THE QUINTERO FAMILY.

"He saw a pattern of black spots and dents and told the neighbor something had appeared on the car," recounts his 12-year-old daughter Aurora. "The word spread quickly to newspapers and TV."

Soon Quintero, who runs an auto repair shop from his home, had built a little shack for the Holy Camaro of Elsa, as it came to be known. "Many people came and are still coming," continues Aurora. "They leave candles, pictures, and flowers." And there have even been healings: "The day the Virgin appeared, a local man was shot in the head. They said he wasn't going to live. His wife came to see the car, and now the man is fine."

Which leaves one burning question: Could the bumper have possibly come from Trevino's auto parts store?

What to Expect

E & E Mini-Market has replaced Trevino's store, although he still owns the land. But the image is still there. "You can barely make it out," he says. He enclosed the area in glass, capturing the mini-shrine for posterity. "Once in a while someone will remember and drop by and ask to see it."

The Quintero family, many of whom do not speak English, welcome all visitors to the Holy Camaro. In fact, they have a celebration around the first week of September to honor the discovery of the image and also on December 12, the feast day of Our Lady of Guadalupe. "We have mariachis and give a dinner for people," adds Aurora.

What They Say

Ray Trevino, Weslaco, Texas: "I didn't think that something like that could actually appear," he remarks of the likeness. "But when it happens, you feel something deep inside, and hear something within yourself, even though you question, 'What would she be doing here?'

"But that's her way. She'll show up in unexpected places—on the floor, in a corner—so you won't forget about her."

Lucio Duque, Elsa, Texas: A reporter for the local paper, *The Delta Chronicle,* Duque covered the Holy Camaro incident. "As a citizen, I feel this is a sign for people to have more faith in God," he says. "Young people especially have lost touch with a Supreme Being and a sense of morals. We no longer have a fear of God. . . . But something like this is positive. The Quinteros aren't asking for money and have no hidden agendas."

How to Get There

To Progreso: Take Highway 281S from San Antonio; follow it through Brownsville to Progreso. Then turn left on Farm Rd. 1015, go six blocks, and E & E Mini-Market is next to a junior high school, at the corner of 1015 and Shelby. Hours: 8 a.m.–9 p.m. For more information, write Ray Trevino, P.O. Box 1047, Progreso, TX 78579.

To Elsa: From McAllen take I-83E to Westlaco exit (Hwy 88); go north until you run into Elsa. For specific directions to the Camaro and more information, contact Santiago Quintero, P.O. Box 1335, Elsa, TX 78543, 210/262-3616.

_____

✝ Stigmata and the Roller Coaster King

St. Elizabeth Ann Seton Church
Lake Ridge, Virginia

How It Happened

Prior to November 28, 1991, James Bruse's claim to fame was that he was a three-time record holder in the *Guinness Book of World Records.* From 1972 to 1978, Bruse and his companions reigned supreme in the category of marathon roller-coastering, riding a Virginia 'coaster for a little more than five consecutive days. Shortly after that crowning achievement, Bruse decided to quit his job repairing trucks and act on a long-held dream of joining the priesthood.

Eventually he landed an assistant pastorship at the St. Elizabeth Ann Seton Church, a "looming modern edifice whose sloping roofs and redwood siding give it the look of an out-of-season ski lodge set among snowless trees," according to *U.S. News & World Report.* While there, he began experiencing the "priesthood's legendary 'seven-year' itch," states the account. Along with "being on call 24 hours a day; the job is not just repetitive, it is lonely. . . . As his daily duties merged into a numbing sameness, Father Jim began to struggle with . . . depression and doubt. . . ." He questioned whether he should be a priest at all, and 'If Christ was real, why couldn't he feel his presence?'"

His uncertainties were about to end. While Bruse was visiting his parents over Thanksgiving, the statues—all the statues—in their home began to weep, especially when Father Jim was in the room. The tears became so copious that his mother put bowls underneath the icons to protect the furniture.

Then, the day after Christmas, Bruse claimed to feel sharp, stabbing pains in his wrists. Blood appeared to seep from unbroken skin there and, in subsequent weeks, from his right side and feet as well.

"When it first started, I thought it was some kind of skin disease," Bruse told *The Washington Post*. Shaken, he consulted the senior priest, Father Daniel Hamilton, on New Year's Day.

Hamilton, "the ultimate cynic," according to the *Post*, was astounded. Not only because statues spontaneously excreted tears and blood in the presence of both men, but because the young priest seemed unfamiliar with the concept of stigmata, injuries similar to those of Christ during the crucifixion. "Didn't they teach you anything at [divinity] school?" he purportedly asked.

By March, statues were crying all over the place—in the church's administrative offices, at schools where Bruse spoke to children, in front of 500 parishioners when he said Mass. Although Bruse had been questioned by the Diocese of Arlington and examined by a psychiatrist and internist, no one could find anything out of the ordinary. When the media got wind of the events, it was a roller coaster marathon all over again.

Soon thousands of people were mobbing the church on Sunday, "spilling out the doors, trampling the daffodils, and jamming the streets, . . ." states *U.S. News*. "Inside, people fell to their knees before the [statue], weeping, praying aloud, and straining for a glimpse of tears." The faithful brought their own icons to be blessed and their loved ones to be healed, although many went away as sick as they'd been before. Even "parishioners began whispering of . . . spinning suns, rays of vibrant colors, statues, and rosaries changing colors. . . ." And this in a town where many of the residents work for the Pentagon, the FBI, and a nearby Marine base.

But it brought out the doubters as well. The president of the Capital Area Skeptics stood before a large fiberglass Madonna at the church and demonstrated how misdirection could make it "appear" to weep. Shawn Carlson, an astrophysicist at Lawrence Berkeley Laboratory in California, who has also made pictures bawl, told the *Post*, "It's very, very easy to do. I've learned that the best solutions are so obvious they're overlooked—the kind of thing that involves a trip to the hardware store and spending no more than $5."

And discounting the fact that fake blood is readily available at any magic or novelty shop, "Dr. Oscar D. Ratnoff, a Cleveland hematologist who has studied more than 100 cases of spontaneous bruising and bleeding . . . says such cases are often psychogenic, linked to severe emotional stress," observed *U.S. News*. Since the 13th century there have been 300 reported cases of stigmata. Most of the victims were women.

Despite the controversy, the Church refused to investigate. "The church does not pass judgment on purely physical phenomena, but only on a purported meaning," said a statement issued by the Diocese of Arlington. The soft-spoken priest seemed to thrive in the limelight and pilgrims arrived by the busload.

However, by the end of summer 1992, much of the uproar had died down, despite the occasional report of tears on a statue or a miraculous healing. Bruse's stigmata had faded months before. Even the huge fiberglass Madonna in the center of the church had ceased crying. Bruse continued to minister to his flock.

Today Father Jim is a full pastor in another parish in a small town in Virginia. Although he seems to shy away from the media, "people still want him to pray for them," says Marie Pelletier, who works in the church office. "They have an incredible attachment to him . . . he always answers their letters and phone calls. He's more than willing to accommodate everyone."

Although physicist Carlson did not talk to Bruse personally nor examine the icons in question, "the thing about these religious statues is that you can't get to touch them," he remarked in the *Post*. "That's blasphemous. You can't pick on religion. But I can honestly say that I've found fraud and I've found wishful thinking. I've never found a miracle."

What to Expect

One of the fastest-growing churches in north Virginia, Elizabeth Ann Seton serves 1,800 mostly prosperous families and recently completed a new building. The 5-foot fiberglass Madonna that attracted much of the attention has a place of honor in a special alcove in the chapel. "We still have quite a few people come to see the statue," adds Pelletier.

What They Say

Jo Ann Cawley, Lake Ridge, Virginia: "God's touched Father Jim," Cawley told the *Post*. "All the strangers want to come and see to believe. Everybody's a little bit skeptical. The Lord is here. I think he is trying to say to his people, 'Believe.'"

Marie Pelletier, Lake Ridge, Virginia: As a longtime employee of the church, Pelletier was taken aback by some of the media coverage, "things like how we didn't have to water the plants. But the truth of it was, the signs were wonderful. And they caused an incredible spiritual deepening in the parish. The experience grabbed hold of my heart and has never let go."

Lucille Ienna and Lisa Ross, Washington, DC: Cancer patients Ienna and Ross took statues to St. Elizabeth Ann Seton to be blessed. According to an account in the *Post,* "First, [Ienna] said Bruse pointed to a statue in his office and said, 'This statue cried today.' Then as she watched, it began to shed tears again, and she smelled a fragrance in the air, like roses. She turned around and saw Bruse cradling her statue in his arms and it too was crying. Her friend reached into her pocketbook to pull out her small figurine, only to find tears falling from its eyes, although Bruse had not touched it."

"I said, 'This is unbelievable,'" Ienna continued. "He said, 'This is unbelievable.' He didn't talk much. We said, 'Thank you, thank you.'"

How to Get There

St. Elizabeth Ann Seton Church is about 25 miles from Washington, DC. Take I-95S to exit 160 (Lake Ridge/Occoquan). At the second light make a left on Old Bridge Rd. Go down nine lights to Cavalier Dr.; make a left. The second street is Valley Wood Dr.; turn left there also. The church is on the right-hand side about a mile down. Open daily from 9 a.m. to 3 p.m. Mailing address: 12805 Valley Wood Dr., Lake Ridge, VA 22192, 703/690-1493.

West Virginia

✝ Jesus Treed

The Holden Schoolyard
Holden, West Virginia

How It Happened

In the year of 1982, in a little mining town,
Upon a hill in Holden, the Jesus tree was found.

Thus begins a poem by local resident Ealois Mullins, detailing an account of a 30-foot poplar covered with kudzu vines. Many believed the tree resembled a side view of Jesus with his hands clasped in prayer, similar to a painting of him in the Garden of Gethsemane. Discovered one spring night in an abandoned elementary school yard, the pious profile drew the eye of several boys who were swigging beer. At least one of the youths gave up alcohol and joined a church.

Soon praying replaced partying as thousands flocked from around West Virginia and other states to view the amazing tree. "It's the biggest thing ever to hit these parts," Jane Watson, editor of the *Logan Banner,* told the *Charleston (WV) Gazette.* "We're getting sacks and sacks of letters asking about it."

This wasn't, however, the first time Holden held center stage. Billed as the Cadillac of West Virginia coal towns, it had been a model community, thanks to the largesse of its major source of income, Island Creek Coal. In the '30s and '40s, the postcard-perfect burg boasted up to 10,000 residents, paved streets, well-tended lawns, a store, a theatre, a bowling alley, churches, schools, a hospital, even a dairy. The company president's mansion was the local showplace and the downtown area had flower gardens, a gazebo, and rows of neatly painted two-story houses. Cleanliness was maintained by garbage crews (almost unheard-of in mining areas); those who wanted to junk up their yard with a cow or other tacky stuff were moved "up the holler" and out of sight. Even neighborhood activities included blacks and Italians.

By the '50s, however, the homes had been sold to a realty company and the coal industry began to decline. Many buildings were abandoned or taken over by independents, although some families—especially those of the original owners—still kept their tracts spiffy. And even though Holden wasn't exactly a ghost town, it did have quite a few residents collecting Social Security. "Young people moved away to look for jobs," observes one old-timer. "There's not a lot in the mines and they wanted something better anyway."

The Jesus tree effected a reverse exodus. Not only did the curious and faithful clog streets and trample yards, but busloads of church groups stopped by for worship and gospel songs, much to the dismay of residents who hoped for some sleep. "Every evening at dusk they'd come, because that was when you could see it best," recalls Ruth McNeil, another longtime resident. As the street lights behind the tree illuminated the profile, "folks would pray, shout, and sing. Or they might sit there all night, just staring at it."

Some interpreted the image as an omen of pending misfortune, but the local gendarmes felt they were already in the middle of a mishap, what with tangled traffic and the crowds. "I wouldn't know about any signs," Lt. James Ferguson of the Logan County sheriff's department told United Press International. "But in my opinion, Jesus ain't going to come in any tree."

Yet others claimed to experience miracle cures. According the *Charleston Gazette,* the knee of coal miner Bill Scaggs suddenly healed while Scaggs prayed in front of the tree. "I couldn't bend my knee at all," he told the paper. "Now it's as limber as wet spaghetti."

Retired miner Johnny McKenzie professed to recover from black lung disease. "I couldn't take a deep breath without coughing myself half to death," he admitted to the *Gazette.* "Now I don't even cough when I get up in the morning."

"As a rule, people really believed in it," observes Delphia Hall, who lived nearby. "They might arrive skeptical, but by the time they saw the image, they knew it was something." (Yet one resident—who asked not to be identified—told UPI that all *she* saw was a half-dead tree covered with kudzu.)

Regardless, by the next summer the crowds had withered even though, according to McNeil, the image looked more like Jesus than ever. "You'd think the growth of vines might have changed the shape but it didn't." However, a chain had been put across the road leading up to the site by a contractor who wanted to store heavy equipment. "And people just didn't come like they used to, although a lot of locals still did." Eventually, the vines distorted the image completely.

Today the tree is no more and the razed school is now part of Appalachian Corridor G (SR 119) which links Williamson to Charleston. "There was some talk of cutting down the tree at the time it was so well-known, but of course that never happened," adds Hall. But those kudzu vines would likely have downed the popular poplar, if progress hadn't gotten there first.

What to Expect

With a current total area population of around 1,500, Holden's glory days appear to be gone. Many buildings—the main company store, the hospital, the theatre—have been demolished or abandoned. There isn't even a traffic light for drag racing. SR 119 paved the way for the destruction of several homes, although a barber shop and post office remain. People go to nearby Logan for shopping and other needs; 119 also expedites travel to the metropolises of Williamson and Charleston.

What They Say

Delphia Hall, Holden, West Virginia: The tree presented a "finely detailed image, all the way down to cut of his hair and beard," recalls Delphia Hall, a lifelong Logan denizen now in her 80s. "His head was tilted upward as if he was gazing at heaven. . . . You could make out an eye if you looked hard enough.

"It might have been the arrangement of vines," she goes on. "But you wonder, if those boys hadn't been up there drinking, no one would have ever noticed. So what moved them to stare at that tree?"

Ruth McNeil, Holden, West Virginia: "All the publicity from the tree didn't help the town much. People have left since 1982, and there's a lot of unemployment."

Still, even her skeptical husband and son thought the tree resembled Jesus. "It was pretty eerie while it lasted, especially when you stood out there alone at night."

How to Get There

Holden is located in the southwest corner of West Virginia, a few miles from Logan. So although you can't see this Jesus tree, the wheels of your car will likely run over the site every time you pass through town. To get to Holden, take 119S from Charleston.

Introduction: Happening or Hoax?

Barrett, Mary Ellin. "How We Worship." *USA Weekend,* March 13, 1991, p. 4.

"Charlatans in the Church." *U.S. News & World Report,* March 29, 1993, p. 51.

Nickell, Joe. "Miracles or Mania?" *Skeptical Inquirer,* Fall 1994, p. 477 (4).

Oakes, Larry. "The Story Behind the Vision that Wasn't." *Minneapolis Star Tribune,* May 30, 1993, 1A.

Ostling, Richard. "Handmaid or Feminist?" *Time,* December 30, 1991, p. 62 (5).

Vara, Richard. "The Mystery of Miracles." *The Houston Chronicle,* April 4, 1992, Religion; p.1.

White, Gayle. "Visions of Mary." *The Atlanta Journal and Constitution,* September 21, 1991, E6.

Alabama

Jasper: Double Exposure at Walker Baptist Medical Center

Byars, Tom. "A Saving Face." *Powergrams* (newsletter), nd, pp.16–17.

"The Door." Jasper *Daily Mountain Eagle,* April 19,1983, p.8.

Hewett, Kelli S. "Mysterious, Divine Image Discovered on Walker County Man's Spinal X-Ray." Jasper *Daily Mountain Eagle,* April 17, 1994, A1 and A10.

―――. "Walker Regional No Stranger to 'Miracles.'" *Ibid.*

Howle, Paul. "The Face at the Door." *The Atlanta Journal,* April 22, 1983, 2A.

"'Image,' Draws National Attention." Jasper *Daily Mountain Eagle,* April 19, 1983, p.9.

Sikora, Frank. "X-Ray Appears to Include Image of Jesus." *The Birmingham News,* June 15, 1994, 2D.

"Thousands Flock to Alabama Town as Christ Mysteriously Appears on Door in Hospital." *The Star,* May 3, 1983, np.

Williams, Tim. "A Miracle." Jasper *Daily Mountain Eagle,* April 14, 1983, pp. 1 and 8.

Sterrett: Medjugorje Pipeline

American History You Never Learned (booklet). Birmingham: St. James, 1993.

Garrison, Greg. "Visionary's Legacy." *The Birmingham News,* nd.

―――. "Visionary's Host Buys Field Where Pilgrims Gather." *Ibid.*

The Reconsecration of the Tabernacle of Our Lady's Messages (booklet). Birmingham: Caritas, nd.

The Tabernacle of Our Lady's Messages (completion report). Birmingham: Caritas, 1992.

White, Gayle. "Reports of Apparitions." *The Atlanta Journal and Constitution,* August 22, 1992, E6.

Wilstach, Nancy. "Tabernacle Marks Site of Virgin Sightings." *The Birmingham News,* March 10, 1995, 1A and 10A.

Witt, Elaine. "Thousands Expected Today at Site of Visions." Birmingham *Post-Herald,* nd.

———. "Vision of Mary Transformed Community." Birmingham *Post-Herald,* November 8, 1989, D11–12.

Arizona

Phoenix: Mary Branches Out

Bearden, Michelle. "Touch of Grace." *Phoenix Gazette,* January 28, 1989, D1 and D3.

Perkes, Kim Sue Lia. "'There Is a Hunger in the Human Heart . . .'" *The Arizona Republic,* November 13, 1994, A1.

Scottsdale: Yuppie Visions at St. Maria Goretti

Faricy, Robert and Rooney, Lucy. *Our Lady Comes to Scottsdale.* Santa Barbara: Queenship, 1993, pp. 1–82.

"Bishop Issues Statement on Scottsdale Locutions." *The Catholic Sun,* January 18, 1990, np.

Moulton, Kristen. "Divine Apparitions Sweeping the United States." The Associated Press, May 1993, np.

Sedona: New Age Vortex or Vacuum?

Chandler, Russell. "Bad Vibes Rock New Age Mecca." *Los Angeles Times,* August 4, 1991, A1 (2).

"Chapel of the Holy Cross" (brochure). Sedona: Chapel of the Holy Cross, nd.

Rabey, Steve. "Welcome to Sedona." *The Ottawa Citizen,* November 28, 1992, L4.

California

Chula Vista: A Strange Twist on the Road of Tragedy

Bratt, L. Erik. "Pupils Graduate; Memory of Laura Goes with Them." *The San Diego Union-Tribune,* July 1, 1994, np.

McDonnell, Patrick. "Some Call Sign a Miracle Image of Slain Girl." *Los Angeles Times,* July 19, 1991, B1.

Lee, Peggy. "Slain Girl's Ghostly Image to Turn to Real." *Los Angeles Times,* August 1, 1991, B1.

Moran, Greg. "Visitors Still Show Up at Billboard." *The San Diego Union-Tribune,* April 2, 1992, np.

"Photo to Replace 'Ghostly' Billboard Image." *Los Angeles Times,* August 1, 1991, A26.

Reza, H.G. "Living with, 'If Only . . .'" *Los Angeles Times,* September 29, 1991, B1.

Smolla, David; McDonnell, Patrick; and Zamichow, Nora. "Vision of Chaos around Chula Vista Billboard." *Los Angeles Times,* July 20, 1991, B1 (2).

Colfax: Mary Visits the Foothills

Seelmayer, John. "Real Life" (editorial). *Grass Valley Union,* December 17, 1990, np.

Trombley, William. "A Beacon for the Faithful and Skeptics." *Los Angeles Times,* December 9, 1990, A3.

United Press International. "Church Wall Image Fails to Appear on Overcast Morning." *Los Angeles Times,* December 11, 1990, A35.

Los Angeles: Faith Shines Through

Andrews, Mays. "Crowds Flock to 'Miracle' of Cross." *Los Angeles Sentinel,* nd.

Dart, John. "The Phenomenon on 80th St." *Los Angeles Times,* nd.

Klein, David. "'It's a Miracle!' Cry the Hundreds." *National Enquirer,* nd.

Techter, David. "A Flap of Glowing Crosses." *Fate* Magazine, June 1972, p. 52.

Santa Ana: A Mosaic Mystery

Lundgren, Kristina. "Word of Apparition Draws Hundreds to Church." *Los Angeles Times*, November 23, 1991, A26.

Santa Maria: Mary Goes "Krogering" in Earthquake Country

Arnerich, John Paul. "Did Mary Speak to a California Woman?" *National Catholic Register,* March 1, 1992, p. 1 (3).

———. "Marian Apparitions: What the Experts Say." *National Catholic Register,* nd, np.

Corwin, Miles. "Vision Quest." *Los Angeles Times,* June 23, 1991, A3.

Finucane, Stephanie. "Santa Maria a Haven for the Quake Fearful." *Santa Barbara News-Press,* April 16, 1992, B2–3.

———. "Disciples Still Have Their Cross to Bear." *Ibid.*

Whitman, Hazel. "The Cross of Peace: Seven Years Later." *Santa Maria Times,* March 18, 1995, A6.

Thornton: Our Lady of Fatima Takes a Hike

Corrigan, Emmett/McClatchy News Service. "Devotees Still Flock." *The Sacramento Bee,* August 20, 1983, B7.

"'Crying Statue is No Miracle.'" Oakland *Tribune,* June 9, 1983, A11.

"Diocese Calls for Return to 'Normalcy.'" *Lodi News-Sentinel,* June 18, 1983, p. 8.

"Madonna's Tears Are No Miracle." *San Francisco Chronicle,* June 8, 1983, p. 3.

Magagnini, Stephen. "Church Officials Skeptical about Statue That Cries." *San Francisco Chronicle,* March 28, 1983, np.

Tachibana, Judy. "Statue of Virgin, 'Cries, Moves.'" *The Sacramento Bee,* November 6, 1982, A13.

"'Weeping Madonna' Ruled a Deception." McClatchy News Service, nd.

Colorado

Golden: Double Vision at the Mother Cabrini Shrine

"6,000 Flock to Shrine." Reuters, December 8, 1991, np.

Kuntz, J. Gary. "What Is Happening at Cabrini?" *Heart of the Harvest,* March 25, 1992, p. 2.

Legge, Gordon. "Stairway to Heaven." *Calgary Herald,* August 14, 1993, B7 (2).

Lignitz, Amy. "Denver Archbishop Exhorts Faithful to Stop Gathering at Shrine." The Associated Press, December 18, 1991, np.

Micheli, Mother Ignatius. *A Short History of the Mother Cabrini Shrine* (booklet). Boulder: D & K, 1992.

Morrow, Lance. "How to Believe in Miracles." *Time,* December 30, 1991, p. 68–9.

"Mother Reports 4-Year-Old's Experience." *Heart of the Harvest, loc cit.*

"Pilgrims Damaged Eyes Looking for Virgin Mary." *St. Petersburg (Florida) Times,* December 21, 1991, 2E.

Scripps Howard News Service. "Probe Finds No Sighting of Virgin." *The San Diego Union-Tribune,* May 15, 1993, B8:1,4; B11:2,3.

"Stafford Discredits Visions." *Rocky Mountain News,* March 9, 1994, 5A.

"Thousands Flock to Shrine." The Associated Press, December 9, 1991, np.

Silverton: Small Town Miracles

"Christ of the Mines." *Silverton-San Juan Vacation Guide* (booklet). 1994, p. 22.

Destination Silverton (booklet). Silverton: Chamber of Commerce, nd.

Miniclier, Kit. "Little Town Blues." *Denver Post Magazine,* March 13, 1994, p. 9 (2).

Swanson, Gerald. "Shrine Brings Miracles." *Silverton-San Juan Vacation Guide* (booklet), 1991, p. 4.

Connecticut

New Haven: Jesus vs. the Devil in Wooster Square Park

Bradford, Arthur. "The Jesus Tree." *The Yale Daily News Magazine,* October 1992, pp. 17–21.

Clark, Edie. "Moss or Miracle?" *Yankee,* June 1994, pp.87–92;132–6.

Walbert, Kate. "This Week in Milford, New Haven." nd, np.

Waterhouse, Don. "Book Probes 'Jesus Trees.'" *Central Maine Morning Sentinel,* March 5, 1993, p. 14.

Florida

Hollywood: Making Room for Mary

Allen, Diane L. "Believers, Nonbelievers Flock to 'See' Virgin Mary." *St. Louis Post-Dispatch,* December 26, 1994, 5B.

Davis, James D., et al. "Our Lady of Florida." *Chicago Tribune,* October 25, 1994, "Tempo" section, p.1 (2).

Georgia

Columbus: Jesus Christ, Crimestopper

Earle, Joe. "Columbus's 'Jesus' Tree Draws the Faithful, Curious." *The Atlanta Journal and Constitution,* May 7, 1994, B8.

Conyers: Visions by Nancy Fowler

Child, Judith. "The Conyers Story." In *To Bear Witness that I Am the Loving Son of God.* Newington, VA: Our Loving Mother's Children, 1991, pp. 1–21.

Dvorchak, Robert, The Associated Press. "Virgin Mary 'Seen' All Around Nation." *The Columbus Dispatch,* October 16, 1994, 3A.

Lancetti, Susan. "Faithful Pray for a Glimpse." *The Atlanta Journal and Constitution,* October 14, 1991, D6.

Smolowe, Jill. "A Heavenly Host in Georgia." *Time,* January 18, 1993, p. 55.

White, Gayle. "Sharing a Vision of Virgin Mary." *The Atlanta Journal and Constitution,* September 14, 1991, B1.

Stone Mountain: Pasta Jesus, Please

"And the Winners Are." *Adweek,* July 8, 1991, "Corridor Talk" section, np.

Applebome, Peter. "A Sign: It's Jesus, or a Lunch Bargain." *The New York Times,* May 25,1991, Section 1, p.8.

Guevara-Castro, Lillian and Viele, Lawrence. "Dozens Say They Have Seen Christ on a Pizza Chain Billboard." *The Atlanta Journal and Constitution,* May 21, 1991, D1.

Hayes, Jack. "You Gotta Have Faith." *Nation's Restaurant News,* June 10, 1991, p. 18.

Jacobson, David. "Icon in the Spaghetti." *Orlando Sentinel,* June 13, 1991, E1.

Illinois

Chicago: The Sorrows of Rosa Mystica

Buursma, Bruce. "Though Skeptical, Church Still Does Believe in Miracles." *Chicago Tribune,* September 22, 1985, Section C, p. 11 (2).

Hirsley, Michael. "'Tears' of Mary Comfort Believers." *Chicago Tribune,* May 8, 1992, Section "Chicagoland," p. 7.

Ries, William. "'Crying' Statue Attracts Faithful, Curious." United Press International, June 10, 1984, np.

Roszell, Stephen. "Rosa Mystica" (documentary transcript). 1992, pp. 1–27.

Schmetzer, Uli. "Souvenir Trade Thrives on Statue's Tears." *Chicago Tribune,* September 16, 1985, "News" section, p.1 (2).

Stamets, Bill. "Roszell's 'Rosa Mystica' Tells Story of 'Weeping' Statue." *Chicago Sun-Times,* April 24, 1992, "Weekend Plus" section, p. 33.

United Press International. "Domestic News" (brief item). August 4, 1984, np.

United Press International. "National News Briefs" (brief item). May 31, 1985, np.

———. "'Weeping' Icon Draws Hundreds to Church." June 2, 1984, np.

Weigl, A.M. *Mary the Mystical Rose.* 2nd ed. Chicago: St. John of God, 1988, pp.1–2.

Chicago/Cicero: Weeping Icons Frequent Orthodox Churches

(Chicago)

Fox, Mario. "Eastern Patriarch Blesses 'Weeping' Virgin Mary Icon." The Associated Press, July 24, 1990, np.

"Inspirational Spiritual Welcome to St. Nicholas Albanian Orthodox Church and Shrine of the Blessed Virgin Mary" (pamphlet). Chicago: St. Nicholas Albanian Church, nd.

Kavvadias, Tasia, "Icon's 'Miraculous Sign' Draws Multitude." *Chicago Tribune,* December 15, 1986, "Chicagoland" section, p. 1.

Locin, Mitchell. "Icon's 'Tears' Bring Smiles to Parishioners." *Chicago Tribune,* December 12, 1986, "Chicagoland" section, p. 1.

———. "'Weeping' Icon Draws Worshipers." *Chicago Tribune,* December 9, 1986, "Chicagoland" section, p. 3.

———. "Visitors to Icon Force Church to Cut Its Hours." *Chicago Tribune,* January 14, 1987, np.

"The Scientist Who Makes Icons Weep." *Newsweek,* October 26, 1987, p. 79.

Tamarkin, Civia. "In an Eastern Orthodox Chicago Church, a Weeping Madonna and Child Bring Throngs to Pray and Hope for Miracles." *People,* January 19, 1987, p. 44.

"'Weeping Virgin' Icon Draws Throngs to Chicago." *The New York Times,* December 22, 1986, Section B, p. 16.

(Cicero)

Banks, Nancy. "Shrine Draws People from All Walks of Life." *Chicago Sun-Times,* May 15, 1994, G1 and G6.

Byrne, Dennis. "Icon Tears? Less Shed, the Better." *Chicago Sun-Times,* April 28, 1994, p. 31.

Gilliland, Pat. "Although Skeptical at First, Priest Sees Painting Weep." *Saturday Oklahoman & Times,* June 4, 1994, pp. 1–2.

Hirsley, Michael. "Icon's Tears Are Turning into a Stream of People." *Chicago Tribune,* May 6, 1994, "Chicagoland" section, p. 1.

"Our Lady of Cicero Proclaimed by Metropolitan." *The Cicero Town News,* May 1994, p. 1.

Rihani, Malek. "The Miracle of St. George of Cicero." *The Word,* June 1994, pp. 4–5.

Zorn, Eric. "Icon Is Still Crying for Our Attention." *Chicago Tribune,* May 15, 1994, pp. 1–2.

Hillside: Mary Visits a Cemetery

At the Cross Her Station Keeping, Vol. II (booklet). Long Grove, IL: At the Cross, 1994, pp. i–v.

Donato, Marla. "In Search for Miracles, Believers Head to Hillside." *Chicago Tribune,* July 24, 1991, p. 1.

Szymczak, P. Davis. "Hillside Apparition Latest in Long List." *Chicago Tribune,* September 6, 1991, "Chicagoland" section, p. 9.

Unsworth, Tim. "Amid a Cemetery's Peace, a Show of Undying Faith." *National Catholic Reporter,* January 29, 1993, p. 18.

Kentucky

Cold Spring/Falmouth: A Woodstock for Catholics

Bartlett, Beverly. "Some Heard Only Silence." *The Courier-Journal,* September 2, 1992, 1B.

———. "Waiting for a Vision." *The Courier-Journal,* September 1, 1992, 1A.

Goldberg, Laura. "Believing Is Seeing?" *The Cincinnati Enquirer* (Indiana-Ohio edition), September 1, 1994, B1.

———. "Thousands to Hail Mary." *The Cincinnati Enquirer* (Kentucky edition), May 8, 1994, B1.

———. "Visions Reported at Midnight." *The Cincinnati Enquirer* (Final edition), September 1, 1994, B1.

Hill, Bob. "Managing a Miracle." *The Courier-Journal,* August 25, 1992, 1C.

Menge, Beth. "Gathering to Mark Kentucky Vigil for Mary." *The Cincinnati Enquirer* (Indiana-Ohio edition), August 30, 1994, B1.

———. "'Vision' Could Attract 50,000 Sunday." *The Cincinnati Enquirer* (Indiana-Ohio edition), May 6, 1994, D1.

Ross, Gerald G., ed. *Personal Revelations of Our Lady of Light.* Ft. Mitchell, KY: Our Lady of Light, 1992, pp. 1–22, 63–67, 102–8.

———. *More Personal Revelations.* Ft. Mitchell, KY: Our Lady of Light, 1993, pp. 1–10, 54–57, 119–32.

Steinfels, Peter. "Cold Spring Journal." *The New York Times,* September 2, 1992, Section A, p. 14.

Louisiana

Tickfaw: Visions amid the Vegetables

Ashton, Linda. "Some Claim Religious Visions as Thousands Visit Tiny Louisiana Town." The Associated Press, March 12, 1989, np.

"Hundreds Looking for Apparition of Virgin Mary." The Associated Press, March 11, 1989, np.

"Our Lady of Tickfaw" (pamphlet). Tickfaw, LA: Our Lady of Tickfaw, 1990.

"Police Say 20,000 Gather to Pray." United Press International, March 13, 1989, np.

"Thousands Expected at Mass Inspired by Virgin Mary." Reuters, March 8, 1989, np.

Maine

Fairfield: Another Knothole for Jesus

Austin, Daniel L. "People Flock to Tree for Sight of 'Jesus.'" *Central Maine Morning Sentinel,* July 7, 1992, pp. 1 and 8.

Beem, Edgar Allen. "Miracle on Burns St." *Yankee,* April, 1993, p. 64.

Klopp, Barbara M. "Miracle on the Market." *Bangor Daily News,* April 15, 1995, np.

Lively, Rob. "Do You See Jesus Christ?" *Maine Times,* August 14, 1992, pp. 1–3.

Rawson, Davis. "We All Want to Believe in Something." *Central Maine Morning Sentinel,* nd, np.

Maryland

Emmitsburg: "Vision Night" at St. Joseph's Catholic Church

The Associated Press. "Domestic News" (brief item). September 21, 1994, np.

Borgman, Anna. "Messages from Mary." *The Washington Post*, October 22, 1994, B7.

Gaul, Christopher. "'Mission' Puts Health Care on Wheels." *The Catholic Review,* May 31, 1995, A1 and A8.

Jasuta, Jill. "'I've Never Seen Anyone So Beautiful.'" *The Catholic Review,* June 22, 1994, A1 and A8.

———. "A Place of Grace." *The Catholic Review,* August 24, 1994, A2.

"Mission of Mercy." *The Emmitsburg Regional Dispatch,* September 1994, pp. 1 and 3.

O'Neill, Kendi. "Miracle Valley?" *Frederick,* June 1995, pp. 22–7.

Snider, Keith. "Messages from Mary Spark Probe." *The Herald Mail,* June 11, 1994, np.

Tasker, Greg. "Heavenly Visions Disturb Small Town's Way of Life." *The Baltimore Sun,* September 15, 1994, 1B.

———and Hare, Mary Gail. "Following the Vision of the Virgin." *The Baltimore Sun,* June 28, 1994, 1B and 3B.

———. "Woman Tells of Melodic Voice and Joyous Beauty." *The Baltimore Sun,* June 26, 1994, 3B.

Massachusetts

Medway: Rock of Jesus

Auerbach, Jon. "Some Still Oppose Nun's Plan." *Boston Globe,* September 25, 1994, p. 39.

Callahan, Mary T. "The Image of Jesus Christ on a Rock in Medway?" *Milford News,* November 15, 1993, pp.1–2.

Carini, Frank. "Framingham Nun Has Vision of Catholic Community in Medway." *Country Gazette,* December 22, 1993, p. 12.

Dixon, Leslie H. "Nun Plans Spiritual Center in Medway (Part One)." *Milford Daily News,* August 26, 1994, pp. 1 and 10.

———. "After 100 Years, Breezy Meadows Has Become a Mecca for Pilgrims (Part Two)." *Milford Daily News,* August 27, 1994, pp. 1 and 4.

Greenwald, Igor. "A Place Where Miracles Happen?" *Middlesex News,* June 9, 1994, pp. 1–2.

———. "Project Faces Long Road Ahead." *Ibid,* p. 1.

Morony, Tom. "Rock Called Spiritual Discovery." *Boston Globe,* November 14, 1993, np.

Ware: Mary Cries at Christmas

Della Valle, Paul. "Mary's 'Tears' Kindle Faith at Ware Creche." *Sunday Telegram,* January 5, 1992, A2.

Gronberg, Kim Ann. "Weeping Virgin Report Draws Crowds to Ware." *Springfield Union-News,* December 25, 1991, pp. 1–2.

"Hundreds Trek to See Teary-Eyed Madonna." The Associated Press, December 30, 1991, np.

Palumbo, Mary Jane. "'Weeping' Madonna Draws Curious to Ware Display." *Boston Herald,* December 31, 1991, p.5.

Shea, Suzanne S. "Madonna Moves Faithful at Ware Nativity Scene." *Ware River News,* January 3, 1992, pp. 1 and 9.

New Jersey

Marlboro: Rough Riding on the Marian Trail

Fussman, Cal. "Miracles." *Harper's Bazaar,* December 1993, pp. 161–63.

Goldman, Ari. "When Mary Is Sighted, a Blessing Has Its Burdens." *The New York Times*, September 6, 1992, Section 1, p. 1.

Hanley, Robert. "Undeterred by Pleas, the Faithful Again Seek Out a Vision of the Virgin." *The New York Times,* September 7, 1992, Section 1, p. 25.

Nieves, Evelyn. "For Thousands, Leap of Faith Is a Drive to a Monmouth Farm." *The New York Times,* August 3, 1992, Section B, page 4.

Parisi, Albert J. "Marlboro Girds for Another Onslaught." *The New York Times,* August 30, 1992, Section 13NJ, p. 1.

Paterson: A Chameleon of a Statue

Kalchthaler, Mary Jo. *If It Didn't Happen to Me* (unpublished manuscript). nd, pp. 145–60, 172–83, 207–8, 213, 218, 223.

"Parishioners at Paterson Church Say Statue of Our Lady Changes Color." *The Beacon,* May 17, 1992, p. 5.

"Paterson Parishioners Say Icon Changes Color." *The Northern New Jersey Record,* June 13, 1992, A3.

Stern, Harry, Associated Press. "Statue Said to Change Color." Morris County *Daily Record,* June 7, 1992, B6.

West Paterson: God Finds a Loophole

Kalchthaler, Mary Jo. "St. Ann's Church" (audiotape). August 1995.

New Mexico

Chimayo: A "Pit" Stop on the High Road to Taos

El Santuario. Silver Spring, MD: Sons of the Holy Family, 1994, pp. 1–28.

Holman: Jesus Up against the Wall

Bullock, Alice and Moscow, Jeff. "I Have Seen the Wall." *Viva,* August 3, 1975, pp. 4 and 15.

Warren, Nancy Hunter. *Villages of Hispanic New Mexico.* Santa Fe: School of America Research Press, 1987, pp. 27–28.

Lake Arthur: Heaven on a Burnt Tortilla

O'Connor, Priscilla. "Hundreds Flock to See Image of Tortilla." *Daily Press,* October 10, 1977, p. 1.

———. "Tortilla Story Draws Wide Interest." *Daily Press,* August 2, 1978, p. 1.

Olmsted, Richard. "Tortilla Image on National TV." *Record,* nd, pp. 1 and 5.

Smith, Toby. "The Face in the Flour." *Impact* (Albuquerque Journal Magazine), December 22, 1987, pp. 5–7.

"Thousands Trek to the Shrine of the Holy Tortilla in New Mexico Home." United Press International, June 6, 1982, np.

Santa Fe: This Old Madonna

Archuleta, Maria Victoria. *Our Lady of Light in Santa Fe.* Santa Cruz, NM: Author, 1994, pp. 3, 11–44.

Canticos, Misas Y Novena De La Conquistadora (booklet). Santa Fe: Cathedral of St. Francis, 1978, pp. 38–41, 52, 61.

New York

Bayside (Queens): Call 1-800-882-MARY

Harpaz, Beth J. "Queens Miracle Claim Keeps Drawing Crowds After 20 Years." The Associated Press, August 3, 1990, np.

Heller, Karen. "Snapshot Miracles." *Chicago Tribune,* December 29, 1989, "Tempo" section, p. 1 (2).

Polsky, Carol. "Our Lady of Controversy." *Newsday,* May 12, 1989, Part II, p. 2 (3).

"Pilgrims Find Vision at a Park in Queens." *The New York Times,* September 5, 1991, Section B, p. 3.

Winton, Ben. "Protesters Remind Pope Not Everybody Is a Fan." *The Phoenix Gazette,* August 13, 1993, A9.

Hempstead: A Divine Wedding Gift

"40 [sic] Years Ago." *Newsday,* July 18, 1992, pp. 16 and 74.

Swift, Maurice and Kahn, Dave. "Archbishop to Examine LI's 'Weeping Madonna.'" *Newsday,* March 21, 1960, pp. 4, 32.

Williamsbridge (Bronx): A Jewel in the Bronx

Gonzalez, David. "At Lourdes of Bronx, Where Cooling Hope Flows." *The New York Times,* May 27, 1992, Section B, p. 3.

Marcus, Aliza. "A Shrine in the Bronx Where the Water Heals." *The Reuter Library Report,* August 21, 1992, np.

Ohio

Barberton: From Magic City to Miracleville

Bako, Carl. "Barberton Church to Commemorate Third Anniversary of Weeping Icon." *The Barberton Herald,* March 9, 1995, A1–A2.

Byard, Katie. "He's Out of the Mainstream, But Faith Is Unwavering." *Akron-Beacon Journal,* March 22, 1992, A1.

———. "Humble Place for a Miracle." *Akron-Beacon Journal,* March 12, 1992, A1.

———."She Prayed at Icon—Her Foot Got Better." *Akron-Beacon Journal,* March 19, 1992, A1.

———. "Tiny St. Jude Church Not Used to Spotlight." *Akron-Beacon Journal,* March 14, 1992, B1.

Haferd, Laura. "Orthodox Church Tough to Delineate." *loc cit.*, A5.

"Janitor Says He Talked with the Virgin Mary." United Press International, March 12, 1992, np.

Kuhar, Patti. "Weeping Icon Draws Thousands." *The Barberton Herald,* nd, np.

"The Madonna Weeps." *National Examiner.* nd, np.

"Miracle Cures" (transcript). "48 Hours," CBS Special, nd.

Nevada, Charlene. "Fate, Curiosity Pack One-Room Church." *Akron-Beacon Journal,* March 16, 1992, A1.

O'Connor, Bill. "Hint of Divine Draws Faithful." *Akron-Beacon Journal,* March 13, 1992, A1.

Richardson, Dave. "One Man's Meat." *The Barberton Herald,* nd, np.

"Second Barberton Icon Sheds Tears." *The Orthodox Catholic Voice,* Numbers 4–5, 1992 (nd), p. 3.

Carey: Conspicuous Communion

"Basilica and Shrine of Our Lady of Consolation" (pamphlet). Carey, OH: Our Lady of Consolation, nd.

Candel, Brother Joseph, ed. *A History of the Basilica and National Shrine of Our Lady of Consolation* (by Brother Jeffrey) 2nd ed. Carey, OH: Our Lady of Consolation, 1993.

France, Bob. "Believing in Miracles." *The Columbus Dispatch,* December 24, 1994, 1–2F.

Harden, Mike. "Carey Ready for Procession of the Faithful." *The Columbus Dispatch,* June 17, 1987, 1B.

Souvenir Guide in Living Color to Our Lady of Consolation (booklet). Carey: Our Lady of Consolation, nd.

"Your Tour" (pamphlet). Carey, OH: Our Lady of Consolation, nd.

Fostoria: Rust Stains on Tank or Sacred Image?

Darr, Kent and Mason, Debra. "Some See Christ's Image on Soybean Oil Tank." *The Columbus Dispatch,* August 21, 1986, 1F.

Jaynes, Gregory. "In Ohio: A Vision West of Town." *Time,* September 29, 1986, pp. 8 and 14.

"'Jesus Image' Damaged, Firefighter Charged." *Chicago Tribune,* September 27, 1986, "News" section, p. 3.

Switzer, John, "They're Seeing Things Again Back Home." *The Columbus Dispatch,* October 8, 1992, 6B.

"Traffic Jams Caused by Religious Image." *Chicago Tribune,* August 22, 1986, "News" section, p. 3.

United Press International. "Second Purported Image of Christ Draws Throngs to Soybean Oil Tank." *Los Angeles Times,* August 24, 1986, Part 1, p. 6.

Lorain: A "Contagious" Icon

The Associated Press. "Lorain's 'Miracle' Icon." 1988, np.

Helgason, Julia. "Faithful, Curious Flock to Gaze at Icon." *Elyria Times,* 1988, pp. 1 and 11.

Matuszewski, Carol. "'I Take It as a Good Sign,'" Lorain *Morning Journal,* 1988, pp. 1–2.

United Press International. "Weeping Icon Still Drawing Crowds." August 4, 1988, np.

Vidka, Ron. "To See Her Cry." Lorain *Morning Journal,* 1988, pp. 1–2.

Pennsylvania

Ambridge: Did He Blink?

Burrell, Cassandra. "No Proof of Miracle, Report Says." The Associated Press, July 6, 1989, np.

Memmott, Carol. "'Miracles' Many, but Proof Hard to Come By." *USA Today,* April 12, 1989, 8A.

Mullen, Sheila. "Catholic Church Panel Scuttles Miracle Report." United Press International, July 5, 1989, np.

————. "Parishioners Say Statue Closed Its Eyes." United Press International, March 26, 1989, np.

Philadelphia: Parochial Vision during the Eisenhower Years

"50,000 Flock to Bush in Fairmont Park." *The Evening Bulletin,* October 26, 1953, np.

Chardak, Burton. "Small Crowd Visits Bush on 2d [sic] Anniversary of 'Vision.'" *The Evening Bulletin,* September 19, 1955, np.

"Children's Report of Vision Draws Big Crowd to Park." *The Evening Bulletin,* October 14, 1953, np.

"Contract Let for Shelter at Vision Bush in Park." *The Evening Bulletin,* October 9, 1956, np.

"Court Asked to Use Donations to Beautify Site of 'Vision.'" *The Evening Bulletin,* November 17, 1954, np.

"Fairmont Park 'Vision Bush' Is Damaged and May Die." *The Evening Bulletin,* March 30, 1954, np.

"Fairmont Park Vision Site Mecca for Sunday Thousands." *Philadelphia Daily News,* November 2, 1953, np.

Fox, Tom. "The Day the Virgin Appeared." *Philadelphia Daily News,* March 13, 1973, pp. 2 and 41.

————. "She Kept Faith in Park 'Holy Bush.'" *Philadelphia Daily News,* March 22, 1973, np.

————. "Vision in Bush Has Affected Her Life, Woman Says." *Philadelphia Daily News,* April 4, 1973, p. 30.

Harry, Lou. "The Miracle in the Park." *Philadelphia,* April 1987, p. 18.

Lee, Adrian L. "Solicitor Rules on Gifts at Bush." *The Evening Bulletin,* March 11, 1954.

Lloyd, Jack. "Some Recall Bush 'Vision.'" *Philadelphia Inquirer,* April 7, 1969, np.

Martin, Jerry. "Another 20,000 Visit Vision Scene." *Philadelphia Daily News,* October 27, 1953, pp. 3 and 22.

Moriarty, Rowland. "5 Recall Vision of Virgin Mary in Park." *The Sunday Bulletin,* April 29, 1973, p. 48.

"Park Bush Gifts to Build Shelter." *The Evening Bulletin,* June 11, 1954, np.

"Photo at Scene of Reported Vision." *The Evening Bulletin,* November 1, 1953, pp. 1 and 3.

Pittsburgh: Seeping Beauty

Butler, Ann. "The Weeping Bronze." *Pittsburgh Press,* February 26, 1980, A9.

Charles, Rodney. *Every Day a Miracle Happens.* Fairfield, IA: Sunstar, 1994, pp. 322–23.

Demetrius, Allen. "The Anniversary of Man's End." Unpublished poem, Pittsburgh, nd.

Lewis, Jim. "Statue Wept for Hiroshima, He Says." *Pittsburgh Press,* March 18, 1979, A10.

"Tears of Doom." *Post-Gazette,* July 14, 1969, np.

"Warning from Weeping Statue." *Midnight/Globe,* May 8, 1979, p. 5.

Texas

Bellaire: Stampede at the Ayob Home

Brunsman, Steve. "'Weeping' Jesus Goes on Display in Bellaire." *The Houston Post,* January 7, 1992, A11.

———. "'Weeping' Jesus Picture Still Draws the Curious." *The Houston Post,* May 17, 1992, A23.

———. "'Weeping' Portrait of Jesus Christ Gets 200 Visitors a Day in Houston." *The Houston Post,* December 4, 1991, A22.

"Jesus Wept" (pamphlet). Bellaire, TX: St. Mark Coptic Orthodox Church, nd.

Jesus Wept (booklet). Bellaire, TX: St. Mark Coptic Orthodox Church, nd.

Vara, Richard. "'Jesus Wept.'" January 11, 1992, *The Houston Chronicle,* "Religion" section, p. 1.

———and Holmes White, Cecile. "Report of Angels Draws Pilgrims." *The Houston Chronicle,* October 3, 1992, "Religion" section, p. 1.

Blanco: Tears in a Trailer

Moreno, Sylvia. "Miracle Icon Brings World to Monastery." *The Dallas Morning News,* February 20, 1994, 42A.

Potok, Mark. "The Miraculous Discovery of Father Pangratios" (reprint). *D The Magazine of Dallas.* December 1992.

"Shrine of the Blessed Virgin Mary" (pamphlet). New Sarov/Blanco, TX: Christ of the Hills Monastery, nd.

Stockbauer, Betty. "The Weeping Icon at Christ of the Hills." *Share International,* October 1992, pp. 11–12.

Vaidhyanathan, Siva. "Faithful Flock to Trailer." *Omaha World-Herald,* November 23, 1989, 12A.

———. "Sacred Tears." *Austin-American Statesman.* October 26, 1989, A1 and A11.

"Weeping Icon Draws Pilgrims." Johnson City *Record-Courier,* November 23, 1989, np.

Lubbock: Lone Star Lourdes

Belkin, Lisa. "Reports of Miracles Draw Throngs." *The New York Times,* August 17, 1988, Section A, p. 14.

Gaussion, Helen. "Domestic News." United Press International, August 15, 1988, np.

Weingarten, Paul. "In the Town Where the Virgin 'Speaks' Thousands Hope to Be Healed." *Chicago Tribune,* April 14, 1988, "News" section, p. 5.

Progreso/Elsa: Mary Appears in an Automotive Context

(Elsa)

Balli, Cecilia. "Filmmakers Examine Holy Sites." *The Brownsville Herald,* July 31, 1994, p. 10.

Durnan, Kimberly. Unpublished article. *Valley Morning Star,* nd, np.

(Progreso)

Nickell, Joe. *Looking for a Miracle.* Buffalo, NY: Prometheus, 1993, pp. 35–6.

Virginia

Lake Ridge: Stigmata and the Roller Coaster King

Curl, Joseph. "Thousands Flock to See Virginia 'Miracle.'" *National Catholic Reporter,* March 27, 1992, p. 3.

Pressley, Sue Ann and Thomas-Lester, Avis. "Treading Softly into the Matter of Miracles." *The Washington Post,* April 5, 1992, B1.

Rossellini, Lynn. "The Case of the Weeping Madonna." *U.S. News & World Report,* March 29, 1993, pp. 46–55.

Thomas, Pierre. "Phenomena Pack Va. Church." *The Washington Post,* March 9, 1992, D3.

West Virginia

Holden: Jesus Treed

Borino, Bob. "Thousands Flocking to Be Cured By the 'Jesus' Tree." *Charleston Gazette,* 1982, np.

"Crowds Drawn to Tree Resembling Image of Christ." United Press International. September 9, 1982, np.

Douthat, Strat. "Mother Nature Resurrects Logan County's 'Jesus Tree.'" The Associated Press, August 8, 1983, np.

"Faithful Flocking to Jesus Tree." The Associated Press, September 9, 1982, np.

Massey, Tim. "Living with Coal." *The (Huntington) Herald-Dispatch,* nd, D1–D2.

Mullins, Ealois. "Jesus Tree" (privately published poem). nd.